ISBN: 9781314305258

Published by:
HardPress Publishing
8345 NW 66TH ST #2561
MIAMI FL 33166-2626

Email: info@hardpress.net
Web: http://www.hardpress.net

The General Post Office.

LIVING LONDON

ITS WORK AND ITS PLAY
ITS HUMOUR AND ITS PATHOS
ITS SIGHTS AND ITS SCENES

EDITED BY . . .
GEORGE R. SIMS

VOL. II—SECTION II

SPECIAL EDITION, WITH FULL-PAGE REMBRANDT PLATES

CASSELL AND COMPANY, Limited
London, Paris, New York & Melbourne
All Rights Reserved

OCT 28 1959

LONDON TYPES: THE ORGAN-GRINDER.
(From the Painting by W. Rainey, R.I.)

LONDON TYPES: THE WAITER.
(From the Painting by H. H. Flère.)

LONDON TYPES: THE FLOWER GIRL.
(From the Painting by H. H. Flere.)

CONTENTS.

	BY	PAGE
LONDON'S DRAPERS	MRS. BELLOC-LOWNDES	209
HOUSE-HUNTING LONDON	GEORGE R. SIMS	216
MUSIC-HALL LONDON	H. CHANCE NEWTON	222
HOOLIGAN LONDON	CLARENCE ROOK	229
HOTEL LONDON	J. C. WOOLLAN	236
THAMES PLEASURES AND SPORTS	JOHN BLOUNDELLE-BURTON	243
ROMAN CATHOLIC LONDON	WILFRID MEYNELL	249
LONDON THRIFT	SIDNEY DARK	254
LONDON UNDER THE WEATHER	GEORGE R. SIMS	261
SCOTTISH, IRISH, AND WELSH LONDON	C. O'CONOR ECCLES	267
LIGHTING LONDON	DESMOND YOUNG	274
SIDESHOW LONDON	A. ST. JOHN ADCOCK	281
BAR AND SALOON LONDON	GRAHAM HILL	286
CHRISTENING LONDON	SHEILA E. BRAINE	293
COUNTY COUNCIL LONDON	FREDERICK DOLMAN, L.C.C.	298
THE LONDON CITY COMPANIES	CHARLES WELCH, F.S.A.	305
LONDON GETS UP IN THE MORNING	GEORGE R. SIMS	311
LONDON'S STREET INDUSTRIES	P. F. WILLIAM RYAN	317
BIRD-LAND AND PET-LAND IN LONDON	HENRY SCHERREN	324
SCENES FROM FACTORY LONDON	C. DUNCAN LUCAS	330
LUNATIC LONDON	T. W. WILKINSON	338
A COUNTRY COUSIN'S DAY IN TOWN	GEORGE R. SIMS	344
SERVANT LONDON	N. MURRELL MARRIS	351
LONDON'S LITTLE WORRIES	GEORGE R. SIMS	358
LONDON'S WASH-HOUSES AND BATHS	I. BROOKE-ALDER	364
SCENES FROM OFFICIAL LIFE IN LONDON	L. BRINDLE	371
SATURDAY NIGHT IN LONDON	A. ST. JOHN ADCOCK	378

LIST OF ILLUSTRATIONS.

	PAGE
LONDON'S DRAPERS:—	
A Work Room	209
A Packing Room	210
At Dinner on a Big Sale Day	211
Left Outside	212
A Cash Desk	212
A Postal Order Room	213
A Sale Day at Peter Robinson's	214
HOUSE-HUNTING LONDON:—	
A Well-Known Establishment in St. James's Street	216
Shown into the Drawing-Room	217
An Inspection by the Dog	218
Let as Fast as Built	219
A Choice of Agents	220
Moving In	221
MUSIC-HALL LONDON:—	
Ready to Pass in ("Wonderland")	223
Waiting to Go on at a Music-Hall	223
Beneath the Arena (Hippodrome)	224
Types of Music-Hall Performers	225
Performing Dogs	226
At the Corner of York Road	227
Before the Doors Open (London Pavilion)	228
HOOLIGAN LONDON:—	
Attacked by Two	229
Pitch and Toss	230
Hooligan Weapons	231
Hooligan v. Hooligan	233
Sandbagging in the Fog	234
A Street Group	235
HOTEL LONDON:—	
Manager Receiving Guests (Hotel Victoria)	236
Page	236
Arrival of an Oriental Potentate (Claridge's)	237
Porter	239
The Palm Court (Carlton Hotel)	239
Smoking Room (Grand Hotel)	239
Chambermaid	239
Lift Man	239
Commercials "Writing up the Mail" (Manchester Hotel)	239
Drawing Room (Hotel Cecil)	240
Dining Room (Oak Salon, Hotel Métropole)	241
Lounge (Hotel Russell)	242
THAMES PLEASURES AND SPORTS:—	
The Oxford and Cambridge Boat Race	243
Doggett's Coat and Badge	243
Excursion Steamers Leaving Fresh Wharf, London Bridge	244
Bathing in the River	244

	PAGE
THAMES PLEASURES AND SPORTS (continued):—	
Ready for a Row	246
A "Penny Sweat"	246
At Practice	247
"Boats to Let"	247
River Steamer	248
ROMAN CATHOLIC LONDON:—	
Leaving the Oratory, South Kensington	249
Arrival of a Cardinal at Sardinia Street Chapel	250
The Red Mass as Formerly Celebrated at Sardinia Street Chapel, Lincoln's Inn	251
Unloading a Cart at Nazareth House	252
Old Women's Ward, Nazareth House	253
LONDON THRIFT:—	
The National Penny Bank (Hackney Road)	254
School Teachers Receiving Pupils' Pennies	255
Salvation Army Reliance Bank, Queen Victoria Street	256
Birkbeck Bank	257
Hearts of Oak Certificate	258
Forester's Certificate	258
A Christmas Eve Distribution of Turkeys, Geese, etc. (Aldenham Institute)	259
Druid's Certificate	260
Post Office Savings Bank Stamp Form	260
LONDON UNDER THE WEATHER:—	
During a Summer Heat Wave	261
On the Kerbstone: Sun Hats	261
High Holborn in a Storm	262
By Torchlight	263
At the Mercy of the Wind	263
Ludgate Circus in a Fog	264
Skating on the Serpentine	265
SCOTTISH, IRISH, AND WELSH LONDON:—	
Playing in the Haggis on St. Andrew's Night	267
London Kymric Ladies' Choir	268
Learning Irish Reels (Athenæum Hall, Tottenham Court Road)	269
Irish Guardsmen	270
Shamrock Seller	270
A London Irish Hurling Match	271
Welsh Paper Published in London	272
Highland Piper and Dancer in London	273
LIGHTING LONDON:—	
Laying Electric Cables	274
Lamp-Lighter	274
In the London Electric Supply Corporation's Works	275
Drawing Retorts by Hand (South Metropolitan Gas Company)	276

LIST OF ILLUSTRATIONS.

LIGHTING LONDON (continued):—

	PAGE
Lamp Cleaner	278
Paying out a Leaden Cable	278
Supplying Arc Lamp with Carbon	278
Lamp Repairing Shop (South Metropolitan Gas Company)	279
Collecting Pennies from a Slot Meter	280
Taking in Coal at Vauxhall (South Metropolitan Gas Company)	280

SIDESHOW LONDON:—

Punch and Judy	281
A West-End Sideshow	282
The Lion Jawed Man	283
A Rifle Range	283
A Tattooed Couple at Tea	284
A Waxwork Show	284
A Fat Lady	285

BAR AND SALOON LONDON:—

Served Through the Window	285
Inside a Public-House on Saturday Night	287
The Chandos Bar and Lounge	288
A City Wine-Bar (The Bodega, Bucklersbury)	289
A Strand Wine-Bar (Short's)	289
At a "Change" in the East-End	290
During Prohibited Hours (Whitechapel): Satisfying the Landlord; Waiting to Enter	291
Outside the "Bull and Bush," Hampstead, on Sunday Morning	292

CHRISTENING LONDON:—

A Christening at a West-End Church	293
A Nurse: New Style	294
A Nurse: Old Style	294
A Scottish Christening in London	295
A Batch of Christenings	295
A Christening at the Italian Church, Hatton Garden	297
A Salvation Army "Dedication"	297

COUNTY COUNCIL LONDON:—

At the L.C.C. Licensing Sessions (Clerkenwell); Examining a Witness	299
Four Days' Work: Pages from a Member's Diary	300
L.C.C. Open Space Notice Board	300
Fire Brigade Committee Starting on an Inspection	301
L.C.C. Stonemasons at Work	302
L.C.C. Wharf	303
A Sitting of the London County Council	304

THE LONDON CITY COMPANIES:—

Dynamo Class at the City and Guilds Institute (South Kensington)	305
Outside a Cell, Bridewell Hospital	306
Court of the Cutlers' Company: Examining the Work of their Apprentices	307
An Examination at Apothecaries' Hall	308
The Copyright Registry, Stationers' Hall	309
A Playing Card Design (Playing Card Makers' Company)	310

LONDON GETS UP IN THE MORNING:—

	PAGE
Mary Jane Descends	311
The Children Awake	312
A Late Riser	313
Welcome News	314
Reading the Press Notices	315
The Bride of the Day	315
In the Condemned Cell	316

LONDON'S STREET INDUSTRIES:—

Net Making; "Sweep!"; Crumpets; Sweetstuff Making; Flags and Windmills; Salt; Bread; Shrimps; Window-Cleaning; Watercress; Fish; Old Hats; Milk; "Scissors to Grind"; Kettle-Holder Making; Saw Sharpening; Chair Mending; Coals; Fly Papers; Woolwork Picture Making; Shoeblack; Old Iron; Step-Cleaning; Greengrocer; Brushes; Clock-Mender; Old Sacks; Yule Logs; Licensed Messenger
317, 318, 319, 320, 321, 322, 323

BIRD LAND AND PET-LAND IN LONDON:—

A Pet Python	324
Feeding Pigeons Outside the Guildhall	325
Gulls near the Thames Embankment	325
Feeding Pigeons in Hyde Park	325
Feeding Sparrows from his Hand (Hyde Park)	325
Feeding the Ducks in St. James's Park	325
A Bird Shop on Wheels	326
In a Bird and Animal Shop (Great Portland Street)	327
Caged	328
Feeding Pet Lemurs	328
A Street Bird Stall	329

SCENES FROM FACTORY LONDON:—

Matchbox Filling	330
Cream Fondant Moulding Room	331
A Cigar Manufacturing Department	333
Marking Soap for Hotels, Clubs, etc.	334
The Potter at Work	335
Wrapping Infants' Food	336
Printing "Living London"	337

LUNATIC LONDON:—

The Bethlem Magazine	338
A Christmas Entertainment at St. Luke's	339
Padded Room in a London Workhouse	340
Cricket (Bethlem)	341
Gardening (St. Luke's)	342
Needlework (Bethlem)	343

A COUNTRY COUSIN'S DAY IN TOWN:—

Preparing Models (Madame Tussaud's)	344
The Artists' Room, Pagani's	345
The Coliseum: From the Stage	347
In the Brasserie, Hôtel de l'Europe, Leicester Square	347
After a Matinée	348
The Empire Promenade	349
"Good-Bye"	350

LIST OF ILLUSTRATIONS.

	PAGE
SERVANT LONDON :—	
In a Registry Office: Servants Seeking Situations	351
Maid-of-all-Work	351
Housemaid	351
Outside a Registry Office: Reading the Notices	352
Club Page	352
Club Waiter	352
In a Servants' Hall: At Dinner	353
Coachman	354
Groom	354
Footman	354
Servants' Fire Brigade at the Hotel Cecil	355
Servants' Recreation Room at the Army and Navy Club	356
Lady's Maid Learning Hair Dressing	356
Smoking Concert at a Servants' Club (St. Paul's, Knightsbridge)	357
LONDON'S LITTLE WORRIES :—	
The Pestering Acquaintance	358
"Lost Ball"	359
"I will Call for an Answer"	360
"I'll Shoot that Cat!"	360
Behind the Smokers	361
"My Purse is Gone!"	362
A Whining Appeal	363
LONDON'S WASH-HOUSES AND BATHS :—	
In a Public Wash-House (Marylebone Road): Washing	364
Men's Private Baths (Hornsey Road Baths and Wash-Houses)	365

	PAGE
LONDON'S WASH-HOUSES AND BATHS *(continued)* :—	
In a Public Wash-House (Marshall Street, W.): Folding and Mangling	365
Turkish Bath (Jermyn Street): Shampooing Room	367
Water Polo Match (Westminster Baths)	367
Teaching Schoolboys to Swim (Kensington Baths)	368
Turkish Bath (Jermyn Street): Cooling Room	369
Ladies Using the Chute (Bath Club)	370
SCENES FROM OFFICIAL LIFE IN LONDON :—	
Awaiting the Arrival of Ministers to Attend a Cabinet Council	371
A Reception at the Foreign Office	372
A Council at Buckingham Palace	374
A Deputation to the Colonial Secretary	375
After a Naval Disaster: Enquiries at the Admiralty	376
Presentation of War Medals on the Horse Guards Parade: Arrival of the King	377
SATURDAY NIGHT IN LONDON :—	
Saturday Night in King Street, Hammersmith	378
Braces	379
Boots and Shoes: Trying on	379
Saturday Night in Whitechapel Road	381
Inside a Big Provision Stores (Hammersmith)	382
China	383
Outside a Public-House	383
Selling Meat by Auction	384

The Illustrations are from Drawings by J. H. BACON, GORDON BROWNE, R.I., R.B.A., JAMES DURDEN, J. S. ELAND, C. H. FINNEMORE, H. H. FLERE, CLEMENT FLOWER, A. H. FULLWOOD, PROFESSOR MAURICE GRÜN, A. P. GARRATT, W. H. HUMPHRIS, E. LANDER, W. H. MARGETSON, F. PEGRAM, H. PIFFARD, VICTOR PROUT, W. RAINEY, R.I., EDWARD READ, A. MONRO SMITH, ISAAC SNOWMAN, ALLEN STEWART, W. R. S. STOTT, L. CAMPBELL TAYLOR, H. E. TIDMARSH, F. H. TOWNSEND, C. D. WARD, ENOCH WARD, R.B.A.; *and from Photographs, nearly all of which were specially taken for this work, by* MESSRS. CASSELL AND COMPANY, LIMITED.

LIST OF REMBRANDT PLATES.

THE GENERAL POST OFFICE	*Frontispiece*
THE HOTEL CECIL	*To face p.* 238
THE ROMAN CATHOLIC CATHEDRAL, WESTMINSTER	,, 249
THE INDIA OFFICE	,, 376

A WORK ROOM.

LONDON'S DRAPERS.

By MRS. BELLOC-LOWNDES.

LONDON has long been, in the business sense of the word, the market of the world; but only comparatively lately have been established, especially in the West-End, the well-known emporiums which now cater successfully not only for Londoners, but for those American and Continental visitors who formerly took the whole of their dress custom to Paris.

A volume might well be written concerning life at the draper's; the more so, that not content with what was originally their mainstay—namely, drapery, millinery, dress-making, and underclothing departments—many now join to these separate sections, where every household want is satisfied, from the morning tea and milk to the costly fruit and liqueurs required for a Lucullian banquet.

The time may come when no drapery business will be able to live without these adjuncts; but there are still many prosperous establishments which, like their French rivals, deal almost entirely with the art of dress. Let us content ourselves with, as it were, taking off the roof of one of the half-dozen busy London hives which cater almost exclusively for the lady customer. It may be doubted whether this can be done more effectively than in tracing the various incidents connected with the brief existence of one of the many pretty items, say a hat or toque, dear to the feminine heart, from the day when it takes its place in the stockroom of a big West-End establishment to the moment when it is finally handed in at its purchaser's door by one of the army of *employés* belonging to the distribution service of the emporium in question.

Paris is still supposed to hold the sceptre where feminine dress is concerned: accordingly, the managers of each great London drapery business have to make a point of being in constant communication with the gay city, and their buyers—many of whom are paid salaries averaging from six to twenty guineas a week—are always on the look-out for new ideas, and huge prices are paid without a murmur for really original model

75

A PACKING ROOM.

gowns, model hats, and even model underclothing.

"What," the reader will ask, "has this to do with the progress of any special article from the workroom to the customer's hatbox?" Everything; for the hat or toque in question owes its very existence to the care exercised by the buyer, whose business it is to keep himself in touch with the great Paris millinery houses; and the piece of headgear under discussion is almost certain to be a clever modification of a Paris model, so arranged by the important lady whose business it is to superintend the millinery department. It is she who decides of what materials the hat or toque is to be made, and what price is to be asked for it.

At the London draper's each day, properly speaking, begins at 8.30, but as early as 7 o'clock the young men assistants, known to the trade as "squadders," have started work, cleaning, dusting, and finally unpacking the goods which are to be shown and offered for sale that day. The young ladies, who, in some great establishments I could name, number as many as 250, have nothing to do with what may be called "squadder" work, although they dress the windows of their departments; and, of course, the more delicate goods—and this especially applies to millinery—are taken out of boxes and from the tissue paper in which they were carefully wrapped up the night before, to display them to the best advantage. It may be assumed that particular care is bestowed on those windows where the newest millinery is displayed, as so much depends, when headgear is concerned, on a first impression. In most good houses every article for sale is marked in plain figures, and there is a "marking-off room," where everything is priced; but this only applies to goods that are not made by the firm. Before a hat or toque, for instance, has left the workrooms it is marked by the head of the department, for she alone can know what it has cost and what the profit should be. It may interest some of those ladies who spend much of their time "at the draper's" to learn that the best and newest goods, especially those copied from the more recent Paris models, are always at once put in the window. It is there that they are first seen by the public.

The best-looking young lady assistants are generally to be found in the millinery department; for human nature being what it is, many a middle-aged plain customer will the more willingly invest in a hat when she has seen it gracefully poised above the pretty face of the young lady who has been told off to attend to her wants. Once the piece of headgear has been chosen, the delicate matter of payment comes. If the customer has an account, and is known to the assistant, the amount of her purchase is simply debited to her; if, on the other hand, she is a casual purchaser, she is, of course, asked to pay ready cash, but it is also open to her to pay on delivery.

The question of payment satisfactorily settled, the hat or toque is packed by the vendor, and sent down to the despatch-room, where—and this is rather a curious fact—the parcel is opened, to see if everything is all right, by one of the many porters and packers whose duty it is to finally do up the hat-box and place it in the delivery cart.

Few ladies seem to care to begin their shopping before 11 o'clock, but by midday business is in full swing, and the outside porters are busily minding the pet dogs which, by a wise rule, are not allowed to accompany their mistresses through the great glass doors which admit them to the modern woman's El Dorado.

The busiest times of the day are from 12 to 1 o'clock and from 3 to 5 o'clock; but time has to be found for dinner, and the shop assistants in most great emporiums take their meals in five parties—half an hour being allowed for dinner and twenty minutes for tea. The mid-day meal consists of an ample supply of well-cooked food—hot in winter and generally cold in summer, everything being done to vary the diet and to make it palatable.

Time was when much of the drapery business consisted of unmade-up goods. Ladies preferred to buy their materials, and have them made up either at home or by their own dressmakers. Now, however, the largest and most profitable side of the drapery business is the sale of made-up goods. Customers will sometimes arrive in the middle of the morning and ask to be shown a gown that they can wear the same evening! Accordingly, an important side of the business is that of altering bodices and skirts to fit the buyer's figure; and the workroom, though never seen by the public, is a very busy department of a modern drapery business.

The half-yearly sales, which play so prominent a part in the lives of those connected with great drapery businesses, and also, it may be added, in that of some of their customers, who are always looking forward to "sale time," take place soon after Christmas and about Midsummer. During the days of the sale everything in a really good shop is, as a rule, "marked down," especially everything in the shape of a made-up garment, for these must be cleared off at an "alarming sacrifice" if need be; and amazing bargains may be secured in the millinery departments, for the simple reason that a winter or summer piece of headgear, if it be put away for

AT DINNER ON A BIG SALE DAY.

LEFT OUTSIDE.

twelve months, always acquires a worn look.

The preparation for a season's sale goes on for many days previous to the date advertised, for, as we have said, in respectable establishments all the articles offered during the days of a sale are "marked down"—that is, their price is lowered—and this means an extraordinary amount of careful work and thought for all those concerned. On the days of a sale, especially when some attractive "line" is offered at what seems to the average shrewd customer an exceptionally low price, it is quite usual for a large crowd of ladies, each and all eager for the fray, to gather outside the large plate-glass doors some half an hour before they are actually opened; and the scene, when the magic hour of nine is struck, recalls nothing so much—if one may credit the remark made by a certain stalwart soldier who had been through more than one campaign—as that of a town being taken by assault! Once the establishment is full the doors are again shut, and impatient customers are often kept waiting half an hour before they also are allowed to join the eager throng.

The more popular "lines," especially cheap footgear—shoes, for instance, at a shilling a pair—and very cheap gloves, are cleared out in the first hour. But there still remains plenty to satisfy the bargain hunter, the more so that, as the day goes on, fresh supplies are brought out; and the woman who is aware of such simple facts as that light silks cannot be stored for any length of time without becoming spotted, or that a very showy Paris model will generally be "marked down" to a third of its value, can often pick up, at any period of a genuine sale, articles for which she would have to pay at least fifty per cent. more under ordinary circumstances.

During the sales weeks of the year the assistants have scarcely time to breathe, and the pleasant room which the managers of most leading emporiums provide as a resting-place for their "young ladies" is practically deserted, the latter finding it as much as they can do to get their meals within an hour of the proper time.

Strangely enough, the *employés* of a drapery emporium rather like sale times, and it may be hinted that those shop assistants with any sense of humour thoroughly enjoy the experience, for all that is eccentric and peculiar in London femininity is there seen to most advantage. Again, the lady customer attending a sale is generally far less hard to

A CASH DESK.

please than she is on ordinary days; the delightful thought that she is acquiring a series of bargains—even if the articles purchased by her will never be of the slightest use to either herself or her family—filling her with unwonted self-satisfaction. Many more sensible people, however, wait patiently for sale time and deliberately buy with a view to what is to fill their wardrobe the following year; yet it is, from the manager's point of view, surprising to note how often a customer who has a chance of securing a real bargain in silk or fur will pass it by, and perhaps spend just as many pounds in purchasing cheap articles of wearing apparel—gloves, veils, and last, not least, blouses—which have only been "marked down" a few pence, or, in the case of a blouse, a couple of shillings.

Although a considerable strain is put on the parcels department, generally situated, by the way, under the showrooms, it is remarkable how many ladies, when attending a sale, are content to take away their purchases, even if the latter be great in bulk. They seem to think that they must secure their bargains at once. One type of customer whom the experienced saleswoman can detect almost at a glance is she who orders a great number of things to be paid for "on delivery," and who then instructs her parlourmaid or butler to refuse the parcels when they arrive the same evening or the next morning.

The shop-walker, that elegantly dressed individual who seems to the casual observer

A POSTAL ORDER ROOM.

to have so little to do, and yet who is considered so important a member of his staff by the managers of each emporium, finds his duties greatly lessened on the days of a sale. It is at ordinary times, when business is more or less slack, that the shop-walker who knows his business shows to advantage. It is he who then indicates to the hesitating customer where she may hope to find exactly what she is seeking, or, better still, where she may be persuaded to purchase some article of which she is not in any sense in want.

It has often been asserted that women cannot be taught the business side of life.

A SALE DAY AT PETER ROBINSON'S.

The best answer to this charge is that in the great drapery establishments the cash desk is almost always occupied by a girl clerk, who does her work well and civilly.

An important and profitable branch of the work performed each day concerns what may be called the shopping by post department. This is carried on in the Postal Order Room. Many country cousins have an account at a London shop, and all such important customers must be answered by return, and their wants, if it be in any way humanly possible, supplied.

On one side of life at the draper's it is not quite easy to touch, yet it plays a part of no small importance. Now and again, under " Police News," appears a paragraph stating that " Mrs. or Miss So-and-so, of such-and-such an address, was charged with stealing various articles, valued at so much, from Messrs. ——, Ltd." Of course, the world at large never hears of the innumerable cases when ladies, detected in appropriating more or less valuable articles from the counters and stands, are not taken in charge, either because they happen to be connected with old and valued customers, or, more often still, because it is extremely difficult to actually catch such persons in the act.

One method, often pursued by an intelligent and well-dressed shop-lifter, is to actually purchase and pay for, say, a pair of gloves, or a piece of real lace, and, while the shopwoman is obtaining change, or even when she is only making out the bill, the thief manages to pull over the counter several other pairs of gloves or pieces of lace, and then, stooping down, stuffs them into her hand-bag, which has been previously placed on the ground in readiness for the operation.

The true kleptomaniac, as differentiated from the ordinary thief, not content with taking a number of valuable articles from one counter, will go through the whole shop annexing pieces of dress material, rolls of silk, half-a-dozen pairs of stockings, veils, and even such articles as pairs of boots and shoes, not one of which will fit her! This type is far more easily detected and punished than her wiser and more artful sister who contents herself with only stealing articles from one counter, and who chooses pieces of valuable real lace, or lengths of beautiful embroidery, in preference to heavier or more cumbersome articles.

In connection with each emporium is a regular detective service, and during a big sale twelve to twenty detectives are present in the shop. At these times every drapery business loses, in spite of the vigilance on the part of the detectives, a great deal of real value, mostly in fur and lace.

It is difficult to over-estimate the responsibility borne during sale days by these detectives. Much is left to their discretion and tact, for it is not too much to say that the making on their part of a "mistake" —that is to say, the arresting of an innocent person—would do the establishment with which they are connected incalculable harm. So true is this, that often when a detective sees a lady walking off with, say, a valuable piece of lace, unless he has reason to suppose that the lady in question is really a professional thief, he simply follows her to the door, and, taking the article, which still bears the ticket on it, from her hand or from under her cloak, remarks suavely, " Excuse me, madam ; I will have this sent home for you." As a rule, the thief quickly disappears in the crowd, but if she is a hardened kleptomaniac she may reappear the very next day.

Once the day's work is over—that is, once the doors are closed—the young lady *employées* have the whole evening to play in or to work for themselves ; they also have Saturday afternoons from two o'clock. They are not, however, allowed to go out from Saturday to Monday unless they can show a letter from their parents authorising them to do so, and stating where they are going. Those young ladies who remain in have pleasant sitting-rooms in which to spend their time, and plenty of books and games ; while the young men have various forms of indoor amusements, including billiards, and on fine Saturday afternoons can enjoy the national games of cricket and football, large pieces of land near London having been secured for that purpose by several of the leading drapery firms.

A WELL-KNOWN ESTABLISHMENT IN ST. JAMES'S STREET.

HOUSE-HUNTING LONDON.

By GEORGE R. SIMS.

EVERY day in the year a certain number of people are consulting agents, or referring to the advertising columns of the newspapers, or driving or walking round the residential portions of London in search of a roof for their heads. The bulk of them are people who are already householders, but who wish to change their addresses. Sometimes the change is due to prosperity, sometimes to adversity, frequently to the increased accommodation required by the growing up of little boys and girls. In some cases, in fact in many cases, it is the mere desire for change. But we have not, fortunately, to concern ourselves with motives—our task is the lighter one of accompanying the Londoner in that series of adventurous expeditions commonly known as "house-hunting."

For the wealthier class there are West-End firms who undertake the whole business. These firms have always in their hands the letting of a certain number of first-class residences in the localities favoured by rank and fashion. The fashionable house-hunter cannot go very far afield in search of his new address. Society has certain quarters in which it keeps itself "to itself" as much as possible in these days of the millionaire, native and imported; therefore the fashionable house-hunter is confined to one of the aristocratic squares or streets of the West or South-West. These houses are not generally advertised, nor do they display as a rule the notice boards which allow the passer-by to know that they are to be let. They are placed in the hands of a firm whose speciality it is to deal in "town mansions." The people who desire such a property send to such a firm and request it to find them a residence. The firm indicates the residences on their books, and the rest is merely a matter for the solicitors of the two parties to the transaction. When the purchase or the leasing is completed the world is informed in the "Society" columns of the daily papers that Lord This or Lady That has taken Number So-and-so, Berkeley, or Cavendish, or Portman, or Eaton, or Grosvenor Square, or Park Lane, as the case may be.

Occasionally photographs are taken of resi-

HOUSE-HUNTING LONDON.

dential properties of the first class and may be seen in the front windows of, let us say, Messrs. E. and H. Lumley, in St. James's Street. The higher-class house furnishers are also house agents, and have generally on hand a number of photographs, thus enabling their clients to see what a house looks like without the trouble of going to it. If the photograph makes a good impression, personal inspection follows; but in some cases houses, principally furnished houses let for the season or a limited period, are taken for clients abroad who see their new home for the first time when they drive to it from the railway station.

But for the great body of house-hunters, the ordinary family folk who have many things to consider before their address is altered in the Post Office Directory, the process of house-hunting is at once more absorbing, more anxious, and more fatiguing.

The time has come when Mr. and Mrs. Horace Brown feel that their present house is not large enough for them. They started housekeeping two in family, with a couple of servants; now they are five in family, and they have three servants. Mr. Brown is in the City, and a busy man. He hates the idea of moving, but his wife has dinned into his ears morning, noon, and night that it is quite impossible they can stay where they are any longer, and has at last induced him to consent to the taking of a more desirable residence.

But he absolutely refuses to take any part in the preliminary search; he has his business to attend to. Once or twice on a Sunday he has been cajoled into taking a drive round the suburban district which Mrs. Brown "fancies" in order to look at the houses which are exhibiting boards; but none of them have seemed quite the thing, and he has declined to make any further sacrifice of his Sunday's rest to the contemplation of house agents' boards stuck up in front gardens; though these boards, as will be seen in our photographic illustration, "A Choice of Agents," sometimes make a brave show and furnish quite a large amount of reading.

So Mrs. Brown has to go hunting alone. Her instructions are to find the place

SHOWN INTO THE DRAWING-ROOM.

that will suit, and then Mr. Brown will try to get away from the City for an hour or two to look at it. It is an anxious time for poor Mrs. Brown. She reads the advertisements in the papers, she calls at house agents', she gets their lists, day after day she hurries off hither and thither to look at this desirable residence and that eligible villa; but there is always a "something." At one house which she would have liked very much there are an absurd number of fixtures to be taken; another, which is all that could be desired in the way of accommodation, is next door to a church with a powerful peal of bells. In

AN INSPECTION BY THE DOG.

he opens the door. Mrs. Brown boldly attacks the situation. She has come to see the house, and hands the man the agent's order to view. The man scowls, goes to the top of the stairs, and calls out, "'Lizer — somebody to see the 'ouse."

'Lizer appears, wiping her hands on her apron, takes the card gingerly, and flings open the dining-room door without a word. Mr. and Mrs. Brown look at the dining-room, exchange a few remarks in a low voice — nobody ever talks loudly while viewing an empty house, for there is always a sense of restraint in the process—and come out into the hall. 'Lizer flings open the door on the other side, and says, "Drorin' room." While Mr. and Mrs. Brown are looking at the drawing-room and mentally measuring it a baby begins to cry in the basement, and 'Lizer goes to the top of the stairs and shouts down some domestic instructions to her husband. When Mr. and Mrs. Brown come out of the drawing-room 'Lizer conducts them upstairs. She walks much after the manner of a clergyman preceding a coffin to the graveside. She flings open the bedroom doors one after the other. Presently she gathers from the remarks of the visitors that the house is likely to suit them, and instantly her manner changes. She becomes more friendly, she volunteers little communications as to the length of time the house has been empty, she thinks that the reason no one has taken it is that it is damp. She even confesses that she and her husband have suffered from rheumatism a good deal since they have lived in it. She doesn't quite *volunteer* this information, she allows it to be *dragged* from her as it were. Mr. Brown is impressed with her candour; Mrs. Brown is grateful. When the inspection is completed 'Lizer is presented with a couple of shillings. "Thank goodness that woman was honest," says Mr. Brown when he gets outside; "I shall save doctors' bills for the next seven years; for I *liked* the house."

another she discovers that the drainage is not above suspicion ; in yet another that a railway runs at the bottom of the garden, and that every ten minutes the " desirable residence " rocks with all the premonitory symptoms of an earthquake.

She goes back to the house agent and enters into fresh explanations, and he supplies her with a list of six houses, each of which he thinks will exactly suit her requirements. This time she insists on her husband accompanying her. She is most anxious to settle ; she wants his moral support in assisting her to a decision. Mr. Brown is grumpy, but eventually consents to sacrifice an afternoon, and they set out together.

The first house is empty, and in charge of a caretaker. The caretaker is a woman with two children and a husband. The husband is out of work, and at home ; he is smoking a pipe, and has it in his mouth when

HOUSE-HUNTING LONDON.

Inside, 'Lizer joins her husband in the kitchen. "They looked like taking it," she says; "but I told 'em it was terrible damp, and that settled 'em." The man heaves a sigh of relief. To have had to turn out just now would have been decidedly inconvenient.

The next house visited by the Browns is occupied. The family are still in it. The housemaid, who opens the door, looks at the card and says, "Oh, to see the house!" and vanishes, leaving the visitors standing in the outer hall.

When she returns she says, "This way, please," and opens a door. Mr. and Mrs. Brown are about to enter when they discover that members of the family are there. The members of the family try to look agreeable, but glare. Mr. and Mrs. Brown remain on the threshold and just peer in. "Thank you, that will do," says Mrs. Brown. The same process is repeated in the next room, where a young lady is practising at the piano. "I—er—think *you'd* better go and see the bedrooms," says Mr. Brown somewhat nervously to his better half; "I'll stay here." And he remains patiently in the hall, like a man who has brought a parcel from the draper's and is waiting for the money. The dog of the family suddenly appears and eyes him suspiciously. Mr. Brown feels rather nervous, especially as the dog approaches to make a closer scrutiny of his legs. For the first time in his life Mr. Brown is sorry he has never kept a dog; he has always understood that if you keep a dog strange dogs discover it quickly, and become friendly. Just as he is wondering whether it would not be wise to call for a member of the family, in order that it may be explained to the animal that he is not there with dishonest intentions, a young gentleman makes his appearance, and, hurriedly seizing the dog by the collar, drags him away and pushes him through the swing door at the top of the kitchen stairs. "Keep Bill downstairs," he calls out; "some people are looking over the house." Then he turns to Mr. Brown half apologetically. "'Bliged to be careful with him," he says; "he bit the washing man yesterday."

Presently Mrs. Brown comes downstairs, looking hot and flurried. "Do you want to go into the kitchen?" says the housemaid. "No—I—er—think not," Mrs. Brown stammers. Mr. Brown is greatly relieved. In a few seconds he and his wife are outside. "Oh, my dear," she says, "I didn't see the house, I only went into two bedrooms. The eldest daughter was lying down in one with a bad headache, and there was an old lady in the other—the grandmother I think—who has epileptic fits. She was in one then, and, of course, I said I wouldn't disturb her." "And I've nearly been bitten by a savage dog," exclaims Mr. Brown. "No more house-hunting for me!"

LET AS FAST AS BUILT.

A CHOICE OF AGENTS.

But the afternoon is still young, and a house *must* be found, so at last he is pacified, and calls with his wife at the next address. Here everything is satisfactory. The house is admirably adapted for their requirements; it is sunny, it is dry, there is an excellent garden, a good view from the windows, and the caretaker says there are two "parties" after it. Mr. Brown says, "Ah! this will do; we'll go to the agent's at once, and see about the fixtures, and settle." The agent is at the West-End. They take a hansom and drive to his place of business at once. On the way they discuss the rooms. Mr. Brown selects one for a smoking-room, Mrs. Brown decides on one with a sunny outlook for her boudoir. In two of the rooms the old carpets will fit, which is a great blessing. They arrive at the agent's, and inform the clerk that they will take Laburnum Villa. The clerk goes into the private office, and returns quickly. "Mr. —— is very sorry, sir, but he has just had a telegram to say a gentleman who looked over the house yesterday, and had the refusal till to-day, has wired to say he will take it."

What Mr. Brown says does not matter. Mrs. Brown feels inclined to cry. It is *so* annoying; and it is getting late. Instead of seeing any more houses, the Browns go home, and the evening repast is a gloomy one. Mr. Brown is "sick of the whole business." He talks wildly about staying where they are—they will have the children's beds moved into Mrs. Brown's room, and he will sleep in the coal cellar.

But with the morning comes reason, and more house-hunting. Eventually the Browns succeed in securing a house after their own hearts, and, after paying for about forty pounds' worth of fixtures which are of no earthly use to them, they move in. And once Mr. Brown declares that he won't move out or go house-hunting again as long as he lives.

Flats, with all their advantages, do not always retain their charm for Londoners. There is a great difficulty in getting good servants, for Mary Jane looks upon life on the third or fourth floor of a huge block of buildings as too far removed from the world below. In many flats the kitchen and the servants' rooms look out on back streets or back gardens, and so the servant difficulty forces many a flat family into house-hunting. Then comes the difficulty that the furniture of a flat does not always suit houses which are differently arranged, and generally much more spacious in their room measurement. The flat house-hunter therefore hunts generally for a house which can be fitted and furnished with the flat "belongings," and makes many anxious inquiries as to rates and taxes, which were covered by the flat rent. The flat people invariably want more garden than anyone else, because they have been without a garden for so long; and, having had the use of a lift, they look at stairs with a critical eye. To find a house that will satisfy the family moving from a flat is one of the house agents' most difficult tasks.

The small house-hunter is perhaps the most genuine hunter of all. She—it is generally the wife, for the husband is in employment and not his own master—covers ten miles in her search to the better class house-hunter's one. She has no agent to assist her, and not only is the rent a great consideration, but she must make sure that the 'bus or train service is convenient for her husband's daily journeys to and from his place of employment. As quarter day approaches the young wife becomes feverish in her anxiety. Notice has been given to her landlord, and another tenant has been secured. Visions of her household goods piled on a van with no address to be given to the driver, and herself and little ones homeless in the street on a pouring wet day, haunt her imagination. At last she is in the condition when she will take anything. She sees a place that will suit—though it is not *quite* what she would have liked—and she hopes and prays that it will remain vacant till Saturday, for on Saturday afternoon her husband can go and see it. If *he* says it will do, her principal terror is removed—men's ideas of houses differ so much from women's. At last the house is taken, and the references given. The references are a worry to many men who have no banker. It is a delicate thing to write to a friend in a good position and say "Will you be my reference?" As a rule, in small properties the last landlord's reference is sufficient. But many landlords ask for two. The second reference keeps many an honest man awake of nights just before quarter day.

The way in which the population of London drifts and changes, and flits from house to house and from neighbourhood to neighbourhood, is always wonderful, but the most remarkable feature of the "general post" which takes place on the great moving days —Lady Day and Michaelmas Day—is that all the new villa residences springing up in every direction around the Metropolis are snapped up almost before the slates are on them. Hardly are the windows in before a large "Let" is whited on them. The old neighbourhoods are still densely inhabited, the boards after quarter day are few and far between; but in some mysterious way a new population is continually entering the capital, and the stream of house-hunters spreads itself over neighbourhoods that a year previously were green fields and meadows and country lanes. A year later they will have their streets of thriving shops, their pawnbroker and hotel, their local Bon Marché, their telephone call office, and their local newspaper.

MOVING IN.

MUSIC-HALL LONDON.

By H. CHANCE NEWTON.

ONE of the most remarkable developments in Living London of late years is that of the modern music-halls—or Theatres of Varieties, as they are mostly called, except when they are described as Empires or Palaces. The variety form of entertainment now so prevalent is a real boon to those amusement-seekers who cannot, even if they would, indulge in playgoing at the so-called "regular" theatres. Working hours have for many to be continued until it is too late to reach home in time to come out again to the play—especially for those who are only able to afford unbookable seats.

For these hampered toilers the music-hall or variety form of entertainment is the only thing of the show kind available. They can take or leave the entertainment at any hour they please—the programme given being, of course, everything by "turns" and nothing long. Besides all this—and it is an important factor—there is the chance of enjoying a smoke, a luxury prohibited in all theatres run under the Lord Chamberlain's licence.

The most striking examples of the modern variety theatres in London are the Empire, the Alhambra, and the London Hippodrome. Next to these would undoubtedly rank those other popular West-End resorts, the Palace Theatre, the Oxford, the Tivoli, and the London Pavilion, together with the more recently established Coliseum and the converted Lyceum Theatre.

The Empire is one of the most beautiful buildings, as regards its interior, to be found in the Metropolis. Its entertainment is of a high class, and its gorgeous ballets and other extensive and expensive spectacular productions are patronised not only, in addition to its large general audience, by our "gilded youth," but by all sorts of society folk.

The Alhambra—a huge Moorish building—is, in its status and its style of entertainment, similar to the Empire, with the difference that it claims—and rightly—precedence of all neighbouring places of the sort. Indeed, its own proud description is, "The Premier Variety Theatre of London." This house was certainly the first to introduce the big ballet and spectacular form of entertainment. For many years a large proportion of visitors to the Metropolis made the Alhambra their first variety "house of call." Nowadays, however, these visitors must perforce take in the Empire and the other important variety palaces.

A few steps from these huge halls is the London Hippodrome, one of the most remarkable buildings in the great city. Although so close to the Empire and the Alhambra, the entertainments and the audiences are of a totally different character. The Hippodrome programme is principally made up of equestrian, gymnastic, and menagerie "turns," plus a burletta or pantomime. This last must include at least one aquatic scene of some sort, in which the comedians (most of them expert swimmers) disport on or in the large lake which, by a wonderful mechanical process, when required, fills up the circus ring. The Hippodrome's audiences are not of the lounging "after dinner" or "round the town" kind, but are in a great measure formed of family groups, headed by pater or mater, or both. Indeed, most of its patrons are of the sedate domestic sort. There is no doubt that the fact of the Hippodrome being, like so many of the new large variety theatres, forbidden a liquor licence, is in itself (however unfair it may seem) an attraction for most of those who take their youngsters to such entertainments. The Hippodrome—the auditorium of which is a sight—resembles the Alhambra and the Empire in one respect, namely that not a few of its artistes are foreigners, and that many of its performances are in dumb show. Our photographic illustration on page 224 depicts a scene beneath the arena of the Hippodrome. Here are heavy wooden

READY TO PASS IN ("WONDERLAND").

WAITING TO GO ON AT A MUSIC-HALL.

"properties" about to be conveyed above, while "supers" and stage hands are crowded together in readiness for their particular duties.

The Oxford, the Tivoli, and the London Pavilion are likewise sumptuous if somewhat smaller establishments. At these resorts, however, comic and "serio" singing, sandwiched with short acrobatic, dancing, and trick cycling "acts," and fifteen or twenty minutes' sketches, are the rule. The best available artistes are engaged at these three houses. Oftentimes the same "stars" appear on the same evening at the three halls, which are virtually run by one syndicate. When a comic or a "serio" "star" books an engagement with this syndicate, he or she is required to stipulate by contract not to appear at any other hall within a radius of so many miles. This "barring out" clause, as it is called, has also of late prevailed in connection with certain of the larger music halls in suburban London.

The Palace Theatre, in Shaftesbury Avenue, is a beautiful building, which was opened by Mr. D'Oyley Carte as the English Opera House. In spite of such excellent operatic works as Sir Arthur Sullivan's *Ivanhoe* and André Messager's *La Basoche*, Fortune frowned upon the enterprise. Ere long Sir Augustus Harris transformed it into a variety theatre, with its present name. Its entertainment is one of the best of its class, not only as regards its singers and dancers, pantomimists, mimics, sketch artists, and others of all nations and denominations, but also its beautiful and realistic biograph pictures.

At the Coliseum, which has an electric revolving stage, four performances are given daily, the entertainment being principally singing and dancing; while the Lyceum, with its two "houses" a night, resembles what are called "Empires." In each cheap seats are the rule.

It is no wonder that the old-time stuffy music-hall has been killed by such places as the splendid variety houses referred to, to say nothing of those other large and admirably conducted halls such as the Royal in Holborn, the Metropolitan in the Edgware Road, the Canterbury in the densely crowded Lambeth district, and the Paragon in the still more densely crowded Mile End region.

Besides these resorts there have sprung up several vast "Empires" such as those respectively at New Cross, Holloway, Stratford, Shepherd's Bush, and Hackney, all

BENEATH THE ARENA (HIPPODROME).

under the direction of the wealthy syndicate that runs the London Hippodrome and a number of "Empires" in the provinces.

If one should desire to get some notion of how the "toiling, moiling myrmidons" (as Béranger calls them) patronise these new "Empires," he has only to watch outside any of them just before the doors are opened for the first or second "house." For be it noted that two entire performances are given at each nightly, and at small prices of admission. Moreover, the programmes always contain several highly-paid variety artistes—whether of the comic singing, acrobatic, canine, or sketch kind. Indeed, it is not at all unusual to find here a favourite performer in receipt of at least one hundred pounds per week; not to mention this or that leading serio-comic lady or "Comedy Queen" at a salary not much lower. Yet, in spite of such princely salaries, the prices of admission are small, ranging, say, from two shillings or eighteenpence in the best parts to threepence in the gallery.

That these "Empires," "Palaces," and similar halls are run not only with excellent programmes but also on strictly proper lines is proved by the fact that, moderate though the admission prices may be, the patrons come from some of the best parts of Hampstead, Stoke Newington, Catford, Blackheath, Woodford, and so forth. Here recreation-seekers may—and do—have placed before them all sorts of "turns" besides those above-mentioned, and comprising many examples, such as conjurers, acrobats, performing elephants, seals, bears, instrumentalists—comic and otherwise. Often will be found old stagers or juvenile performers of dramatic sketches, sometimes made up of boiled-down plays—even of *Hamlet*, in a twenty-minutes' version of that play.

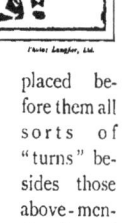

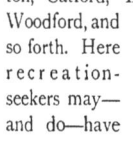

To those amusement-seekers who may prefer to take their variety entertainment in a rough-and-ready form there are still such haunts as that Whitechapel resort fancifully named "Wonderland." In this big hall are provided entertainments of the most extraordinary description. They include little plays, songs, and sketches, given first in Yiddish dialect and afterwards translated into more or less choice English by, as a rule, a Hebraic interpreter. This interpreter often improves the occasion by calling the attention of kind—and mostly alien—friends in front to certain side shows consisting of all sorts of armless, legless, skeleton, or spotted "freaks" scattered around the recesses of this great galleryless hall. When once the "freaks" have been examined, or the "greeners" and other foreign and East-End "sweated" Jew toilers have utilised the interval to indulge in a little light refreshment according to their respective tastes, the Yiddish sketches and songs—comic and otherwise—are resumed until "closing time."

TYPES OF MUSIC-HALL PERFORMERS.

It is, however, on its Boxing Nights (which in this connection means

Mondays and Saturdays) that "Wonderland" is to be seen in its most thrilling form. Then it is indeed difficult either to get in or to get out. In the first place it is hard to get in because of the great crowds of hard-faring—often hard-faced—East-End worshippers of the fistic art; several types of which are to be seen in our photographic illustration on page 223. In the second place, if you do contrive to get in you speedily find yourself so hemmed in by a sardine-like packed mob that all egress seems hopeless.

Several other extremely typical East-End variety resorts, each of a totally different kind, are close at hand. One is the huge Paragon Theatre of Varieties, further east in the Mile End Road. Another is the much smaller Cambridge Music-Hall, which is in Commercial Street, a little way westward from Toynbee Hall. There are also the Queen's Music-Hall at Poplar, the Royal Albert at Canning Town, and the Eastern Empire at Bow.

In spite of its cheap prices and its seething audiences, the Paragon entertainment is exactly on a par with those given in the West-End and South of London Variety Theatres. Indeed, the entertainment at the Paragon is mostly identical with that supplied at the Canterbury, Westminster Bridge Road, and is under the same syndicate. As for the Canterbury, the better class South London tradesfolk and toilers go there, excepting, of course, when they visit the newer and equally well managed South of London variety shows.

The Cambridge Music-Hall, between Spitalfields and Shoreditch, deserves a few special lines. In point of fact, ever since the time when, years ago, it was converted from a synagogue into a music-hall, the Hebrew residents of the locality have made it a point of honour to attend the Cambridge. With them they often bring not only their wives, but also their black-curled, black-eyed infants, who may often be seen toddling calmly about the stalls — especially during the earlier of the two "houses" per night.

Round the corner in Shoreditch is the London Music-Hall, wherein the stranger who pays his first visit will undoubtedly fancy for the nonce that he has lost his way and has by accident strayed into one of the best West-End halls.

PERFORMING DOGS.

Further north there are several more or less large and more or less "classy" variety houses: for example, the two "houses" per night resort, the Euston, opposite St. Pancras Station; the Bedford, in Camden Town; the Islington Empire, which is next door to the Agricultural Hall; the old-established music-hall, Collins's, on Islington Green; and the newer Palaces at Walthamstow and Tottenham.

The west-central district and southern suburbs are also well provided for in a music-hall sense. Among others, one notes the old Middlesex, or "Mogul," in Drury Lane; the Granville, at Walham Green; Empires at Balham and Deptford; an Empress at Brixton; a Royal Standard at Pimlico; and a Star at Bermondsey; and Palaces at Camberwell, Chelsea, the London Road (Southwark), and Croydon. To add to the number, the old Surrey Theatre is now run on music-hall lines. Besides these may be mentioned Gatti's in Westminster Bridge Road, a Grand at Clapham Junction, and a Palace at Hammersmith.

Like the halls themselves, the agents who supply the managers with artistes at so much per cent. commission on the salaries have, too, not only much improved in character, but have in many cases migrated from their former dingy haunts in the York Road, Lambeth, to more commodious—not to say palatial — offices in or around the Strand, the Haymarket, and elsewhere. Some few of them, however, still have their offices near a well-known tavern at a corner of York Road; and at certain hours a large number of minor music-hall entertainers and their agents may—as shown in the above illustration—still be seen congregating near this old-established hostelry.

Music-hall "artistes" (as they love to call themselves) have also vastly improved. Not many years ago these were mostly shiftless and thriftless from the "stars" downward.

Nowadays the music-hall ranks include large numbers of the worthiest of citizens. And, what is still better, they have combined together of late years to organise several protective associations, such as the Variety Club and the Music-Hall Railway Rates Association, as well as to found some excellent charities for benefiting their brethren out of health—or out of work—and to provide for the widows and orphans of comrades who have fallen by the way.

The chief of these charities is the Music-

AT THE CORNER OF YORK ROAD.

Hall Benevolent Fund, a very fine organisation, the committee of which consists of many of the most important and most honourable men to be found in any department of life. From time to time the smaller associations assist their parent fund, or the Music-Hall Home for the Sick and Aged, by arranging matinées or sports. In the case of the Music-Hall Railway Rates Association all the surplus of the money subscribed thereto for the purposes of getting the fares reduced for travelling "artistes" is handed over to one or other of the aforesaid charities.

And though the members of the smaller music-hall societies delight to call themselves by such names as "Water Rats," "Terriers," and "J's," and to dress themselves as ostriches, savages, cowboys, Red Indians, and so on at their annual sports, or to disport as comic cricketers in all sorts of extraordinary costumes—what does it matter, seeing that they do it all for charity's sake? Thus, by drawing vast crowds of the general public, they add substantially to the funds of their excellent charities.

As will be seen from the photographic illustration on page 223, the "behind the scenes" life of Music-Hall London is not without its humours. In "Waiting to Go On" we have, indeed, a motley throng of variety "turns." These include a famous "serio" in Early Victorian "dandy" costume; a popular "comic" in the usual battered hat and ill-fitting clothes which such comedians always adopt; a celebrated conjurer, a couple of clever "descriptive" singers, a noted strong man, and several others. This "Waiting to Go On" represents, of course, quite a different state of things from the arrangements in a regular theatre, where every entrance and exit is fixed, and where the players have to report themselves, as a rule, some time before the curtain rises. Music-hall entertainers must, if they wish to earn a remunerative amount per week, do three or four "turns" a night; and in order to travel from hall to hall, a brougham—or, in the case of a troupe, a private omnibus —. has to be provided. When they arrive they are naturally in a hurry to get their work over, and are apt to get in each other's way, either in the dressing-room or at the wings. As most music-hall entertainers start from home already "made up," and even sometimes "change" in their vehicles *en route*, it does not take them long to be ready for their respective "turns"; and their punctuality is remarkable.

To sum up, it may in common fairness be said that without its Palaces of Variety and its Music-Halls Living London would only be half alive.

BEFORE THE DOORS OPEN
(LONDON PAVILION).

ATTACKED BY TWO.

HOOLIGAN LONDON.

By CLARENCE ROOK.

IF you will take a walk—it will be a pretty long one—round the inner circle of London, and keep your eyes open, you will see many interesting things. And, if your eyes are open for human character rather than for buildings or historical associations, there is one type that will probably remain as a lasting impression. Start from the Elephant and Castle, and work westward through Lambeth, cross the river to Chelsea, fetch Notting Hill in the circuit round by the Euston Road and Pentonville, and then take Bethnal Green on your way down to the Commercial Road, and back again across the Tower Bridge for a glance at the Old Kent Road and Walworth and the Borough.

Whatever else you fail to notice on that walk, you will scarcely fail to notice this: the persistence of a particular type of boy. He is somewhere between fourteen and nineteen years of age, but he is undersized and underfed. You will find him selling newspapers, or sitting on the tail of a van, or loafing among the cabs at a stand; you will find him playing pitch-and-toss, with a sentry on the look out for prying policemen, on any convenient bit of waste ground; or you may spy him at a game of cards—more especially on Sunday—on a deserted barge in the Pool. But you will not find him among the crowds that come at twelve and six o'clock out of the factories, or filter at odd hours from the big printing establishments. The boy of this special type which you cannot fail to notice has no fixed purpose or permanent employment, and he shows it in his face. He has found no place in the orderly evolution of society. He is a member of his Majesty's Opposition—the permanent Opposition to law and order which every big city develops.

Before you cross the river again on your return journey, look a little closer. It is Saturday night, when half London is at leisure, and the other half ministering to its demand for "bread and games." The man who keeps the big coffee-stall near the end of the bridge is making ready for his customers; and the policeman who stands hard by stamps his feet to keep them warm. He is not permitted to take a walk, for it is his business to see that the disorder about the coffee-stall does not pass reasonable limits. But things are quiet enough at present, and the man in a reefer jacket, shoulders slightly hunched and elbows close to the side, which marks the London street boy. The policeman at the coffee-stall looks knowingly at them as they pass. He knows well enough that the belt which this boy is carefully tightening serves other purposes

PITCH AND TOSS.

bowler hat, and thick boots, who ostentatiously ignores the policeman, is quite conspicuously a plain clothes constable. Now and then, among the strollers and the women returning from market, there passes along a boy—sometimes two or three together—walking swiftly and with evident purpose. They are not nicely dressed; though the night is cold there is not an overcoat among them; but their jackets are buttoned tight, neckcloths supply the place of collars, and they walk with the curious light tread, than that of dress; he knows that the unusual stiffness of that boy's arm is probably due to the presence of an iron bar up the sleeve. But there is no law which compels the wearing of braces instead of belts, and the policeman, from experience of his own, deduces the task which lies before some of his colleagues across the river.

On the other side of the bridge these furtive figures scatter through the streets to left and right; for they are moving to an attack on Pentonville, all directed by one master mind. These are the boys from the Borough who have developed a feud with the boys of Pentonville, and their leader, a lad of seventeen, with a chopper in his breast pocket and some notion of tactics in his head, has foreseen the position of the enemy and designs to place him between two fires. A quarter of an hour later the movement has been developed. The Pentonville boys have been caught in one of those little streets off the Goswell Road. Belts are off, and the buckles swinging; sleeves lose their stiffening of iron; here and there a fortunate boy has a cheap pistol, which startles quiet citizens and occasionally kills them. The fighting is independent of the Geneva Convention; there are no rules, only a general desire, born of the instinct of self-preservation, to get at once to close quarters, for fist and muscle are less deadly than buckle and bar and pistol. Then come the police— if there are enough within earshot. But that is generally after the fight is decided, and only the wounded appear next morning at the police-court and give texts for letters to the papers. The rest scatter and run, to gather again at the river. And if you are at the aforesaid coffee-stall at one in the morning you may see and hear the whooping victors wheeling back the disabled leader on a barrow—doubtless borrowed.

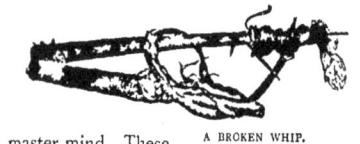

That is a typical instance of the feuds which rage between the street boys of the various London districts. In this case the cause of war was the oldest in the world, a Borough Helen abstracted by a Pentonville Paris. But these mysterious feuds exist, and are fought out, between many London districts, and there are times when a Lisson Grove boy would go east of Tottenham Court Road at his peril. All round London these gangs are ready for provocation. The organisation is loose, and depends mainly on some masterful spirit of lawlessness in direct succession to the original Patrick Hooligan, of Lambeth. But whether at Bethnal Green or Wandsworth, Pentonville or Fulham, so soon as the King of Misrule arises the ground of quarrel is assured.

Sometimes the leader of a gang develops qualities of organisation and command which inspire respect among the police, who know quite well that the Hooligan is always on the verge of crime, and often topples over. Such was the head of a gang which terrorised Lambeth. He was only about seventeen years of age, but he had had a thoroughly good criminal education, and, while he had effected a burglary or two, picked up his living mainly by petty thieving. But he had acquired a remarkable influence over the boys of Lambeth. He made it a point of honour for every boy who aspired to membership of his gang to show a shattered window, a smashed door, or a broken head—the broken head opened the way, as it were, to a commission in the gang. He had no settled residence; that were unadvisable; but the boys knew where to find him and ask for their orders for the day. And he collected about him as enterprising and capable a horde of young ruffians as you could wish to avoid on a winter's evening.

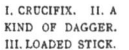

For this lawlessness inevitably leads to crime. Street fighting is fun; but why should not the lessons it teaches be turned to profit? From cracking heads for love to bashing "toffs" for gain is a short step, and the boy who has served his apprenticeship in a gang—such as that of Lambeth—is quite willing and able to commit an unprovoked assault on another's enemy for half-a-crown down and another half-a-crown when the job is done. And we often read the result in the "police intelligence" without a thought of the power of the capitalist who has five shillings and an enemy. Nor is the step from street fighting to highway robbery much longer. Imagine a couple of boys, brought up to the street fighting in which there are no rules, with no fear of God, man, or constable before their eyes, and with no money in their pockets—imagine them face to face with a lonely wayfarer in evening dress, carrying presumably a watch and a sovereign purse. It is the simplest thing in the world. One boy whips the overcoat back and imprisons the victim's arms; the other goes through the pockets. The work of a moment, and so easy! No wonder the Hooligan turns his sport to account! The sandbag, too, is handy. It is an American importation, and has made some reputation in New York. Unlike the bludgeon, it leaves no visible mark; unlike the cheap pistol, it makes no noise. It is easily hidden up the sleeve till required; and a well-directed crack over the head with a sandbag—especially if the sand has been damped—will stun the strongest man for several minutes. Not only gain, but also revenge, is a motive for the Hooligan assault, and the existence of a gang which had not been suspected was proved by the following letter which—marked "urgent"—turned up beneath the nose of an editor of a morning paper:—

"Sir,—For your ——— cheek in put one of our gang away we have Past a Rule that we will have your Life you will not know when we will be in your Liver tomorrow Saturday."

This note, grubby from the hand that delivered it, was signed by the name of the boy who was "Secterary" to the Camberwell gang. The editor is still alive. But shortly afterwards, in the small hours of the morning, one of the compositors was set upon and nearly killed by a gang of boys who caught him at the southern end of Blackfriars Bridge.

The Hooligan is a worshipper of muscle, quite apart from criminal application, and to him the latest hero of the ring is a god. His saints are the wearers of the gloves in those obscure boxing contests which take place, mostly on Saturday night, in all kinds of dim holes and corners of London, where if you wear a collar you are assumed to be a detective. There is one of these places tucked away under a railway arch in a certain dark street off Lambeth Walk. You enter through a sort of hole in a big gateway, and after stumbling forward tumble into a square room, lighted by a flaring gas-jet swung from the roof. Space is limited, and you sit close packed around the square—which is called a ring. Row upon row of eager faces; eyes fixed on the proprietor, in whose breast is locked the secret of the next fight. The lowest row is composed of the youngest—those who came first. Above are men who have fought their fights and apparently lost them. Highest of all appear the cap of an inspector of police and the helmet of a constable, for we are within the rules. The boys step into the ring; their names are announced—not their real names, for the ring's traditions are as insistent as those of the stage, and with better reason. But the inspector, cocking an eye at the boy who turns out in fighting tights with a torso as clean and bright as a new pin, recognises the boy he knows as a grimy, grubby loafer in the street. Absolute cleanliness and neatness of attire are a point of honour in the obscurest boxing saloon, and that is something in its favour.

It is a disillusion to see these boys, so lithe and clean in their fighting trim, huddle on their trousers and coat—they do it in a corner raked by the eyes of the audience —tie the wisp of cloth round their necks, and revert to the slavery of their usual habit. But the most remarkable feature of this saloon—and of others of its kind—is the expectant row of juniors, who got the front places by waiting. At the least hint of a hitch, if an expected combatant delays a moment in facing his antagonist, half-a-dozen coats are off, half-a-dozen shirts are pulled over head, and half-a-dozen clean, trained, eager boys are calling out "I'll tike 'im on." For these boys who sit patiently night by night are waiting to get a foot

HOOLIGAN *V.* HOOLIGAN.

on the first rung of Fame's ladder, and are not going to miss a chance. Some day, if luck is theirs, they will box at "Wonderland" in the Whitechapel Road, where the audience is numbered by hundreds and wears collars; and if the luck holds at the National Sporting Club, where the audience wears evening dress.

To catch the street boy in his softer mood you need not wait for a Bank Holiday or travel so far as Hampstead, much less to Epping Forest. On Saturday evenings they stand in long lines at the gallery doors of the less fashionable theatres and music-halls, having somehow acquired the price of two seats apiece. For every boy who has started life on his own account considers it a point of honour to possess a girl. The girls who stand at the gallery door waiting for the treat which they demand of their cavaliers are neither particularly clean and tidy nor very picturesque. They wear the clothes in

SANDBAGGING IN THE FOG.

which they work all the week at cardboard-box making, jam packing, match making, and so on—with the addition of the feathered hat which is the glory of a woman in this rank of life. But, on the whole, they are reasonably good. And it is a curious fact that the Hooligan boy seldom finds an ally in his girl when he wants to be flagrantly dishonest. She does not ask too many questions—she does not, for instance, inquire where he got the money to pay for a hot supper after the entertainment; but she would prefer to think that her boy is "in work" and "earning good money," and she is perfectly capable of maintaining that proposition—with tooth and claw, if need be—against any other lady who presumes to doubt it.

The street boy of the type I have tried to describe is full of a certain spasmodic nervous energy, but he has neither ballast nor settled purpose in life beyond the present day. Long ago the Ragged School Union set to work to catch this continual growth of possible criminals and train it aright; and to-day the energetic Secretary from the centre influences many institutions and workers. Our illustrations suggest some of the difficulties encountered in Hoxton by a devoted teacher who to this day is engaged in making silk purses out of unpromising material, with no little success. The waist-belt near the top of page 231, for example, was laid about the teacher's head by a voluntary scholar who had changed his mind about the charm of education. The loaded stick at the foot of the same page is a relic of a great street fight outside the school; the missing piece was broken off over a victim's head. But perhaps the quaintest of this little collection is the crucifix. It is the offering of an apostate of eleven. He had joined a High Church club. But the world called him; he enlisted under the leader of the Hoxton gang at the time, and, having chosen the life of disorder, presented his teacher with the symbol which had ceased to symbolise.

A further impetus to the movement started by the Ragged School Union was given by the institution of Toynbee Hall, in memory of Arnold Toynbee, of Balliol. The public schools and the universities caught up the idea of "boys' clubs" which should be impregnated with something of the public-school spirit. At present East, South-East, and North-East London are the main seats of these settlements, while London is breeding boys from Wimbledon to Leytonstone whom careless parents throw upon the streets so soon as they can run alone. Oxford House is a notable centre. It owes its success to Dr. Ingram, who before becoming Bishop of London was Bishop of Stepney. Go down to Bethnal Green—on a Saturday evening for choice—and at Oxford House you will find an interesting dining-hall and common-room. They are all of them young graduates. Some are barristers or journalists at work all day at their own affairs; others are intending clergymen who wish to take a close look at the souls they shall save. A hurried meal, a snatched smoke, and they scatter to the clubs where they have to take control.

We will go to one, typical of many, within a short walk of Oxford House. It is in a quiet street, but near the door boys with knitted brows are hanging about. The entrance fee is sixpence; and just inside a genial official is receiving this sum—usually in pennies—from a new member. We go upstairs, and find a room full of boys playing billiards and bagatelle. There is an evident effort for cleanliness and neatness in attire. One lad with a note-book marks down the games and takes the money; for the club is run, under supervision, by the members, and public spirit is strong against peculation or disorder. We go further, led by the sound of tramping feet, and find the newest recruits to the cadet corps at their drill. One of them, in an interval, tells you he has just joined the football club, having secured an income of a halfpenny a week. He is fifteen, he says. He would pass for twelve on a railway, and for eleven in an Eton preparatory school; the London street boy is terribly undersized. In the basement we reach the theatre, where the minstrels of the club perform; here, too, we find a boy solemnly punching the ball —for as boys will fight anyhow, they may as well join the club and learn to box at an initial and final outlay of one shilling, under the sanction of the Church and the Queensberry rules. But the boy who joins the Webbe Institute may get a great deal at cost price. He may even get a week in a seaside camp every August. This is only one of the clubs which are scattered about the confines of the inner circle. And music, too! The drums and fifes cease for a minute, and you see the contingent of cadets join the main body and march off to the evening service at St. Matthew's Church, clean, erect, and enlisted from the forces of disorder on the side of law and right.

A STREET GROUP.

MANAGER RECEIVING GUESTS (HOTEL VICTORIA).

HOTEL LONDON.

By J. C. WOOLLAN.

PAGE.

HOTEL London is great and growing. Perhaps no feature of London life was more conspicuous for a smart advance in the closing years of the last century and the opening of the new than hotel accommodation of every variety, and what might be called the hotel habit — the living in hotels of even Londoners themselves. There was a time, not so very long ago, when London had to bear the reproach of giving less satisfaction in the hotel way to the visitor than almost any other great city. Even yet the foreigner has his complaints to make, especially when he comes to settle the bill, but in a general way the Metropolis has responded excellently to an increasing demand To-day she can fling at the cities of the European and American continents a boast that she will name twenty of her hotels, and challenge each of her rivals to produce twenty that are better, or even as good.

You may never have reflected, and perchance may not have had the materials for reflection, upon how vast and of what infinite variety is the Hotel London of to-day. Let us consider the first of the two points just named, and estimate in some small way the dimensions of Hotel-land within the confines of the capital.

The most careful of calculations brings one to the safe conclusion that there are daily no fewer than 120,000 visitors in the Metropolis. Not all of these stay over a single night, and of those who do a fair proportion welcome the hospitality of friends in private houses. Yet, when all deductions have been made and we have fined the figures down to those of the net hotel and boarding-house population, it is discovered that there are, on an average, between 50,000 and 60,000 people who daily come within this category. Of this great number it is reckoned that the recognised hotels, licensed and of varying pretensions, are capable of accommodating just about half, and the boarding-houses and private hotels are well able to account for the rest, existing as they do in their thousands. It has been found in actual practice that over 8,000 guests have slept in twenty of the chief hotels on busy nights of the season. One single hotel has about 1,000 bedrooms, and there are five others with 500 or more. A dozen of the chief hotels make up an aggregate of only a few short of 6,000 bedrooms, a proportion of which contain a couple of beds, so that in the whole these sleeping apartments will very likely accommodate 12,000 people—the population of a small town. And the directory gives you the names of over 300 big licensed hotels in London.

The story of the growth of Hotel London to these vast proportions is tinged with not a little of romance. Once upon a time there was an enterprising servant in a West-End mansion, which he forsook in order that he might start a boarding-house. The latter in due course developed into an hotel, and the hotel so thrived and grew that to-day it is one of the biggest in the Metropolis, whilst the quondam servant, for his part, is a rich country gentleman with large lands. He is not alone in his great success. And on the other hand, showing again the vast outcome of the enterprise of the pioneers in the making of modern Hotel London, it may be cited that a score of the chief hotels among them represent a capital of about eight millions of money, and even the little group of Gordon Hotels are capable of accounting for three and a-half millions.

But it is not our purpose to weary with statistics, though such few as are in the foregoing lines will be pardoned for the tale of immensity which they alone can tell. We will discover now the variety of our Hotel London, and the even greater variety of its patrons. Each hotel is not for every patron. The Americans have claimed the biggest; and have, indeed, made the success of some of them. The Germans preponderate at others, and there is another where we may find a regular *potpourri* of highly respectable foreigners of different nationalities. Such is De Keyser's Royal, at the eastern extremity of the Victoria Embankment. Do not even the names of the hotels of the west tell their own little tales of foreign individuality and of cosmopolitanism? There are the Hotel Continental and the Hotel de l'Europe with expansive titles; but there are so many others, many of which you may not know, but all by their names alone making a mute and often successful appeal to particular classes.

However, with this brief general survey, let

ARRIVAL OF AN ORIENTAL POTENTATE (CLARIDGE'S).

us particularise. With the duty we owe to rank let us return to the kings and nobles, and see where they most do congregate.

You may find their majesties at two or three places in the fashionable west. Some time or other they are certain to be at the pre-eminently aristocratic Claridge's, in Brook Street, away from all the din and bustle, and in an atmosphere which is positively scented with exclusiveness and distinction. There are not many hotels in the world which have the extremely restrictive peculiarity of Claridge's. This is no place for the mere man of money, who is nothing more than that—with not even a social aim. Whatever king he be, he may live here and move about in no disguise and with perfect freedom from any vulgar gaze. For here, tenanting the grand and costly suites of rooms, are men and women who are numbered amongst the foremost of their respective lands, men and women who would make up for this king a court of which he might well be proud. There is an English duke, a Spanish princess, a Russian grand duke, a variety of counts, several leaders of London society, and, generally, a collection of people in whose veins runs the best blue blood of every nation. Wealth, rank, and power are represented. On a winter's evening, as we pass along the street, a carriage with a fresh arrival rattles up to the entrance, and with a passing fancy that we will stake the reputation of Claridge's, as it were, on this one haphazard throw, we pause a moment to discover the new comer. Claridge's wins. The American Ambassador has just arrived from Washington, and has driven straight to Claridge's, where he will stay for a few weeks. Another time an Oriental potentate comes driving up, and with some form and ceremony and his own native servant in attendance he passes within.

Yet even Claridge's has not a monopoly of the greatest. You may find royalty and nobles at the Albemarle, in Piccadilly, or at Brown's, in Dover Street, or at the Langham, in Langham Place, upon which King Edward, when Prince of Wales, set the aristocratic stamp by opening. The grand and highly fashionable Carlton is, again, one of the most likely places in London for the foreign potentate or the social star of home to be temporarily housed in, especially if there is a desire to be, in the colloquial term, "in the thick of it." In the Palm Court here one may lounge to perfection amongst the best-known people of at least two continents. Different celebrities, too, have their own conservative tastes and their own hotels; and there are old-fashioned country families, most highly respectable, who would prefer to pay Claridge's and Carlton prices at hostelries of far less renown but of guaranteed "tone."

To leave the rank and fashion pure, and seek the greater rendezvous of wealth and luxury we must proceed a trifle eastward and southward, dip down to Trafalgar Square and Northumberland Avenue, and walk a few score paces along the Strand. In the maintenance of such hotel luxury as we are speaking of the American contribution preponderates. Our cousins of the States are a very notable factor indeed of Hotel London. At the opening of the bright summer season they arrive with their trunks and their money in thousands, till the Transatlantic accent hums in the region to which we have just passed. Always for the biggest, their first thought is for the Cecil; and so pass into the courtyard any fine morning in the season, and walk up to the tables and chairs at the foot of the steps, where the loungers recline preparatory to their day's assault upon the lions of London, and you will not need to search for the man with the American voice, or for the girl with American smartness. They are everywhere—here outside, inside, there still dallying at the breakfast table, penning picture postcards in the writing-room, and—just a few thirsty souls are these —sipping iced concoctions downstairs at the American bar. There is special accommodation for the American, even to the chef. This middle-aged man, with the kindly face and the grey moustache, stepping into a hansom is a great American railroad king who means to revolutionise railway London; the slight dark figure in the porch is that of a man who is an engineer of monopolies and trusts. These are men who are feared. The richly-apparelled lady who is sweeping along a corridor is an American society woman who recently gave a dinner in New York which cost twenty pounds a head.

You will discover also a great American

THE HOTEL CECIL.

I. PORTER. II. THE PALM COURT (CARLTON HOTEL). III. SMOKING ROOM (GRAND HOTEL).
IV. CHAMBERMAID. V. LIFT MAN. VI. COMMERCIALS "WRITING UP THE MAIL" (MANCHESTER HOTEL).

contingent, as well as a fine smattering of other nationalities, at the Métropole, the Victoria, and the Grand—all Gordons, all in Northumberland Avenue, and all palatial and luxurious. The great First Avenue in Holborn and the Grosvenor at Victoria are also Gordons. Well-to-do Frenchmen, well-to-do Germans, and many besides are here in numbers; but then, as has been said, De Keyser's Royal, on the Embankment, is the particular resort of the Continental visitor. Germans are here in force, and if you move still more eastward and come to Finsbury Square you will find a further batch of hotels with great German reputations. Klein's and Seyd's are in the Square, and Buecker's is also there. In Finsbury Square, where beef is "bif," the sons of the Fatherland may live precisely after the manner of the German fighting cock.

Other nationalities, other hotels; and many more, especially in the east, could be added to this already long list. In these followings of the foreigner we are neglecting the strangers of our own country who are temporarily within the hospitable gates of the Metropolis.

Whence comes the provincial? We discover that he comes very largely viâ the termini at Euston, St. Pancras, and King's Cross, and here we find the great railway companies have raised palaces for his temporary residence. The railway hotel is essentially the hotel for the busy man who must live in style and comfort, but who is always catching express trains, or who in catching but a few must make a quick certainty of them. Of course, such hotels as the Midland Grand—truly grand—the Euston, and the Great Central are for other people besides—for families and for pleasure folk as well. All sorts and conditions of British people, but especially business people, are here. One of the greatest financiers of modern times has worked his deals from a suite of rooms in the Midland Grand, and such is high commercial loyalty that in another suite may be found a celebrated director of the Midland Railway itself. At Charing Cross Station is another railway hotel, and at Cannon Street, in the heart of the City, one more—which is perhaps the most businesslike of all, for a long programme of big company meetings is negotiated here every day. Shareholders have

DRAWING ROOM (HOTEL CECIL).

rejoiced and sorrowed, congratulated and stormed, in the Cannon Street Hotel as in no other. Then there is the more purely commercial hostelry, of which the Manchester, in Aldersgate Street, the Salisbury, off Fleet Street, and Anderton's, in the middle of newspaperdom, are great examples. You may witness a busy scene at the Manchester in the evening, when the commercial travellers, their City wanderings over, send their reports and instructions to headquarters, or, as they call it, "write up the mail."

DINING ROOM (OAK SALON, HOTEL MÉTROPOLE).

Forsaking commerce, we will seek out the hotels of the studious, and we shall find them in Bloomsbury, hard by the British Museum, busy hive of brainworkers. The Thackeray, Kingsley, and Esmond trade, one might almost say, upon the Museum; even the telegraphic address of one of them is "Bookcraft." These three are temperance hotels; so, too, are Cranston's Waverleys; and, in passing, let it not be forgotten that London accommodates excellently the people who prefer the teetotal establishment. Wild's, in Ludgate Hill, and the Buckingham, in the Strand, are two more among many.

If we tried we could not before leaving Bloomsbury miss the magnificent Russell, fashioned on the Gordon system, and bearing the Frederick name. For patrons of a different character, in the long street arteries which feed Bloomsbury are countless private hotels, which faithfully serve a mission of cheapness. Mostly they are numbered, but some of them take names to themselves; and, being bound by no traditions, desiring only to be up to date,

fearful and wonderful specimens of hotel nomenclature are prepared in a single night. What was a modest title at eventide glares forth pretentiously as "Hotel Pretoria" next morning, wars and patriotism just then making the blood to leap. And by the same token when there was a scamper for Alaskan gold fields an "Hotel Klondyke" came topically forward. In these days, from highest to lowest, it is Hotel this and Hotel that—*à la mode* "hotel" comes first.

Away in the farther West-End are many other hotels of great reputation. Beginning at Westminster, there are the cosy St. Ermin's, the Windsor, and the Westminster Palace. At South Kensington there is Bailey's; overlooking Rotten Row is the Alexandra, of most pretentious appearance; hard by is the Hyde Park Hotel, carried on in conjunction with the Carlton Hotel; whilst the Buckingham Palace, the Royal Palace, the De Vere, and many others are all institutions of the Metropolis, and there are others, such as Morley's in Trafalgar Square, the Holborn Viaduct Hotel, and the Queen's in Leicester Square, which a London visitor can hardly help but see.

Of the oddities, peculiarities, individualities

of Hotel London—ah! they are so many, too many for one short survey. The trades and the professions have their own hotels. To take two widely different examples, one might point out that, whilst all who attended the great wool sales from the country and abroad would stay at the Great Eastern, country lawyers and clients whose business is at the Law Courts would favour Anderton's or the Inns of Court, which vie with each other in proximity to the great headquarters of Justice. And the space in between these two could be well filled. Come with me to Covent Garden, and I will show you a big hotel with 200 rooms which will not admit ladies—it is "for gentlemen only." There is another not far away which has obtained a peculiar patronage from persons arriving in London by P. and O. steamers, who know nothing whatever of Hotel London, and have gratefully accepted a hint that was given them. There is a clerical hotel; ships' captains have their own in dock-land; there is a Jewish hotel; and in the neighbourhood of Regent's Park there is even one which is advertised as "the only Spiritualist hotel in London." After that, it would be futile to attempt a further illustration of the possibilities of hotel individualism in the great Metropolis.

We will go back to the Strand, and see that each street as it runs from the great thoroughfare southwards to the Thames is honeycombed with hotels of different sorts and sizes. And in perambulating westwards again we may this time note the Savoy, with its abundance of fair fame, which we could on our last journey hardly couple with the Cecil, though they adjoin. The Savoy is as æsthetic as it is big.

Such is Hotel London in all its magnitude and with all its wonders. And in the enumeration of so many wonders we dispel at least one. There is such a variety and such a choice in hotel life that more and more are Londoners of means forsaking their homes and living only in hotels, with all their careless freedom.

For years Hotel London has been passing through an interesting process of evolution, and the end of the process will not be in the twentieth century.

LOUNGE (HOTEL RUSSELL).

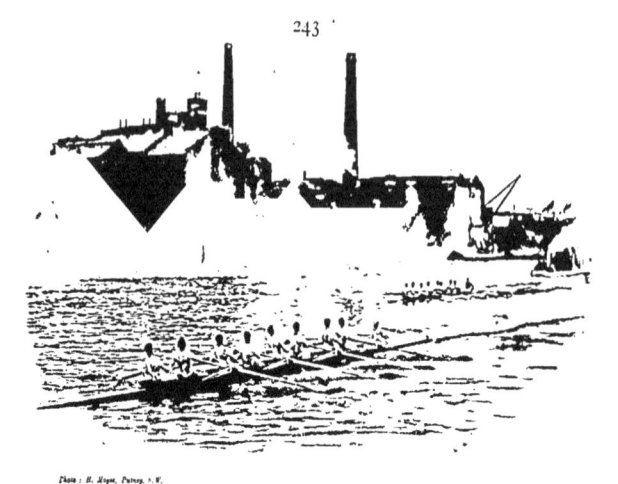

THE OXFORD AND CAMBRIDGE BOAT RACE.

THAMES PLEASURES AND SPORTS.

By JOHN BLOUNDELLE-BURTON.

THE pleasures and sports of the Thames are principally above bridge; the business part lies below. Yet let none forget that there is plenty of pleasure and sport and fun to be obtained below bridge also, and found at Greenwich, Gravesend, Southend, Margate, Ramsgate, and elsewhere. But, even to start for these places beloved of a certain portion of Living London's population—and visited often enough by a totally distinct stratum of that population, whose cry, as a rule, is "anything for a change"— one sets out by water from above-bridge: *i.e.* from the Old Swan Pier. Whenever one does so in the summer time, and providing the weather is fine, the cruise is certain to be an amusing as well as an enjoyable one. There is always a band on board (harp, cornet, and flute), refreshments may be obtained, all are determined on enjoying themselves, and lovers are abundant and shed a rosy glow around. In the case of the "husbands' boat" —for Margate on Saturdays —it is the married men, hastening to join their wives until Monday, who represent the votaries of Hymen, late Cupid; yet they too are happy.

But we will turn to the absolute subject of this sketch, the pleasures and sports of the Thames.

By priority of age comes the race for Doggett's Coat and Badge, a sum of money having been left by Thomas Doggett, a Drury Lane actor of the early Georgian period, to commemorate the accession day of the first Hanoverian monarch, *i.e.* August 1st, 1715. This furnishes a waterman's coat and a silver badge—the latter as large as a pie-dish and bearing the white horse of Hanover on it—and is open to any six young Thames watermen who desire to compete, the course being originally from the "Swan" at London Bridge to the "Swan" at Chelsea. As the event has existed for nearly two hundred years, the old actor's loyalty and enthusiasm have been pretty well stamped

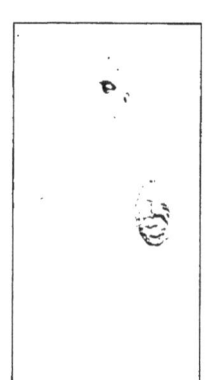

DOGGETT'S COAT AND BADGE.

EXCURSION STEAMBOATS LEAVING FRESH WHARF, LONDON BRIDGE.

BATHING IN THE RIVER.

into the minds and memories of several generations of Londoners. The ground, or rather water, covered by this course, and the shores from London Bridge to Chelsea, not only comprise almost all the chief historical portion of the river as regards sport and pleasure, but also the grandeur and might and power of the greatest city in the world. And—which should give us further food for reflection—Father Thames is still adding to our history while even now serving the purposes of recreation and amusement.

Lean for a moment over Chelsea Suspension Bridge on a summer day and look around and below you. Passing under the bridge is a steamer on its way to Kew and Richmond and Hampton Court. Here, too, you may see, especially if it is Saturday afternoon, single, double, treble sculling boats with young maidens, and, of course, their swains, prepared for an outing, or jaunt—for a Saturday "up the river." You may observe, also, men of sterner metal and intentions passing beneath you—brawny and muscular oarsmen sculling in wager boats, and practising for some race the stakes of which may be well worth winning—stakes that may enable whosoever gains them to set up in business as a boat-builder and a man who will have "Boats to let," or as the landlord of some riverside public-house, which, as every riparian resident knows, is the "be all and end all," in the majority of cases, of the professional sculler's existence.

On one side of this bridge is Chelsea Hospital, where once stood, close by, the celebrated Ranelagh Gardens: on the other is Battersea Park, formed out of what was originally a marshy, undrained piece of submerged land. Now it is a very pretty place, much given up to cyclists, especially beginners who do not care to roam too far afield at first or to encounter the dangers of street traffic.

In this park, especially in summer—since it is then green and leafy and at its best—youths and maidens make and keep their rendezvous, as they have always done and always will. The nursemaid loves to saunter on its paths with the inevitable perambulator, whilst the warriors from Chelsea Barracks across the river cast admiring glances at her. Once, in the early sixties, the West-End terminus of the Brighton line was near here, before the railway came farther into town and before Victoria terminus and the railway bridge were built. Beyond this, as we proceed up the river, there is nothing much to call for special remark in the present day until we come to Putney.

Putney is the metropolis of boating men; and on its embankment are the boathouses of the Thames, Vesta, Leander, and London Rowing Clubs—world-renowned establishments, if not for their own celebrity, which is considerable, then because, also, it is from one or other of these that the boats of the Oxford Rowing Club and the Cambridge Rowing Club put off for their practice daily during the fortnight before the 'Varsity Race, and also on the momentous morning of the race. This they have practically done since the year 1849, when, in consequence of there having been no race in 1847 or 1848, two races were rowed in the former year, while previous to 1849, with one solitary exception, the race was rowed from Westminster to Putney.

We witness a busy scene when the start for the great race takes place soon after the steamers for the Press and the Universities arrive from London; when the river is cleared for what the reporters call the great "aquatic contest," much as the Epsom course is cleared for the Derby, and when hansoms, drags, char-a-bancs and omnibuses line the esplanade, as they line every spot where vehicles can go. The ladies all wear favours and rosettes of their favourite University, or, as the cynics say, of whichever blue suits their complexions and toilettes the better; and it has been whispered that some who have sported the losing colours before the race change it for the winning colour afterwards. This is, however, probably scandal.

Once off and the start made, horsemen and light vehicles, such as hansoms, tear off from the starting-point, make a dash across Barnes Common to the "White Hart" at Barnes or the "Ship" at Mortlake—the huge bend north of the river favouring the short cut—and so get in in time for the death, or, rather, the finish: the result being made known by the hoisting of the winning colour above the

READY FOR A ROW.

losing one on Barnes Railway Bridge, after which a scene of wild excitement takes place. Old Blues—and young ones, too—clergymen from distant parishes and lawyers from town shake hands and nod pleasantly to each other if their 'Varsity has won, while those belonging to the losing side swallow their disappointment as best they can. The negro minstrels commence their soothing strains and the men who swallow hot tow or allow stones to be broken on their bare chests give their performances; the adjacent public-houses become crowded; a few fights take place; pigeons are let loose for distant villages; air-balloons bearing the names of theatres and their performances, or of enterprising newspapers or Turf-tipsters, are sent up. The vehicles either speed back to town or take their occupants to Richmond; the steam-launches turn their heads Londonwards, and the sight-seers on foot stream off to the railway stations; while the "sportsman" who invites you to back the "'art, the hanker, or the diaming," or find the queen as he performs the three-card trick, packs up his traps and departs. The boat race is over and done with for another year.

Only a passing line of reference need be made to Hurlingham. So long connected with pigeon-shooting—for which it was principally founded in the early 'sixties, while water-polo was introduced ten years later—it still stands at the head of other associations of a similar kind, that, while they may eventually rival it in its beauty and aristocratic associations, are never likely to surpass it. Here the visitor, or guest, finds all that can minister to his enjoyment. Excellent bands discourse sweet music beneath the ancient trees that grow down almost to the water's edge; and during the London season the best dressed women of fashion may be seen attended by men equally well known.

The river—especially its pleasures and, in a smaller way, its sports—would not, however, have full justice done to it if attention were not called to one of its most popular haunts —*i.e.* Kew. For here, indeed, the home of pleasure for many holiday-makers is established, and there are those who think that the succulent winkle and shrimp may be found at their best in this resort. Bread and

A "PENNY SWEAT."

butter, too, are, as all the world knows—or should know—partaken of in large quantities, accompanied by the health-giving watercress while washed down by a strong highly-flavoured tea, good for promoting digestion after a stroll in the celebrated gardens. Who has not seen the mystic legend inscribed over many a riverside door here—the legend announcing "Tea and hot water, 9d."? and who has not gently wondered why the hot water should be so emphatically mentioned, since, to make tea without hot water, is at present regarded as an almost unattainable feat?

Kew has its visitors, however, for other things besides the Botanic Gardens and the above appetising refreshments. Anglers come here to fish for barbel, of which there is still a famous "swim" even lower down, namely, at Barnes; and there is an eyot where skeleton leaves can be obtained in large quantities—the kind of leaves our grandmothers pinned and pressed between the pages of books with, often enough, an auspicious date marked against them and the initials of what was, doubtless, a masculine name. Here, too, are rowing clubs capable of producing crews and scullers of no mean prowess, quite fitted to contend for victory in any regatta or water contest which the river can provide. And here is the spot where sweet-scented and beautifully variegated bouquets have been sold near the steamboat pier and the south side of the bridge—the old bridge—from long past days, and are still sold.

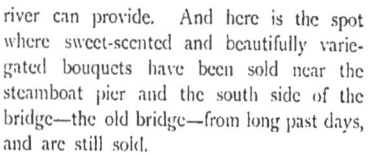

One wonders sometimes what Londoners would be like if it were not for the river. Its waters have not, it is true, been pellucid for many a day; salmon is no longer caught at Putney as it was in the middle of the eighteenth century, and the nightingale no longer sings outside Barn Elms or Craven Cottage, where Bulwer-Lytton lived some time. But boys have bathed from time immemorial in the stream, and will continue to do so; they have also for a long while hired boats in which to take what is called "penny sweats"—*i.e.* enough of them band together to hire a boat (not generally the best the boatman has to let), and so get their modicum of exercise. Who, too, has not rowed on the classic stream, either in outrigger, racing-boat, or randan?—who that is a Londoner has not plunged "the labouring oar" into its waters and rowed his lady-love up river, or, if the tide is very strong, gone ashore and towed the boat containing the fair one, the luncheon-basket and the tea-kettle, as well as other things? Who, too, has not

I. AT PRACTICE.   II. "BOATS TO LET."

fed the swans that abound on the river, and alternately teased or played with them, while some, perhaps, have even witnessed the ceremony of swan-upping, which is occasionally called "swan-hopping"? This ceremony consists in marking the birds on the upper mandible of the bill with nicks; the Royal swans, of which there are many, having two diamonds, those of the Dyers Company one nick, and those of the Vintners Company two nicks. From this old practice comes the corrupted inn-sign, "The Swan with Two Necks."

Of late years old customs have been revived on the Royal River which had quite sunk out of fashion, and they now share with the boat-clubs of men and women the office of furnishing both pleasure and sport upon it. Regattas have much increased and multiplied; so, too, have water carnivals. Richmond, amongst other places, organises several of the latter, and the beautiful and brilliant scenes on the illuminated water and the river banks on a summer night are not unworthy competitors with those of Venice. Indeed, the Thames above bridge, while having its fair share in utility, is the greatest contributor to the Londoner's open-air enjoyment, and is without a rival. For the pleasure-seeker can bathe and row, if he chooses; he can, on the other hand, if he is not athletically disposed, be conveyed upon it in steamers or launches or sailing-boats, and he can dwell on its shores at any point which he chooses to select; while, when he has left London a few miles behind him, he can, if an angler, fish to his heart's content. Moreover, no part of England is better furnished with good hotels and inns where everything that the heart of man can desire is to be found, so that, as one poet has remarked, the holiday-maker can "take his ease at his inn," and, in the words of another, "find his warmest welcome there."

RIVER STEAMER.

THE ROMAN CATHOLIC CATHEDRAL, WESTMINSTER.

ROMAN CATHOLIC LONDON.

By WILFRID MEYNELL.

LONDON entertains, perhaps unawares, some half-million of persons professing the Roman Catholic faith. Not all of this multitude actually practises its religion cover a larger total area of earth, and Westminster Cathedral boasts the broadest nave of all. A bold man is he who builds a cathedral; he has about him the tongues of Babel, and

LEAVING THE ORATORY, SOUTH KENSINGTON.

by going to mass on Sundays and to its "duties" (confession and communion) at Easter. "The world is too much with us" is a Wordsworthian sigh upon the lips of nominal adherents of every creed.

"Nominal Catholics," therefore, exist; otherwise the antithetical term "practical Catholics" would not need to be very commonly heard among them. Of the number of these practical Catholics, failing an official census, nothing can be certainly known. But London has no fewer than eighty churches for their accommodation—and in nearly all of these a succession of masses on Sunday morning, so that every seat may have been occupied twice or thrice. The Westminster Cathedral, dreamt of by Cardinal Manning and realised by Cardinal Vaughan, possesses that ideal conjunction—an actual as well as an official pre-eminence. Only the Abbey and St. Paul's of all churches in London

in this Westminster case nearly Babel's tower. Cardinal Vaughan heard, and, more difficult still, did not hear. He wasted on idle discussions none of the energy which was otherwise required. Fortune and generosity supplied the £200,000 that had to pass into the bare outwork of bricks.

Next to the Westminster Cathedral in size comes the Oratory Church at South Kensington. It is served by over a dozen fathers. These do not belong to an "order" in the sense in which Franciscans or Benedictines do; but they live in community. Their rule is that of St. Philip Neri, adapted to English life by Cardinal Newman. He (from Birmingham, too!) was the nominal founder of the London Oratory; but its actual founder was Father Faber—he whose hymns, sung within their native walls at Sunday and week-day evening services, are echoed in churches and chapels of every other creed

—in truth, a great "conspiracy of song." Its site lies where several ways meet and part — types of the many crises of the spiritual life its walls have witnessed—the farewells involved by "conversions," the meetings, the marriages, the last rites over the dead. In this church, or in its predecessor on the same site, Lothair (the third Marquess of Bute) was married (but not to Corisande), Lord Beaconsfield languidly looking on. Here, too, the Marquess of Ripon laid down his wand as Grand Master of the Freemasons, Mr. Gladstone metaphorically observing anything but languidly; forging, indeed, out of that hot mood, a famous new arrow-head for his quiver as an anti-Vatican pamphleteer. Here was the Requiem sung over beloved Cardinal Manning's bier; here was held the Victorian Diamond Jubilee service of 1897; here Edward VII., when Prince of Wales, has assisted at a nuptial mass; and here, too, is a bench which has been the judges'—all gathered together to pay the last tribute of homage to Lord Russell of Killowen.

History gets made quickly, you perceive; for it is only about fifty years since the first Oratorians in England (most of whom were Oxford and clerical converts) settled on this site, and were stoned in the streets for their pains. Their own pile of stones is that which remains, and the noble dome which crowns the edifice is an admitted adornment—amid a hundred modern defacements — of London. Apart from its memories (and a full share of sad ones) the church is a "show" one, by reason of its size, its abundance of marble, its many altars, its saints and cherubs, with all the flourishes and flying draperies of the Italian Renascence.

I dwell on this very representative church because what is said of it can be more or less applied to the other seventy and nine churches which need, for the most part, no special description. But "Farm Street"— the church of the Jesuit Fathers, planted amid the mundane glories of Grosvenor Square —demands a word. Between Oratorians and Jesuits may be supposed to exist a certain "holy rivalry," which the westerly and south-westerly trend of the social stream, perhaps, intensifies. But the sons of St. Ignatius, who are sometimes called the "Apostles of the Genteels," are really of no fixed time or place. They are a floating population, sent hither and thither by their superiors —it may be to martyrdom in Japan, or in the London slums, or in the fumes of Widnes. They come and go. At one of these altars, where members of the devout female sex, and of the sex that is not devout, may be seen kneeling at all hours to-day, Manning said his first mass. Only a few weeks earlier he was "charging" Chichester as its archdeacon; and in later years, by another great change of domestic sentiment, he ceased to love Jesuits.

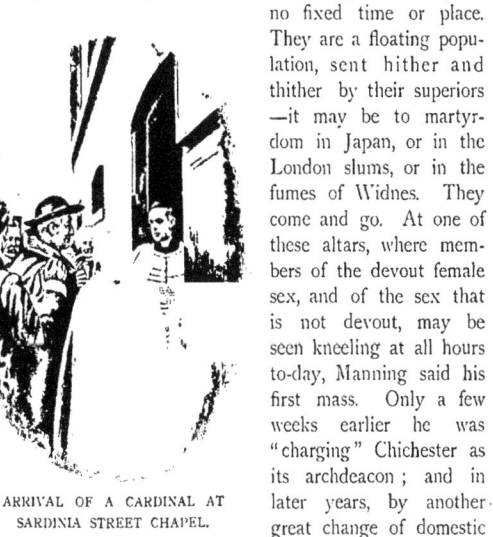

ARRIVAL OF A CARDINAL AT SARDINIA STREET CHAPEL.

The mention of Manning recalls his saying that pulpit oratory is one of the three wounds of the Roman Catholic Church in England. Sermons, in fact, take a secondary place to-day, as ever, in Catholic services; preaching is not practised as an art. "Farm Street," however, has its eloquent preacher in Father Bernard Vaughan, as the Oratory has in Father Sebastian Bowden (formerly an officer in the Guards) its direct one. Of this Mayfair church Mrs. Craigie ("John Oliver Hobbes")—herself a worshipper there—says, in "The Gods, Some Mortals, and Lord Wickenham," that her hero "used to sit near the altar of Our Lady of Lourdes, where he could see, at the end of the aisle, another altar and the pendant lamps before it. The odour of the flowers, incense, melting wax, and that something else, like the scent of goodly fruit stored away for

THE RED MASS AS FORMERLY CELEBRATED AT SARDINIA STREET CHAPEL,
LINCOLN'S INN.

the hungry winter, gave him a welcome. The little silver hearts which hung in a case by the altar had each some story to tell of a faithful vow." This is the literature of fiction. The literature of fact has its devotees inside the large red-brick house adjoining the church; and among the busiest researchers at the British Museum are sons of St. Ignatius.

To the east and to the west, two miles each way from the Marble Arch (the site of old Tyburn, where many a Jesuit was hanged, drawn, and quartered, lie the churches of St. Etheldreda and of St. Mary of the Angels, served by sons of St. Charles Borromeo. The "Tube" covers in a few minutes the four miles between them. In Ely Place, an enclosure on the very confines of the City, and within sight almost of La Belle Sauvage Yard, stands St. Etheldreda's Church, with its thirteenth-century crypt—an ancient fane, and one of the few of the actual churches of "The Old Religion" restored to the ancient rites. It somehow got into the market, and was bought by Father Lockhart, a relative of Walter Scott's son-in-law, and himself the first of Newman's young community at Littlemore to secede from the Anglican Church. Long will the memory remain of his handsome face and figure, as he stood in the surrounding streets preaching on the teetotalism he practised. He belonged to the Fathers of Charity; and there was full accord between his aim and name. The sons of St. Charles Borromeo (he was an archbishop of Milan, who loved the poor and fought the plague and established Sunday schools) were planted by Manning among rather mean streets in Bayswater. You note the meanness, because it contrasts with the reputed "ambition" of its founder. Hither to him came the world to which he would not go; and "receptions into the Church"—the only receptions he ever loved—have not ceased to be an order of the day.

To churches with specialised congregations—for Italians, in Hatton Garden, and others—reference is elsewhere made in this work. The Sardinia Street Chapel, Lincoln's Inn, once tolerated and protected only as a chapel of an ambassador, became in the fulness of time the scene of the Red Mass (so called in Paris from the colour of the legal robes), where Roman Catholic members of the Bar gathered at the beginning of a term to invoke a blessing on its labours —a notable gathering in which might be seen, at one time or another, Lord Brampton, Lord Russell of Killowen, Sir John Day, Sir James Mathew, Sir Joseph Walton, and Lord Llandaff. Cross the water to Southwark, and you find its own cathedral, famous for its congregational singing, and the centre of a circle of spiritual and temporal activities for the amelioration of the lot of the poor who, as Charles Booth shows, are poorest of the poor in that region.

The Religious Orders are dotted about London, which loses in picturesqueness by the non-appearance in the streets in their own religious dress of Friars of Orders Grey and of monks who make their habits, though habits do not make the monk. By Act of Parliament they are forced into the coats, trousers, and headgear that mean despair for the artist. The Carmelites abstain from flesh, and rise by night to sing the Divine Office, in Church Street, Kensington; the Dominicans are at Haverstock Hill, the Capuchins at Peckham, Franciscans at Stratford, Passionists at Highgate, Benedictines at Ealing, Augustinians (whose habit Luther wore) at Hoxton Square; and there are Canons Regular, Redemptorists, Servites, and many more. Congregations of women abound; and their habits are seen

UNLOADING A CART AT NAZARETH HOUSE.

OLD WOMEN'S WARD, NAZARETH HOUSE.

in the streets, for in this matter of the religious dress, as in most others, it is women who lead. Carmelite nuns, with St. Teresa's habit, and Poor Clares, do not come from their enclosure. But Sisters of Nazareth will call anywhere in their carriage—they name it a cart—on anyone in "the world," and they do not always wait for invitations. They beg in fact from door to door for food for the six or seven hundred poor whom they entertain at Nazareth House, Hammersmith. In this great family are young children and old men and old women, into one of whose wards our illustrator has taken no idly intrusive peep. The Little Sisters of the Poor are of their kindred; and there are Sisters of Mercy, who, among their works of the same kind, include the Hospital of St. John and St. Elizabeth for suffering children at St. John's Wood; nuns of the Good Shepherd, with their great laundry worked by penitent women; the nuns who manage the French Hospital; the Sisters of Zion, those of the Sacred Heart, and those at the Convent of the Assumption, to all of whom flock girls of Catholic parents for education—these and many more; the Sisters who go out to nurse (and do not refuse a small-pox case), and the Sisters who carry on the great night Refuge in Crispin Street; those who assist the Rescue Crusade among boys, and, last but not least in a list not easily exhausted, the Sisters of Charity, in whose great house, in Carlisle Place, Lady Etheldreda Howard amid other all noble women has chosen the life of sacrifice.

Come, finally, to Archbishop's House, Westminster, where Archbishop Bourne rules, and preserves a stately solitude, though surrounded by a large working staff.

He has a word for everyone—well judged, shrewd, fatherly. Forms and formalism are not necessarily related. The Archbishop is a young man among the Bishops over whom he presides. These include Bishop Hedley, a literary man and a Benedictine; also Bishop Amigo, from Southwark, like the Archbishop himself, a teetotaller. Then you see an ex-Army chaplain, wearing military orders; and you have been able, perhaps, before you have taken your leave, to tell Monsignor Johnson how indebted to his "Catholic Directory" is any writer (and therefore any reader) of a paper such as this—crumbs gathered from his abundant table.

THE NATIONAL PENNY BANK (HACKNEY ROAD).

LONDON THRIFT.

By SIDNEY DARK.

IT is doubtful whether, both from the nature of his being and the character of his environment, the Londoner of any class can be said to be unduly addicted to thrift. In the sense in which the French peasant and the Paris bourgeois, the Scotsman and the Cornishman, always save a little, however small may be their income, the Londoner is a monument of extravagance. It must, of course, be remembered that expenses of living in the Metropolis are immeasurably greater in proportion to income than they are almost anywhere else, and the storm and stress of life in a great city practically compel a man to spend a certain part of his income in amusement and distraction which in healthier circumstances he would not require. At the same time, alongside the manifold agencies for spending money that exist in our city, there are innumerable agencies for the encouragement of thrift, from great institutions like the Post Office Savings Bank, with its millions of depositors, to the humble Slate Club held in the top room of a public-house, with its constant difficulties of obtaining subscriptions from its members and sometimes of getting them back from its treasurer!

The baby's money box may be said to be the beginning of thrift; but in these progressive days the money box, from which ingenuity and a dinner knife can extract the pennies, is naturally regarded with suspicion. So the modern baby obtains, presumably through his legal guardians, a form from the nearest Post Office, turns his pennies into stamps, and sticks them on to the form, and then, when he has collected twelve, lodges them at the nearest Post Office, where the money, instead of lying idle and unproductive like the talent of the unfaithful servant hidden in a tin money box instead of a napkin, earns, as soon as a pound has been accumulated, two and a-half per cent. for the thrifty infant. Or, if the legal guardian to whom I have referred is a person of individualistic tendencies who regards the enlargement of governmental action with suspicion, the child may take his pennies to the nearest branch of the National Penny Bank, which receives deposits from a penny upwards, and there the directors will guard his money for him, and also give him a certain rate of interest. There is even for the budding capitalist a third alternative. The Salvation Army Reliance Bank will provide him with a money box not of unsubstantial tin or brittle wood which will enable the greed for chocolate of to-day to break through and steal the careful forethought of yesterday, but a strong receptacle, recalling in a miniature manner the masterpieces of the great safe-makers. This box is supplied with a strong padlock, the key of which is in the hands of the Salvation Army agent, who at certain periods visits the house, unlocks the box, counts the pennies, for which he gives a receipt, and, going one better than the Post Office allows the youthful depositor three per cent.

In any account of the way London saves, the Post Office, both from the magnitude of its transactions and its governmental position, naturally claims first consideration. More than £140,000,000 are deposited in the Post Office Savings Bank, and of this huge sum, though there are no official figures, London may be assumed to own a quarter. Of the total number of depositors sixty per cent. are women and children, ninety per cent. own less than fifty pounds, and probably seventy-five per cent. belong to the industrial classes. It is natural and inevitable that amongst the folk, who in their most prosperous times are only removed one hair's breadth from semi-starvation, the women should be the most thrifty. This fact is illustrated in the figures issued by institutions similar to the Post Office Savings Bank. There are a thousand branch savings banks in London. At the central office 3,000 persons, of whom nearly half are women, are engaged in managing the savings of the poor man. The Post Office encourages youthful thrift by allowing school teachers to collect the pennies of their pupils either by the use of stamp forms or by instituting penny banks, the funds of which are placed in bulk in the Post Office Savings Bank.

Somewhat similar in aim and method is the National Penny Bank, founded by Mr. (now Sir) George C. T. Bartley, M.P., with the late Duke of Westminster, the late Earl of Derby, and other friends, in 1875. The Penny Bank, which began as a philanthropic institution, has by careful management been put on a thoroughly sound commercial basis, and its depositors have the satisfaction of knowing that they are obtaining the benefits of a genuine business and not of a mere charity. The National Penny Bank has

SCHOOL TEACHERS RECEIVING PUPILS' PENNIES.

SALVATION ARMY RELIANCE BANK, QUEEN VICTORIA STREET.

thirteen branches, of which that in the Hackney Road is one of the busiest. As an illustration of its operations, during one week before Christmas £150,000 was withdrawn by its depositors, while during the week previous the weight of money paid over the counters was 1 ton 18 cwts. 111 lbs., of which ninety per cent. was silver. The ledgers are probably the most remarkable documents owned by any banking house. Here is a typical account. It began on the first day of a month with the deposit of a penny, which was increased four days afterwards to eightpence. Two days later it was brought down to twopence by the withdrawal of sixpence. It then rose again in three jumps to one and twopence, fell again to threepence, then to a penny, and after an interval of three months the account was closed. This is an instance of the intricate nature of the bank's account. Some years back there was, for various reasons, a run on the bank. Customers poured in demanding their money. Everyone was paid, including two costermongers, who drew out between them in gold and silver something like fifty pounds. About an hour afterwards they returned and asked the cashier if he would kindly take their money back again. "What has made you alter your minds?" said the cashier. "Well, guv'nor," said one of the costers, "me and my mate, w'en we got outside, didn't know wot to do with the stuff, so Bill sez to me, 'Let's tyke it to Coutts's.' We went dahn the Strand, guv'nor, and blowed if Coutts's man didn't refuse to tyke it! So we've come back to you."

The Salvation Army Reliance Bank, which has its headquarters in Queen Victoria Street, is, as far as its deposit side is concerned, worked in much the same manner as the Post Office. The bank itself, with its counters and brass railings, flanked with clerks in red jerseys with "S.A." on their collars, has a novel and unexpected appearance; and on my visit I could not help being impressed by the unusual cheerfulness and civility of everybody, from the happy-looking old gentleman acting as hall door porter, who directed me when I entered, to the able and courteous manager—also in a red jersey—whose manner and appearance were about as unlike one's ideas of a financial magnate as well could be. The curious mixture of spiritual fervour with business acumen which is characteristic of a great deal of General Booth's organisation was exemplified by the fact that this officer was reading when I was shown into his room a copy of the latest Stock Exchange prices, to settle, no doubt, in which direction to invest his bank's money.

Turning to another branch of the subject, it would be impossible to attempt even to enumerate the different benefit and friendly societies of one sort or another that exist in the city of London. Inquiries go to prove that in almost every large business—railway companies, foundries, manufactories, and so on—there is, in addition to the larger outside societies, some sort of benefit fund attached to the firm itself, in which the men's subscriptions are often augmented by subscriptions from the masters. These funds are looked upon with a very great deal of distrust by the trade unions and friendly societies' leaders, and there seems some reason to believe that in certain cases they are administered too much by the master and too little by the men, though I am inclined to think that this is rather the exception than the rule. A large number of publicans and licensed grocers in working class localities also start goose clubs and Christmas clubs amongst their customers, in which, again, the few pence or shillings put by every week for the Christmas festivities are often increased by the publican.

Perhaps more important and more interesting are the great friendly societies and their host of small imitators. Briefly, the object of a friendly society may be stated to be the payment of a certain weekly sum to the members in time of sickness and sometimes, also, when out of work, and of a certain sum to the widow or orphans on the decease of a member. No one unacquainted with the London poor can have any idea of the extraordinary desire, especially amongst the women, for what is called a decent funeral; and I find by inquiries amongst clergymen in the poorest districts of London that the burial club is a far more popular institution than the organisation which provides funds to tide its members over bad times, whether from sickness or from want of employment. There is a well known story of a poor woman who dearly loved her son, but who, rather than spend certain money in buying port wine and risk his having a pauper's funeral, left him to die without the wine, and had a burying which astonished the neighbourhood. I myself once overheard a conversation in an omnibus between two elderly matrons, one of whom said to the

BIRKBECK BANK, SOUTHAMPTON BUILDINGS.

HEARTS OF OAK CERTIFICATE.

the Sons of Temperance, and the two Orders of Sons of the Phœnix—the last four being teetotal organisations. Their ramifications are very difficult to follow, and much of their proceedings is kept secret from the outsider. But generally they may be fairly accurately said to be a combination of freemasonry and an ordinary friendly society. The Foresters, for example, which is the most interesting of them all, is said—I do not vouch for the accuracy of the statement—to have been founded by Robin Hood. Anyhow, a court was in existence in Leeds in 1790, and Forestry was introduced into London in 1837. It consists of nearly a million members, male, female, and juvenile, and its funds are approaching seven millions sterling. The admirable objects of the Foresters, which again may be taken to be fairly typical of these societies, are:—

> To establish and maintain benefit funds, from which, on satisfactory evidence of the death of a member of the society who has complied with all its lawful requirements, a sum shall be paid to the widow, orphans, dependents, or other beneficiary whom the

other, "Oh, it was a beautiful funeral! After we come back we had wine and biscuits and sangwitches; and it must 'ave done 'er 'eart good, pore thing, to 'ave been able to bury 'er 'usband so nice." Of course, it is easy to philosophise over the wastefulness of money spent on elaborate funerals, but it is all very human and very touching.

Christmas goose clubs are held in connection with many institutes and clubs. The Aldenham Institute, St. Pancras, has a club consisting of nearly 2,500 members, who pay weekly contributions towards a Christmas dinner, the distribution of the good things taking place on Christmas Eve. Thanks perhaps to Dickens, putting by for Christmas Day is one of the most popular forms of London Thrift.

Among the friendly societies having branches in London are the Foresters, the Buffaloes, the Druids, the United Patriots, the Oddfellows, the Rechabites,

FORESTER'S CERTIFICATE.

member has designated, or to the personal representative of the member, as laid down in the said laws.

To secure for its members such other advantages as are from time to time designated.

To unite fraternally all persons entitled to membership under the laws of the society; and the word "laws" shall include general laws and byelaws.

To give all moral and material aid in its power to its members and those dependent upon them.

To educate its members socially, morally, and intellectually.

To establish a fund for the relief of sick and distressed members.

A characteristic of the Foresters and most of the other societies I have mentioned is found in their picturesque regalia.

The older trade unions also very largely act as benefit societies, and offer much the same advantages to their members. But it will be remembered that when the new Unionist movement started after the Dock Strike, it was made a great feature that the trade union should be exclusively a fighting body, and that its power to fight for higher wages and better conditions of labour should not be weakened by including within its functions those of a friendly society.

The Hearts of Oak, which has its headquarters near Fitzroy Square, is a benefit society worked from a central office. It, too, offers to its members sick pay and what is called "death money." Young men in good health in receipt of a wage of not less than 24s. per week are eligible for membership between the ages of eighteen and thirty. The entrance fee is 2s. 6d., and the subscription about £2 a year. For this the benefits include 18s. a week in case of sickness, £20 for a member's funeral, and £10 for the funeral of a member's wife—ladies apparently costing less to bury than gentlemen—30s. for a wife's lying-in, and £15 for loss in case of fire. The tremendous business done by the Hearts of Oak, as well as the fertility of its members, may be gauged

A CHRISTMAS EVE DISTRIBUTION OF TURKEYS, GEESE, ETC. (ALDENHAM INSTITUTE).

by the fact that from 1842, when the society was founded, to the end of December, 1904, no less a sum than £1,190,628 was paid for lying-in claims alone, while the total money disbursed for all benefits amounted to over seven and a half million pounds.

Before leaving this branch of the subject it is interesting to notice that the Jewish and the foreign quarters of London have their own friendly societies, with their own peculiar names, of which the following may be taken as specimens:—The Podumbitzer Friendly Society, United Brothers of Kalish, Sochetibover Sick Benefit, Grand Order of the Sons of Jacob, and so on.

The building society is the favourite means of thrift among the artisan and clerk classes.

DRUID'S CERTIFICATE.

There are innumerable building societies all over London, some of which are, rather oddly, connected with Dissenting chapels, and often have the minister of the chapel as one of the trustees. The method of the building society is to collect money in small sums from a large number of persons and lend it to others upon real security. The method has many variations. Usually after a member has deposited a certain amount with the society sufficient to pay a proportion of the price of a house the directors, after an investigation by their surveyor, advance the balance of the purchase price, holding the deeds as security, and this advance, together with interest, has to be repaid in instalments over a specified number of years, the result, of course, being that the borrower pays probably rather less a sum than would be demanded of him for rent, and in the course of a few years owns a house of his own. In one instance which has come to my knowledge a doorkeeper of a factory in the Euston Road has in the course of forty years acquired about twenty houses in this manner, and has become possessed of a comfortable income which he will, of course, be able to bequeath to his heirs.

There are between 2,000 and 3,000 building societies in England and Wales, and the amount of business they do may be gauged by the fact that in the Birkbeck—one of the best known London societies—during a recent twelvemonth 8,700 persons became depositors, and the total cash received during its first fifty years of existence amounted to over £290,000,000 sterling. Our photographic reproduction on page 257 depicts the interior of the well-known Birkbeck Bank, where the business both of the building society and of the bank itself is transacted.

Among interesting minor thrift societies mention may be made of a very admirable idea which has been started in West London by one or two ladies, whereby servant girls contribute a small sum monthly to the funds of what is called a Clothes Club, and are provided with rather more than the value of their subscriptions in garments.

I have endeavoured to give a kaleidoscopic view of the many varied organisations, some entirely engineered by the members themselves, others guided and fostered by clergymen, philanthropists, Government officials, and employers of labour, which have for their aim the encouragement of putting by for a rainy day — the enunciation or the doctrine that to look after the pennies is a sure and certain way of finding that the pounds will look after themselves, and that by the help of that marvellous institution called interest, if you cast your bread upon the waters, it will come back to you largely increased in bulk.

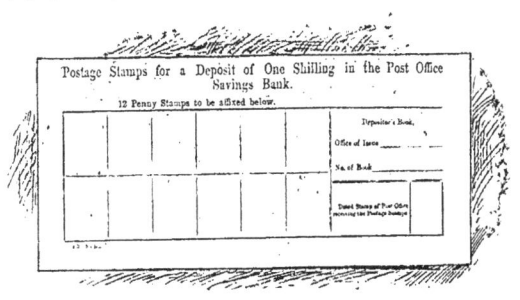

POST OFFICE SAVINGS BANK STAMP FORM.

DURING A SUMMER HEAT WAVE.

LONDON UNDER THE WEATHER.

By GEORGE R. SIMS.

ON THE KERBSTONE: SUN HATS.

THE staple commodity of London conversation is the weather. In the street the usual greeting among passing acquaintances is "Fine day," or "Wretched weather," as the case may be. At the social gathering the weather is the subject which usually breaks the ice, and at the clubs the members meeting in the hall, or gazing out of the big front windows, invariably refer to the atmospheric conditions. Of late years it has been the fashion to describe most of the seasons as "trying," and to-day the newspapers have taken to headlining their meteorological paragraphs. The word "phenomenal" has come into vogue for the autumn that is hot and the spring that is cold. The Londoner seems to be always hardly used by the atmosphere, and the elements are continually against him. If it is hot, it is a "heat wave" and unbearable; if it is cold, it is a "blizzard" and murderous.

Having made up their minds that the weather is extraordinary, Londoners comport themselves under its variations in a more or less extraordinary manner. They are never prepared for heat or cold. A few days of blazing sunshine fill the streets with eccentric costumes for man and beast alike. A few days of snow drive the borough councils to the end of their wits, and paralyse the traffic of the busiest city in the world.

But though only the extremes of heat and cold emphasise the Londoner's helplessness to the point of ridicule, the weather in all its phases frames a picture of serio-comic suffering which is well worth the attention of the student of men and manners.

London in the heat wave is always interesting. The streets suddenly become white with the straw hats of men and women. The waistcoat of civilisation is abandoned, and daring young men wear sashes of colour around their waists which are dignified by the name of "cummerbunds." The ladies in their lightest array anxiously shield their complexions beneath umbrellas or parasols of sufficiently large dimensions to be of use as well as ornament. Aristocratic London in the heat wave—so much of it as remains in town—seeks the shade of the Park at an early hour. Occasionally it breakfasts in Kensington Gardens; it dines at night with its windows wide open amid shaded lights; tattered humanity reclines in the streets, after the manner of the Neapolitan *lazzaroni*. The steps of St. Paul's in the height of a heat wave are frequently used for the *al fresco* siesta of worker and loafer alike.

London in a thunderstorm is a scene of panic. At the first clap women utter a little cry of terror in chorus, and make hurried darts into drapers' shops or convenient doorways. Presently the heavens burst, and a terrific storm of rain sweeps over the town. Instantly, as if by magic, the streets are cleared: where the pedestrians have vanished to is a mystery. But the 'buses and the cabs cannot escape. The 'buses are full inside; the outside passengers bend their heads to the pitiless storm, cowering under umbrellas if they have them.

The cabmen turn up their coat collars, and the wet reins slip through their hands; but the cab horse plays no pranks in the heavy downpour. The rain rattles against the lowered glass; a small Niagara pours off the brim of cabby's hat and further impedes his view; the wheels splash through small rivers of muddy water; and presently the shop windows and the adjacent rails are mud-bespattered, as if they had been pelted by an indignant crowd. When the storm abates, macintoshed stragglers appear in the streets, but the outlook seems dank and miserable. The ladies compelled to be abroad tread gingerly on the tips of their toes. A cat has no greater horror of wet under foot than a female Londoner.

HIGH HOLBORN IN A STORM.

and the balconies of the west have an Oriental character until the midnight hour.

Ordinary London—working London and loafing London—maintains no dignity in the heat wave. Its coats come off in unaccustomed places; the business man carries his Panama in his hand, and mops his brow; the 'busmen and the cabmen adorn their horses' heads with straw bonnets, and tuck handkerchiefs under their own hats, after the fashion of the Indian puggaree. "Ice" becomes the legend in the public-house windows; the sale of white linen hats becomes a trade of the kerbstone; and

London in a fog! The "scene" is unique; no other capital in the world can show the equal of "the London Particular." When the yellow, choking mist commences to roll up in the daytime, London is filled with Rembrandtesque effects even at high noon. The lights in the shops are flaring, the lights in the private houses are full on. You see more of the "domestic interior" on a foggy day than at any other time, for the blinds are not drawn. There is no more picturesque peep-show than the London "domestic interior" lighted up in the daytime with the firelight flickering on the walls.

AT THE MERCY OF THE WIND.

Towards night, when the fog has not lifted, the situation becomes tragic. Fog signals explode with startling detonation on the railways; Dante's Inferno seems to have been transported to the town upon the Thames. Boys and men wander here and there with torches, and lend a diabolical element to the Cimmerian gloom; the warning shouts of 'busmen and cabmen, as they move slowly forward, now getting on to the pavement, now colliding with a lamp-post, come from the unseen. Wayfarers, business men returning from their occupation, belated travellers bound for distant parts of the Metropolis, grope their way blindly along, clutching at the railings of the houses to make sure that they do not wander into the roadway; when they come suddenly upon something that looks like a policeman, they ask in plaintive voices for topographical guidance. But somehow or other everybody gets home—the cabmen find their stables, the 'busmen their yards. On the morrow, when the gift of sight is once more of practical use, we relate our adventures as humorous experiences to our friends who had the good fortune to remain indoors during "a London fog."

London in a gale. London, when the wild north-easter blows over a wind-dried city, is trying alike to the temper and the dignity. As the sign-boards swing the nervous pedestrian glances uneasily aloft. At times he ceases to glance anywhere, and, turning his back on the blast, closes his eyes;

BY TORCHLIGHT.

LUDGATE CIRCUS IN A FOG.

for the dust which has eddied and swirled in the roadway comes on a sudden gust, in a thick cloud, straight at him. In this position the male pedestrian is uncomfortable enough, but the female pedestrian is an object to melt the heart of a woman-hater. To keep her hat on and stand her ground, as the wind blowing fifty miles an hour spends its fury on her ample skirts, is a feat that requires long practice. If she is wise she clutches at a lamp-post or a railing; if she trusts to her own unaided efforts she is generally blown along in a series of undignified little jumps.

When the wind blows furiously in London the pavements and roadways are strewn with rubbish and torn paper, fragments of news-paper contents bills, and shop sweepings. It is as though a caravan of dust-carts had strewn their contents about the Metropolis. The newspaper bills have a partiality for the middle of the roadway, where they frighten horses or, occasionally rising like kites in the air, wrap themselves round the face of a carman or an outside 'bus passenger. The theatre boards and newspaper boards outside the shops are blown down here and there with a sharp little bang, and the spectacle of a gentleman wildly careering among the traffic after his hat is common. A gale is usually more prolific in accidents than a fog, and there is always a long list of casualties.

London in a drizzle—the damp, warm drizzle that goes on and on and colours all things a gloomy drab—is a misery unto men and a woe unto women. There is a penetrating dampness about the London drizzle that seems gradually to mildew the mind. The weather is repeated in the countenance of everybody one meets. The pavements have become gradually like the sea sand at low tide. They are a series of small puddles relieved by pools where the stones have been removed for repair. The nice conduct of an umbrella is not within the genius of the Londoner, and so where the crowd waits for the 'buses that are always full inside, or in the busy streets where there are always two opposing streams of pedestrians, there is constant collision and apology, and occasionally one man's umbrella drips down the neck of his neighbour. The bestowal of wet umbrellas in omnibuses and tram-cars is a fertile source of trouble. With twelve saturated umbrellas all draining at once on to the floor of a crowded vehicle, and frequently down the garments of the passengers, the inside of a public conveyance closely resembles a bathing machine.

There is a peculiar blight that descends on London occasionally and lies heavily upon it for days. The skies are of a smoky grey, a yellowish haze narrows the horizon; in the parks and open spaces a light blue mist hangs upon the grass and envelops the trunks of the trees. The birds are silent, the church clocks strike with a muffled sound. The depression extends alike to beast and man. The cab and 'bus horses go lazily, the crowds of human beings move about as though they had a silent sorrow. It is then the words "Beastly weather" are heard everywhere, and men yawn publicly. There is even a pessimistic note in the public Press, and if Parliament is sitting a dyspeptic tone pervades the debates.

But it is when London has had a snowstorm that the Londoner is seen under the most depressing conditions of all. The beautiful snow of the Christmas number has no joys for him. Short spells of frost may come now and then, but they are marred by the dread anticipations of the thaw that must follow. London under a rapid thaw is the paradise of plumbers, but it is the other place for everybody else.

Yet London half-flooded by thaw is but a minor evil compared with the flooding of certain low-lying districts that follows a long period of heavy rain. South London is sometimes the scene of an extensive inundation. Lambeth Marshes are under water; houses in this neighbourhood are flooded in cellar and basement, founda-tions are rendered unsafe, and the inhab-itants are for many days amphibious. The Thames once extended as far as the Elephant and Castle and Newington Butts, and at times of heavy downpours the dwellers in this district are unpleasantly reminded of the fact.

But to return to the snow. When the Londoner wakes up in the morning and sees that it has fallen heavily in the night —when the Londoner looks out upon a "white city"—he for a moment appreciates the poetry of the picture. But directly

London begins its day's work the scene is changed. The traffic, foot and horse, rapidly crushes the snow into a slushy paste resembling chocolate in the early process of manufacture. The pavements become slippery, the wood and the asphalt are skating rinks. If the snow still continues and the roads freeze hard, or only partially thaw, London does nothing. The unemployed are immediately remembered, and indignant citizens rush into print, demanding an army of men for the relief of the situation.

Presently the authorities summon up courage to attack the difficulty. The householder has felt compelled to clear so much of the pavement as lies in front of his habitation, or has employed the men with spades who perambulate the suburbs shouting, "Sweep your doorway." But the municipal officials have "waited." When they set to work they generally clear the roadway by shovelling the snow into great heaps on either side. London then becomes a miniature Switzerland with a small Alpine range running along its roadways.

If the frost holds and the London lakes freeze over, then the Serpentine and the ornamental waters in Regent's Park revive for a day or two the vanished glories of the Ice Fair. The banks are lined with men who bring old cane-bottomed or Windsor chairs with them, and do a roaring trade in affixing skates to the boots of the select. Sliding is the sport of the small boy, who is largely represented on these occasions. Picturesque figures are the Royal Humane Society men in their cork jackets, and not infrequently their services are required to rescue an adventurous skater who has disdained the warning notice-board of danger.

London while the frost holds and the snow is hard is exhilarating for the young and the idle; snow-balling is indulged in in spite of police prohibition, and in some parts of the suburbs you may come upon the juvenile sculptor's effort at a snowman. But snow disorganises the traffic, and the business man suffers and growls, while the poor feel their situation acutely. Many trades cease. Frozen-out gardeners and bricklayers make their appearance in slowly walking little groups, and seek to open the purse strings of the charitable by chanting doleful ditties.

But London under the snow that is half snow and half slush—London under a week of alternating snow and frost—is a piteous spectacle. A general paralysis attacks the whole working organisation. The train service gradually dissociates itself from the time tables, the omnibus service is cut down to infinitesimal proportions, and the newspapers are filled with sarcastic comments concerning "The Beautiful Snow." Then indeed is London "Under the Weather."

SKATING ON THE SERPENTINE.

SCOTTISH, IRISH, AND WELSH LONDON.

By C. O'CONOR ECCLES.

EVERY year from Scotland, from Ireland, and from Wales young men flock in hundreds to London. They are of all classes, all degrees of education, united in one common aim, that, namely, of making a living. The new-comers find employment in many different ways. Scotland and Ireland largely recruit the ranks of the police force. The Civil Service, too, in all its branches employs many Irishmen, whose brilliant talents often enable them to rise from small posts to places of high emolument and power. Mercantile clerkships attract the Scot, who has a happy knack of coming South with the traditional half-crown in his pocket, and by thrift, ability, and industry amassing a fortune. Scottish and Irish doctors, too, abound, from men who have made a name and dwell in fashionable squares to struggling practitioners in Whitechapel and Southwark. Irish barristers are numerous, and, thanks to the eloquence which is their birthright, win fame and fortune in their profession. Journalism likewise attracts large numbers of Scotsmen and Irishmen so that it is a saying in Fleet Street that English editors are kept simply to correct the "shalls" and "wills" of their colleagues.

Welshmen in their pursuits are usually either musical or mercantile, and frequently both. Many of London's leading singers, both men and women, are Welsh, though both Ireland and Scotland contribute their quota of musical talent. Indeed, perhaps, the gayest and most picturesque figure to be seen in London streets is the itinerant Scottish piper with his bagpipes, a man who, if he does not rank in the eyes of the

PLAYING IN THE HAGGIS ON ST. ANDREW'S NIGHT.

LONDON KYMRIC LADIES' CHOIR.

world with the musical celebrities of his nation, would seem to have a "guid conceit" of himself, and to enjoy mightily the interest he rouses in quiet residential quarters.

From music to milk is an easy transition, if we may judge by the innumerable old Welsh ballads which begin by stating that "Winnie" or "Nesta" was a milkmaid. It is consequently interesting to learn that the milk trade of London is to a great extent in the hands of the Welsh. Several drapery establishments, too, are owned by enterprising Welshmen.

Very many Irishmen of the poorest class likewise drift to London in search of employment. Debarred by lack of means from lodgings where the rate of payment is high, and yet compelled to be near the great industrial centres where chance jobs may be most easily picked up, they and their families are automatically forced into slum dwellings in such neighbourhoods as Poplar, Islington, and Southwark, where they form colonies of people wonderfully good and helpful to each other, but over-crowded, deprived of all that brightens and beautifies existence, and compelled to bring up their children under circumstances that give the little ones but a slender chance of developing their highest possibilities.

The Scot who comes to London is sure sooner or later to find himself in touch with the Scottish Corporation in Crane Court, Fleet Street. This body occupies No. 7, a spacious building at the extreme end, with high-pitched roof, small turrets to the front, and other features of Scottish architecture. Scottish life in London centres round the spot. It is the headquarters of many county associations, of the Highland Society, the Caledonian Society, the Gaelic Society, and various other organisations. Because of the innumerable activities and interests concentrated there, 7, Crane Court, has been called "The Scottish Consulate." The house is modern, having been rebuilt in 1880 on the site of the old hall purchased at the end of the eighteenth century by the Corporation from the Royal Society. Sir Isaac Newton's presidential chair was saved from the fire which destroyed this original building as well as many valuable paintings and records; it now stands in the board room.

Ever since 1665 the Corporation has held an annual dinner on St. Andrew's Night, where the guests in full Highland costume are marshalled to their places by skirling pipers, who later in the evening head a majestic procession of cooks, each bearing on a trencher a haggis, "great chieftain of the pudding race," the national dish which to the palate of the true-born Scot surpasses all that the South can offer. At this festival

SCOTTISH, IRISH, AND WELSH LONDON.

some prominent Scottish nobleman presides, and on the walls appear Scottish emblems, "the ruddy lion rampt in gold," the banners and shields of Highland clans, with claymores, dirks, and pistols. Funds are collected for the relief of distress, and thanks to Scottish benevolence many a humble home has been kept together, and many a decent body, brought low by misfortune, has been pensioned and enabled to spend his last days in peace. It is an interesting sight

clad in the Stuart tartan, and ready at their teacher's word to sing plaintive Jacobite ballads in sweet childish trebles. Their soft notes have more than once melted the hearts and loosened the purse-strings of Scottish visitors. Practical good sense is shown in the training given.

Scottish gentlemen of position, officers of Scottish regiments and others, foregather at the Caledonian Club, 30, Charles Street, St. James's. The house is roomy and old-fashioned, with wide corridors and lofty, spacious apartments. The Club, though only established in 1898, numbers over a thousand members, and, like the famous

LEARNING IRISH REELS (ATHENÆUM HALL, TOTTENHAM COURT ROAD).

to see the old people come for their pensions once a month.

Should an indigent Scotsman die in London, or a Scottish soldier, sailor or marine be disabled when on active service, his children will be received at the Royal Caledonian Asylum, which has now its headquarters at Bushey. It is worth while to go down any morning and, escorted by the kindly Secretary, see the kilted boy pipers march up and down skirling bravely, or watch the little lads dance the Reel, the Highland Fling, and the Sword Dance. There are about ninety of them, all well-fed, well-cared-for, well-taught, and bright-faced. Along the corridor, on the girls' side of the building, are some sixty bonnie lasses,

giantess, is "still growing." Ladies are admitted as guests daily to lunch and tea, and once or twice a week to dinner. The fine reading-room with its panels of dark green silk brocade is given over to them, and a special dining-room is reserved for them and their hosts.

The Scottish Golf Club at Wimbledon, founded in 1865 by a group of London Scotsmen, has a large body of members, devotees of the national game.

Seldom is a London winter sufficiently rigorous to admit of curling, but when the ice bears, the members of the Shinto Curling Club are there, ready to take advantage of it for this exciting game.

The Irishman finds in London his own

literary, athletic, political, and social institutions. He may join the Irish Literary Society, and stroll down to its headquarters, where he can read all the Irish papers, have luncheon, tea, or dinner, and meet his friends, since this organisation combines the advantages of a club with lectures, concerts, and other attractions, and is becoming more and more the chief centre of social intercourse for the Irish in London. It is non-sectarian and non-political, and, as its primary object is the advancement of Irish literature, appeals to all parties. To it belong many literary men and women of Irish nationality. Several of these are members of a kindred association, the Irish Texts Society. This was established to publish, with English translations, glossaries, and notes, the large and interesting body of Irish MSS. which still exists.

The most Irish of the Irish belong to a flourishing young organisation which is friendly in its relations with the Irish Literary Society, though quite independent of it. I allude to the Gaelic League, which attracts a number of the most energetic and practical of the younger generation, and has its headquarters at Duke Street, Adelphi. Its direct object is to extend the living Irish language, and preserve the store of fine Irish songs and traditions that, without such timely help, might die out; indirectly—being based on principles of national self-reliance—it stands for the revival of Irish industries, for all that is at once national and progressive. The visitor to the Athenæum Hall, Tottenham Court Road, will find on any Monday evening some two hundred young men and women assembled to study Gaelic. There is always a large mixture of Irish speakers who make it a point of honour at these meetings to speak in Gaelic only. Amongst them are some who, though born and bred in London and speaking English without a trace of accent, are well acquainted with the sweet native tongue of their forefathers. The League has fifteen Irish schools in the Metropolis. Recreation, on traditional lines, is not lost sight of. The Irish dancing classes are always popular, and in addition there are in summer pleasant *Seilgi* and *Scoruidheachta*, or excursions and social gatherings, with now and then a *Pleraca* or dance, while an annual musical festival is held at the Queen's Hall. This has a large number of Gaelic songs on the programme, and the music is exclusively traditional. This festival is now considered the central event in the Irish musical year. It is distinct from the Irish concert now held at the Queen's Hall on St. Patrick's Night, which is on the lines of the popular Scottish concert on St. Andrew's Night, and attracts the same kind of audience. On St. Patrick's Day there is a wonderful sale of so-called "shamrock" in the London streets—most of it, alas, pure clover that grew probably in Surrey meadows. It is often decorated with sparkling bits of gold foil, and to the uninitiated looks cheap at a penny a bunch. The expert, however, notes the white dot on each leaf and the hairy stems, and prefers to get his button-hole direct from Ireland, where, indeed, there is a considerable export trade in the genuine article about this time. The religious service in honour of St. Patrick at the Roman Catholic Church, Dockhead, is

SHAMROCK SELLER.

IRISH GUARDSMEN.

unique, the hymns, sermons, and responses being respectively in Irish and Latin. It attracts a crowded congregation.

The Gaelic Athletic Association possesses some eight or nine clubs, mostly in North London, devoted to hurling, football, and athletics generally, their chief grounds being at Muswell Hill and Lea Bridge. They hold no matches or competitions with English clubs. The "G.A.A." has its headquarters in Ireland, and Great Britain ranks as one of its provinces, London being considered a county. There are in the Metropolis a large body of members, of whom over 200 belong to the Hibernian Athletic Club, the oldest of the group, which was founded in 1895. Hurling, as practised by Irish teams, differs in certain respects from hockey, and is a more dashing game; while the Gaelic Athletic Rules for football prohibit handling, pushing, or tripping, which are permitted by Rugby rules. When the grass is very wet, however, some of the players discard boots and stockings. The various G.A.A. clubs in London challenge each other, and then the winning team challenges some other county, as, for example, the Manchester and Liverpool G.A.A. The winner in this latter match is always expected later to play All Ireland for the championship.

In Holborn there is an Irish club the members of which are civil servants, medical men and others; the medical men having also an association of their own at 11, Chandos Street, one of the objects of which is to secure the recognition of Irish degrees by London hospitals, which in distributing appointments often refuse to accept Irish qualifications, however capable may be the men holding them.

A LONDON IRISH HURLING MATCH.

While the various Irish counties have no such societies as the Scottish for bringing natives together, a province, Ulster, has its own association. It owes it origin to the casual encounter of two or three enthusiastic Northerners who lamented that, proud as was the position of their compatriots in London, they had no general meeting place. Its inaugural banquet was held in January, 1897, when many recruits joined the Society, and, thanks to excellent management, the membership has since greatly increased. Balls, concerts, cinderella dances, banquets, and a river trip are among the entertainments offered. The headquarters of the association are at the Hotel Cecil.

In the days of Parnell, the Westminster

PUBLISHED IN LONDON.

Palace Hotel was a favourite rendezvous of the Irish Nationalist Members of Parliament. Nowadays, however, they have no recognised centre, but hold their meetings sometimes at one place, sometimes at another. Some of them have town houses, others live in apartments, others again chum together and have rooms or chambers in common, whether in localities like Kensington or Chelsea, or on the Surrey side, which, if less fashionable, is within easier reach of the House of Commons. There are, it may be added, many purely political associations for Irishmen in London.

The above may be taken as covering Irish Ireland in London, but there is also fashionable Ireland, which, if the bull may be pardoned, is not Irish at all, since it includes wealthy non-resident Irish landlords who, for the most part, like the Duke of Devonshire and the Marquess of Londonderry, are Englishmen born and bred, but hold estates across the Channel. Many wealthy women, however, in this circle do good work in buying Irish manufactures, and no trousseau of an aristocratic bride is complete unless the dainty stitchery, the fairy-like embroidery, and the costly lace are provided by workers in some Irish convent. The Irish Peasantry Society at Stamford Street, Blackfriars, offers a free education to a certain number of the London born children of Irish parents, preference being given to those whose fathers were soldiers or sailors. This Association also offers small prizes in Ireland for the best kept cottages.

Since the establishment of the Irish Guards by Queen Victoria, in compliment to Irish valour in South Africa, the uniform and the flat cap with its green band have become familiar in the London streets. The three figures in our photographic illustration on page 270 are shown standing in front of a coat of arms affixed to a wall in the Tower of London. There is also a well-known Irish Volunteer regiment, the London Irish Rifles, already mentioned in the article on "Volunteer London."

The Welsh inhabitants of London, though they number some fifty thousand, have no such central meeting places as the Scots and Irish. True, they possess an admirable literary society, the Cymmrodorion, which gives aid to necessitous members of the community, but Welsh life in London centres chiefly in the chapels, and its activities for the most part are religious, or, at any rate, connected with religion. To gain some idea of its true inwardness, one cannot do better than attend the New Jewin Chapel or the Welsh Tabernacle in the Pentonville Road some Sunday evening when a popular preacher has come up to address the congregation. The stranger will find the building thronged with well-dressed people, for the most part prosperous business men and women, the number of the former sex being remarkable. The majority are Calvinistic Methodists, for to this body the bulk of the London Welsh population belong, though there are also many Welsh Congregationalists, Baptists, and Wesleyans in the capital, while the Established Church finds a certain number of adherents. The sermon, the hymns, the announcements are all in Welsh, so that the visitor feels himself an outsider and a foreigner, despite the familiar aspect of everyone and everything. As might be expected where a race is so musical, the congregational singing is exceptionally good. The organist at the Welsh Tabernacle, Mrs. Frances Rees-Rowlands, is conductress of the London Kymric Ladies' Choir, of which Lady Puleston is president. The members are selected from all the Welsh chapels, the best voices only being picked out, with the result that this choir was awarded the first and second prizes at the Royal National Eisteddfod of Wales, and has appeared before Royalty. All the singers are dressed in their national costume, with the Welshwoman's characteristic hat.

On St. David's Eve Welsh people have special services at the City Temple and St. Paul's; and on St. David's Day, though few of them sport the leek as the Irish sport the shamrock, they eat it at their annual dinner in the form of Cawl Cenin, a favourite soup. The Welsh in London possess a political society, the Cymru Fydd, which is Radical in its tendencies, and to which most of the Welsh Members of Parliament belong. Moreover, they have a newspaper of their own printed partly in their own language, and bearing the title of *The London Welshman (Cymro Llundain)*. Thrifty, cleanly, industrious, neighbourly and united, the London Welsh form an important and valuable addition to the population.

Indeed, the Scottish, Irish, and Welsh elements do and have done much towards making London a world city, and in leavening the Anglo-Saxons with Celtic impetuosity and mental alertness have, with other causes, given to metropolitans a width of outlook and a receptivity not to be found in provincial towns where these elements do not bulk as largely or act as potently.

HIGHLAND PIPER AND DANCER IN LONDON.

LAYING ELECTRIC CABLES.

LIGHTING LONDON.

By DESMOND YOUNG.

IF one could only hover in a balloon over Central London as night falls! To see, as the man with the long stick makes his round and switches are turned on and levers pulled behind the scenes, the transformation scene gradually unfold and the myriad lights spurt out of the grey gloom beneath: the sinuous Thames become outlined by moonlike arc lamps; the bridges start up as if set pieces of fireworks; Leicester Square assert itself as the hub of Pleasure London in a blaze of bluish-white refulgence, more than ever eclipsing its sedate neighbour, Trafalgar Square; long lines of stars shoot out from the busy, pulsing heart below, radiating in all directions, beginning with steady white orbs and fading away in glimmering specks of yellowish luminosity —what a picture it would be!

Innumerable are the lights of London and well-nigh inconceivably vast is the system by which they are produced and maintained. Scores of private companies, as well as a number of public bodies, including the County Council, are engaged in the work; the capital sunk in it is fabulous in amount; and the pipes and cables connected with it form an amazingly complex subterranean network, of which Londoners get a glimpse when the streets are "up."

Electricity is generated in the Metropolis at scores of points. The oldest company distributing the energy is the London Electric Supply Corporation, whose station at Deptford was long the largest in the world. Whether it is now or not, its capacity is enormous. To obtain even a superficial knowledge of the lighting of London these works must be visited. Here we are, then. A bewildering maze of engines and machinery fills the large

LAMP LIGHTER.

engine house. To the right is the older plant — powerful engines connected to dynamos by rope pulleys. To the left are some of the newer engines, coupled direct to huge dynamos which are revolving so rapidly and noiselessly that but for the little sparks that come and go they would seem to be motionless. At present — it is 11 a.m., with a bright sky overhead — there is a light load on, not much electricity is being consumed. Hence there are only two engines running. As the demand increases others will be started to keep pace with it. There is no drawing on reserves when the rush comes about dusk, as at a gas works. As electricity is wanted so it must be generated and supplied, because storing it, while possible, is not commercially practicable. And, as a consequence, some engines are always running.

On a gallery to the left the switch-board is situated. It has as many rows of dials as a clockmaker's shop, and underneath are ranged levers like those in the signal cabin on the iron road. The quivering hands of the gauges show the attendants the pressure, etc., of the mysterious current that is passing through the cables below, and the handles enable them to regulate it. Though they seem to have it completely in harness, this is the most dangerous part of the works.

Among the municipal corporations which supply electricity St. Pancras and Shoreditch occupy important positions. Of the London authorities St. Pancras led the way in opening a station, while Shoreditch was the first borough in the country to combine on a large scale the destruction of dust and refuse with the production of electricity. The two things often go hand in hand now. Still, to Shoreditch is due the credit which should always be given to the pioneer.

Let us take a peep at its station. Begin at the yard, into which the refuse—household, trade, and street—is brought. Little mountains of clinkers from the furnaces are here a feature of the scenery. The economic disposal of this waste is one of the most important problems connected with the undertaking—which is not creditable to us as a commercial nation. Among it, for one

IN THE LONDON ELECTRIC SUPPLY CORPORATION'S WORKS.

DRAWING RETORTS BY HAND (SOUTH METROPOLITAN GAS COMPANY).

thing, are some articles which would pass as relics from Pompeii.

Cross the yard, and we are at the lift which raises the rubbish to the top of the furnaces (already described in the article on "London's Toilet"). Through the engine house, along the gallery in front of an elaborate switch-board, and into another room containing a switch-board for public lighting. If you pulled down one of those levers projecting from it, all the arc lamps on one side of a street would go out. The lights are, except when fog envelops the borough, switched on and off according to a time table. And that points to the coming doom of the man with the stick as well as of the lamp cleaner with his light, portable ladder. Electric lamps, of course, do not need their attention. Both will be superseded by the now familiar figure who supplies the arc lamps with carbon, which is consumed in the production of the light.

Electricity is coming more and more into use in London for lighting. Hundreds of miles of streets are laid with cables, and yet it is impossible to walk very far without seeing more being put down. The road is up. In the gutter stands a huge reel of leaden cable. Presently this is rolled nearer the hole, and then the passers-by stop and gaze expectantly. At last they are going to behold that famous little dog which rushes through the earthenware pipe with a string tied to its tail and thus makes a connection between two lengths. But, alas! this sagacious animal is purely mythical. No dog is used, no member of the brute creation, though there is a tradition that a rat was once pressed into service, and that to ensure all possible speed a ferret was sent after it to tell it to hurry up. Instead of resorting to any device of this kind, the men put an ordinary drain rod through the pipe. To the end of this very prosaic tool a string is attached, and to the end of the string a rope, and to the end of the rope the beginning of the cable. It is all very simple. Londoners, however, are likely to see much of it in the near future.

Gas is supplied to the great city mostly by two corporations. One, the Gas Light and Coke Company, has more than sixty square miles of territory north of the Thames and makes, in round figures, 22,211,000,000 cubic feet of gas per annum. Its works are scattered all over London, though the output at Beckton is as large as at all the others combined. The other great company is the South Metropolitan, which supplies an enormous area on the south side of the river with 11,272,916,000 cubic feet per annum. These companies, with the Commercial Company, supply most of the gas used for street lighting, as well as that consumed by the "flares" on theatres and other public buildings. There are, however, a number of minor companies—the Crystal Palace, the Tottenham, the West Ham, the Wandsworth and District, and others.

To see one of the sources of the old-fashioned light we cannot do better than journey up the Old Kent Road to the headquarters of the South Metropolitan Gas Company. Through the gateway past towers, stacks of pipes, heaps of coke, shops in which lamp-repairing and other work is being carried on, and enormous gas-holders, and, behold! the egg stage of gas-making—taking in the coal. Below, the Surrey Canal, to our side of which three barges are moored. High above, a number of cranes. With a rattle as the chain runs over the wheel at the end of the arm, an iron tub descends, lights on a heap of slack in the hold of one of the craft, opens like a pair of scissors, and closes on the top of the mass. Then a signal, and away the big bucket swings aloft. It is as if a giant's arm had reached down and seized a handful. The illustration on page 280 shows the coal being taken in at the Vauxhall works of the South Metropolitan Gas Company.

Next, the retorts—the old type of retorts, fed by hand, and not the modern gas-extracting chambers that are stoked by machinery, though there are some of these in the works. And now it is hot, scorchingly hot. Mounted on a platform that runs on rails, a half-naked stoker, black, shiny, arms and face so beaded with perspiration that they catch and hold every speck of dust, stands in front of one of a whole series of doors something like those of an ordinary steam boiler, from the top of each of which a pipe runs upwards. Mopping his brow with one hand, he takes

278   LIVING LONDON.

LAMP CLEANER.

a light from a jet close by, and applies it to the door. Pop! A flame bursts out all round it, burns for a few moments, and then dies out. That gets rid of the gas in the retort.

And now there is a blinding, searing glare of light that casts the muscular worker into vivid relief. He has thrown the door open. One glance, with his hands shading his eyes, and, having cleared the opening of the pipe of the tar which has been deposited in it, he plunges a rake into the retort, and draws out the carbonised contents, from which smoke ascends in clouds as they fall down between the platform and the retorts on to sloping iron shelves below where we stand, there to have water played on them and assume the appearance of the coke of commerce. Soon the retort is empty, an incandescent tube, whose sides are white with the intensity of the heat.

Perspiration pours from the silhouetted figure of the stoker. You can see it oozing out of him in great beads. But on! on! there is no time to lose. The retort must be charged speedily, else the cold air will bring about a certain loss of efficiency. So he wheels round to a long scoop like an enormous cheese taster that has been filled with coal from a heap in the rear. By the help of his assistants, he raises the end of this implement to the mouth of the retort, runs it in and turns it over, thus discharging the contents. Again and again does he repeat this operation till the retort is charged.

PAYING OUT A LEADEN CABLE.

There! the work is done — done for six hours. Remember, however, that only one-half of the process has been visible to us. An exact duplicate of the scene we have witnessed has taken place on the other side, for the retorts are drawn and filled from both ends. And, of course, some of the retorts are emptied and fed without using the movable platform, as shown in the illustration on page 276.

We cannot follow the gas from the retorts to the mains. That were too long a journey. Enough that it is drawn off by engines, known as "exhausters," which send it through the works—through plant where it is cooled, washed, etc.; through the meters, which are of the size that the harassed householder sometimes sees in his dreams at the end of the Christmas quarter (they are as big as a railway carriage and register up to hundreds of millions of cubic feet on seven dials); and, lastly, into the huge, towering gasholders, the largest of which—the famous telescopic "Jumbo"—has a capacity of 5,500,000 feet. Vast as this monster is, however, there are two larger at the South Metropolitan Company's works on Greenwich Marshes One of these is actually double the size of "Jumbo"!

From the huge holders the gas passes, at a pressure regulated just inside the gates, into the mains, to be distributed among hundreds of thousands of customers. Within recent years these have increased

SUPPLYING ARC LAMP WITH CARBON.

enormously. Thanks to that beneficial invention, the coin-freed meter, gas companies have tapped a new public—a public which purchases gas by the pennyworth; and now consumers of this class are numbered by the million and are being added to daily. The South Metropolitan Company alone has more than 120,000 slot meters in use, and is installing others at the rate of 250 or 300 per week.

Not that these figures represent so many new customers. No; some people who feel the pinch of poverty acutely clear out their ordinary meter and get a slot one in its place. The advantage is obvious. They pay as they go on. There is no bill running up, no looking forward with anxiety to the end of the quarter, no risk of receiving the company's terrible ultimatum, "Pay up, or your gas will be cut off." It is true that this threat is not often carried out, even when an unfortunate consumer cannot scrape together enough to wipe off the debt; but how many thousands there are in this great city who expect to hear it four times a year! In general, however, the installing of a slot meter means the gaining of a new customer.

Round that special instrument tragedy and comedy centre. It gives the gas industry a human interest which it did not possess in the old days. Let us take a short walk with one of the officials who collect the coppers from meters of this class. Before we reach his round—and matters are so arranged that every person who buys gas by the pennyworth is visited once every five weeks—he tells of a Mrs. Jones who sent a message post-haste to the works the other day. That message, as delivered accurately enough by her daughter, was this:—

"Mother wants you to send a man to open our meter at once. She's put some money in, and she can't get father's dinner."

Now the collector begins to make his calls. For a while he proceeds without incident; but presently he picks out a two-shilling piece from among a lot of coppers. What is it doing in that galley? Accident? Ignorance of the principle of the meter? No; the occupier of the house deliberately put it there to prevent herself from spending it. So she is not surprised when the collector hands her 1s. 11d. Slot meters, that official observes afterwards, are very popular as money boxes.

LAMP REPAIRING SHOP (SOUTH METROPOLITAN GAS COMPANY).

COLLECTING PENNIES FROM A SLOT METER.

And so we go on till we come to an unoccupied house, the late tenant of which has not given the gas company notice of removal. Perhaps the collector will find that he has been anticipated—that one of those ingenious and enterprising gentry who make a speciality of entering empty dwellings and breaking open slot meters has been here before him. But no; the money is safe.

By this time the collector is burdened with copper. We will satisfy our curiosity as to how he gets rid of his load, and then will leave him. There proves to be no great mystery about the matter, after all. He has shopkeepers who take the bronze from him in small quantities, and such as he cannot dispose of in this way he leaves at a branch of the company's bank.

But the mass of coin he and his fellow collectors—nearly a hundred in all—handle in the course of a year is enormous. Conceive, if you can, £320,000, the takings per annum from the slot meters, in pennies. Seven hundred and fifteen tons of bronze!

What mind can grasp the vastness and the infinite ramifications of the lighting system of London? None. The subject is too large, too complicated, and is yearly becoming larger and more complicated.

TAKING IN COAL AT VAUXHALL (SOUTH METROPOLITAN GAS COMPANY).

PUNCH AND JUDY.

SIDESHOW LONDON.

By A. ST. JOHN ADCOCK.

TO repeat a highly respectable platitude—London is one vast Vanity Fair. You can walk about and see most of its shows and sideshows for nothing, but there are proprietorial sideshows in it that you cannot see without first paying a penny at the door or putting at least a halfpenny into the slot.

This "slot" variety is a recent development, and managers of the older sideshows find it such a formidable competitor that they adopt it now as a supplement to their customary exhibits; hence the pleasure-seeker is tempted in some busy London thoroughfare by a display of automatic picture machines ranged round an open-fronted shop, at the rear of which a shooting range yawns like a gigantic baker's oven, with gas jets shining in the depths of it; while for a penny paid to a vociferous showman he can go upstairs and admire a bearded lady seated in an otherwise empty drawing-room, and look into the unfurnished dining-room where, for his delight, three reputed Africans lick red-hot pokers that sizzle on their tongues, and quaff boiling lead out of rusty ladles with manifestations of keen enjoyment.

These upstairs exhibitions do not commence, as a rule, until evening, so if you are bent on a round of visits to Sideshow London you begin with the automatic shows, the shooting galleries, and the penny waxworks, which are open all day.

Shops devoted wholly to automatic shows have multiplied rapidly, and are as popular in Blackwall, Kentish Town, and Lambeth, as in Oxford Street and the more select ways of the West. Some drape their doors with crimson hangings and are ornately decorated inside, others are unadorned to very bleakness; but it is a rare thing to see any of them without visitors, and of an evening they are all crowded.

The public enter gratis and, sooner or later, succumb to the fascinations of one or other of the machines, and drop in a penny or a halfpenny as the case may be, to set little leaden figures under glass playing cricket or football, or peer down a glazed opening and turn a handle to witness, in a series of biograph views, a scene from a familiar melodrama, the changing of the guard at Buckingham Palace, or some ludicrous episode of domestic life.

Suppose, however, you make Piccadilly Circus your starting point, and, pacing one of the most fashionable streets thereabouts, drop into a typical West-End sideshow of more catholic pretensions.

It is a frontless shop in which well-dressed people stroll among groves of automatic machines; at intervals a coin rattles into a slot and the whirr of the handle turning breaks the quiet of the place, or the sharp crack of a rifle sounds from the select shooting gallery at the end, where a marksman is disbursing a penny on two shots at the target.

Near the shooting gallery is a curtained appears on a cramped stage to astonish all beholders with tricks of parlour magic.

On your way to this sideshow, if in your north-west passage you navigated the sombre old backwaters of Bloomsbury, it is more than likely that, as you turned into Russell Square, you were greeted by reedy tootlings and that quavering nasal chatter that is the birthright of Punch, and there you beheld his striped theatre erected against the railings and a semi-circle of auditors, mostly juvenile, spreading out before it.

A WEST-END SIDESHOW.

doorway, with "Pay here" on a label pinned to the curtain, and if you hand sixpence to the lecturer waiting there he will usher you into a small lobby and call your attention to the beauties of a huge painting that is less patronised by daylight critics than by young and elderly connoisseurs who swagger in and out in evening dress after the gas is lighted.

Across London, in the north-west, is a similar sideshow, larger but less aristocratic, noisy with the jolly ripple and rumble of a piano playing popular airs by machinery, and possessing, instead of the shooting gallery, a dapper juggler who periodically

Of course, you have known his preposterous drama by heart since childhood, yet you were constrained to linger shamefacedly and laugh at it again, looking over the children's heads, and when the solemn showman, piping and thumping his drum, shook his little bag insinuatingly under your chin, your hand went involuntarily to your pocket for old remembrance sake.

Perhaps, if you are a well-to-do father or grandfather, when the performance ended and the other showman was walking off with the theatre, you stopped the man with the drum and retained Mr. Punch and his company as a sideshow for an imminent children's party;

in which event there will be work to do in the way of rehabilitating the puppets to-night when the show gets home.

There are peripatetic waxworks that wander about London restlessly and, conscious of their own artistic deficiencies, occasionally acquire alien attractions by leaguing themselves with a cheap palmist or phrenologist and keeping him on tap, as it were, in a bower among the effigies. But our half-dozen permanent penny waxworks are superior to this, and we will take a peep at a typical one of them. The window tempting you with a waxwork nurse soothing a wounded waxwork soldier by showing him a bottle of physic, you pay at the turnstile in the doorway, the lady

A RIFLE RANGE.

THE LION-JAWED MAN.

attendant discontinuing a fantasia on the barrel organ to take your penny.

The shop and the floors above are rich in waxen allegories symbolising the might of the British Empire; also in wax models of statesmen, warriors, thinkers, with here and there distributed among them renowned ruffians who have been crowded out of the Chamber of Horrors, which galaxy of great criminals is on the third floor here, though in some of the other waxworks it is down in the basement, and gains an additional horror from its situation.

The chief object in the principal room is a waxwork Cabinet Meeting, obviously called together at a supreme crisis, for three Ministers have risen to speak simultaneously, and a choice collection of British generals is crowded into a tight corner in the immediate background ready for any emergency. You may not recognise everybody, but that is immaterial, as each gentleman has his name written on a scrap of paper pinned to his chest.

As for the shooting galleries, like the automatic shows they are everywhere. A few are attached to cutlers' shops; a few to barbers' shops, where customers improve their marksmanship while they wait to be shaved; most of them, however, are independent

A TATTOOED COUPLE AT TEA.

of such trade connections. The primitive type with rows of bottles for targets still survives, but the better equipped, thoroughly modernised gallery is more generally favoured, and not infrequently flourishes under the special patronage of local rifle associations.

There is one of this latter class at Islington; it is a fixture there all the year round, and at the right time of year the proprietor enlarges his enterprise by engaging travelling showmen to set up their shows in his first-floor apartments.

The right time of year is in the winter. Throughout the summer living skeletons, midget families, and such like celebrities tour about in caravans and are to be viewed in tents at country fairs; but winter drives them into London and the big provincial cities.

Here their showmen sometimes hire untenanted shops at low rentals till they are re-let, and run shows on their own account; oftener they are glad to get engagements for successive weeks at regular show places, such as the two at Islington, those in Whitechapel, in Kilburn, in Deptford, or in Canning Town.

Wherefore, while the Cattle Show and later the World's Fair are in progress at the Agricultural Hall, you may pay your penny and be entertained over the shooting gallery at Islington by a pair of Oriental jugglers in one room, and in the other by a gentleman and his wife who are tattooed from necks to heels with ingenious designs in half the colours of the rainbow.

Going again next week you find the front room appropriated to an elegant "electric lady," who communicates electric shocks to those who touch her; while the back room is the happy hunting ground of a noble savage. Good living and little exercise incline him to obesity, but he exerts himself in a war dance when enough penny spectators are present, and performs the feat that has won for him the proud title of "The Lion-jawed Man." Having crammed four bones as large as human fingers crosswise in between his teeth, he inserts the

A WAXWORK SHOW.

mouth of a tankard into his own, closes his thick lips all round it like a sucker, and thus holding it defies mankind at large to pull it out.

During this same period the Whitechapel establishment is graced by the presence of a fat woman of stupendous girth and weight. Here the shows are held in the shop itself, the rearward half of it being temporarily curtained off just now and transformed into a living-room for the stout lady, she taking no pleasure in going up and down stairs.

Her showman shouts at the door, while one of his subordinates manipulates the barrel organ with masterly skill; and as soon as a satisfactory percent-

Next week she is bewitching Islington; the tattooed people have transferred themselves to Canning Town; and the noble savage is earning fresh laurels with his tankard in the wilds of Kilburn.

One of the regular show shops has a weird predilection for dead skeletons. Two or three of them have a touching belief in the attractiveness of freaks preserved in spirits; and these are plentiful, whereas the living article is by way of becoming scarce in London, for good live freaks gravitate to Barnum's nowadays unless a minor showman is lucky enough to hear of them in time and intercept them. It is true you may even yet be

A FAT LADY.

age of the crowd outside has come in and paid its pennies, the organist stops to breathe, and the showman, posing by the drapery that conceals his treasure, cries impressively, "Ladies and gentlemen, the young lady will now appear!"

She is always a "young lady," whatever her age may be, and she dawns on our expectant eyes from between the curtains, gliding with a solid and queenly dignity that is only slightly marred by the fact that she carries an oyster shell in which she will presently take a collection for her private exchequer, the taking of private collections being a weakness inherent in all freaks and living sideshows from time immemorial.

startled by seeing in a shop window a presentment of an elephant-headed man larger than life, with one leg elephantine and the other human, and a writhing trunk of the first water; but inside you discover that he dwindles to a leathery-looking object pickled in a glass jar, and having the appearance of a fossilised small boy playing a flageolet.

Nevertheless there was once a real elephant-headed man about town; likewise an elastic-skinned man, and other personages equally gifted, and you may go and see them immortalised in wax to this day in one of the permanent penny waxworks; but in the flesh, Sideshow London knows them no more.

SERVED THROUGH THE WINDOW (WHITECHAPEL ROAD).

BAR AND SALOON LONDON.

By GRAHAM HILL.

WITH the exception of one particularly privileged house in Covent Garden —which is permitted to be opened on three days of the week for twenty-one and a-half hours out of the twenty-four—the licensed hours within the Metropolitan area are twenty and a-half a day. The public-house is the first to open its doors in the morning; it is the last to close them in the early morning following. Mid-day and midnight are both embraced in the working hours of the London licensed victualler. There are suburbs in which the closure is applied at 11 p.m., and bars in the West-End where the presence of a customer before eleven o'clock in the day would be regarded as an intrusion. London has been styled the city of great contrasts, and the truth of this remark is emphasised to the visitor who regards the Metropolis from the "licensed to be drunk on the premises" point of view. Luxury and squalor, gilded affluence and shame-faced dinginess, the marble entrance-hall and the swing doors, stand shoulder to shoulder through the heart of the town.

If we would obtain a comprehensive impression of Bar and Saloon London we must be astir with the dawn. All through the night the market carts have been jogging into town, and although it is not yet three o'clock Covent Garden Market has been long awake. Already a small crowd is gathered around the portals of the market house. With the first stroke of three the doors are unbolted, and the business of the day commences. For the next four or five hours the smart-looking, alert barmen will, literally and figuratively, have their hands full.

The buffets at the terminal railway stations are among the earliest saloons to open, and as we make our way to Piccadilly through the smaller thoroughfares signs of activity are everywhere observable in the licensed world. Tubs of bar refuse, which repose on the kerbs against the coming of the dustmen, attract the scrutiny of the early prowler, potmen are polishing the huge swinging lamps and plate-glass windows, and barrels of beer are being lowered into dark yawning cellars. The four thousand licensed houses and beer shops of the Metropolis are being put in order for the daily round.

Let us pause for a moment in the security of the island pavement in Piccadilly Circus. Here such well-known bars as the Piccadilly and the Leicester Lounge are in sight, while behind the solid blockade of buildings that hedge about the Circus half a hundred licensed houses are within a few minutes' walk of our halting place. We proceed along

INSIDE A PUBLIC-HOUSE ON SATURDAY NIGHT.

Cranbourn Street, glancing at the Haymarket as we go, and if we decide to pass through Leicester Square and thence walk on to Maiden Lane—we have no time to look into the handsome bar of which cover the walls. Stageland in the more exalted form of leading actors and theatrical capitalists is to the fore again at Romano's, which rears its striking yellow frontage in the Strand. Other well-known

THE CHANDOS BAR AND LOUNGE.

the Queen's Hotel, or dive into the beer saloon of the adjacent Brasserie on our way—we shall find at Rule's an interesting gathering of people. There is a distinctly theatrical flavour about the company, and the theatrical traditions of the house are recalled by the pictures and playbills resorts are also in this part of the town, including the Gaiety and Short's famous wine-house. The Garrick is a somewhat newer theatrical rendezvous, and facing it, hard by St. Martin's Church, is yet another, the Chandos, with its imposing bar and lounge, a morning house of call for ladies who have paid their diurnal visit to one or other of the dramatic and musical agencies that flourish in the locality.

In the wine houses a different class of customer is usually encountered. At Short's, whose chief branch is just east of the Gaiety Restaurant in the Strand, port is the favourite beverage. A few wine shops are conducted by a privileged class called "free vintners"—men who have completed service under indentures with a free vintner—who require no licence, and who have the consolation of knowing that, on dying, their businesses can be carried on by their widows with the same immunity from restrictions.

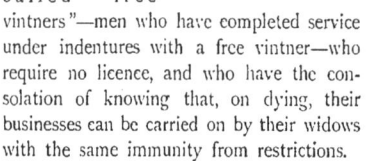

The Cheshire Cheese, rich in tradition of Dr. Johnson and his contemporaries, still retains its ancient form. We approach the sanded bar through a narrow court, and warm ourselves before the old shell-shaped iron grate in a company that is representative of journalism rather than literature, the journalism of sport predominating. The Rainbow Tavern, which for scores of years did one of the most serious, select, and conservative businesses in London, is now a Bodega. The Bodegas adapt themselves to circumstances. They cater for men and women or for men only, according to locality and environment. Let us drop into the commodious branch in Bucklersbury, sometimes known as the "Free Exchange." The heavy swing doorway is flanked on either side by a sandwich counter and a cigar stall. The circular bar occupies the centre of the shop, and on an adjacent stand reposes a whole Cheddar cheese of noble proportions; while baskets of plain but wholesome lunch biscuits are within reach. Besides the above, mention may be made of Henekey's wine house in High Holborn, which was established as far back as 1695.

The Stock Exchange has for years resorted to Mabey's, in Throgmorton

A STRAND WINE-BAR (SHORT'S).

A CITY WINE-BAR
(THE BODEGA, BUCKLERSBURY).

Street, for both meat and drink. It is a hatless and hustling crowd that one encounters in this famous establishment, a note-book and pencil-carrying crowd, that converses in figures and argues in vulgar fractions. Mabey's from the outside has the appearance of a City sale room; some of the other bars of the neighbourhood are small and dimly lighted offices, fitted up with a counter and stocked with good liquor. There are half a dozen such within hail of Shorter's Court.

Going further east into Bishopsgate Street Without we come to "Dirty Dick's," so named after its original proprietor, who found a grubby consolation for blighted matrimonial projects — his intended bride died on the morning appointed for the wedding — in a protracted abstinence from soap and water. Dirty Dick is' also known to history on account of the rule, that was rigorously enforced at this house during his lifetime, which denied a customer more than one drink at each visit. At an adjacent hostelry in Artillery Lane this "one call, one cup" system still obtains, and a printed copy of the rules of the house is presented to each new customer. Formerly another curious East-End public-house — which was merely a wooden building — stood, detached and apart, like an island, in the middle of Mile End Road. Near by, in Whitechapel Road, there is to be seen an open bar — the only one of its kind in London — where, as shown in our photographic illustration on page 286, customers stand on the pavement about the pewter-topped window-ledge, and imbibe their refreshments in sight of the passers by.

Discussion halls, which constituted a popular feature of public-house life some fifty years ago, are now almost extinct, and the time-honoured practice of formally celebrating a change of ownership of licensed property is fast falling into disuse. The Cogers' Hall, near Fleet Street, still holds discussions; but the custom of inviting some of the nobility and gentry of the neighbourhood to spend a long damp day at the joint expense of an outgoing and an incoming tenant is now seldom observed. A modified form of "a change" is still occasionally to be witnessed, but the proceedings are marked by their brevity and orderliness. The gaugers employed by the two contracting parties having completed their duties of checking the stock, the legal deeds are signed, the money is paid over, and an adjournment is then made to the bar. A fund is started by the new and the old landlords, the other interested parties also contribute, and the proceeds are devoted to the disbursement of champagne and other liquors among the assembled well-wishers of the new management.

Sunday closing in London, though rigorously paraded, is rarely strictly observed.

AT A "CHANGE" IN THE EAST-END.

Many houses in the City proper and the West-End are held on the six days' licence, which precludes a Sunday trade, but by far the greater number of publicans are entitled to open on Sundays between the hours of one and three in the afternoon and from six to eleven in the evening. The licensing law permits a traveller, who has journeyed a distance of three miles, to obtain refreshment during closed hours, provided that he has not travelled for the express purpose of obtaining the drink to which he is legally entitled. But this provision is seldom enforced.

For example, on Sundays during the summer months the Bull and Bush at Hampstead is a very popular resort with pedestrians, cyclists, horsemen, motorists, and travellers in every description of conveyance. All the morning there is a continuous stream of visitors, and the broad roadway is filled with a great variety of vehicles, from the neat dogcart to the stately four-in-hand. Stylish gowns mingle with cycling suits and immaculate frock coats, the outer walls present a network of spokes and handle-bars, and the snorting motor is oftentimes the centre of an interested group apart.

In the poorer parts of the Metropolis the authorities assume a more precautionary attitude towards travellers who demand to be served with liquid refreshment out of licensed hours on Sunday morning. The same law applies to both Hampstead and Whitechapel, but in the latter neighbourhood it is dispensed with rigid formality. In the Clothing Exchange, locally known as "Rag Fair," which lies off Middlesex Street (*née* Petticoat Lane), thousands of people assemble on the Sabbath to sell and purchase ready-made and re-made clothes. The doors of the local hostelry are open for *bonâ fide* travellers, but they are zealously guarded. The proprietor, with note-book in hand, interrogates every aspiring customer. If he is without a railway ticket, his name and address are duly entered upon the landlord's tablet; if he produces his "return half," it is subjected to close scrutiny. Should the date be obliterated—by accident or otherwise—the policeman on point duty is consulted. The precaution is adopted at all the houses in the neighbourhood.

It was an observant Frenchman who, arguing from insufficient information, was deluded by the obvious into the reflection that the omnibus system of London was arranged for the purpose, when it was not taking travellers from a public-house to a railway station, or from a railway station to a public-house, of conveying passengers from one public-house to another. It is, of course, a fact that the termini of the majority of 'bus routes are made at public-houses, and that the average Londoner, in pointing out the way to a stranger, will punctuate his directions with references to well-known taverns. Tell the most puzzled cabman the name of the nearest hostelry, and you give him his bearings in a word. Wonderful structures are these establishments that give individuality to neighbourhoods. Islington has its "Angel," Cricklewood its "Crown," Kilburn its "Lord Palmerston," Newington its "Elephant and Castle," Camden Town its "Mother Red Cap," Hendon its "Welsh Harp," Finsbury Park its "Manor House," Finchley its "Bald-

DURING PROHIBITED HOURS (WHITECHAPEL): I. SATISFYING THE LANDLORD. II. WAITING TO ENTER.

Faced Stag," Kentish Town its "Mother Shipton," and Pimlico its "Monster," while "Swiss Cottage" is named after its distinguishing hostelry. No Londoner could associate any of these houses with any other neighbourhood. Structurally they may be widely different, but in their general plan and their working arrangements they are so much alike that a description of one will stand as a description of all.

Let us glance into this palatial building that runs like a headland into the sea of traffic and divides the current of it into two streams. Omnibuses are drawn up against the kerb on both sides of the house, and a dozen huge lamps throw a flood of light far across the roadways. The interior is divided into some half-dozen compartments, which are duly labelled, and the printed announcement, "Parlour prices charged in this department," or "Glasses only," signifies that a practical purpose is served by these partitions. There is a great deal of noise, but no technical disorder, in the "four-ale" bar, where a small crowd of omnibus drivers and conductors are making full use of their short respite. In the corresponding bar opposite the "horny-handed sons of toil" are interspersed with lady customers; and in the bottle and jug department more women are to be descried, who while their vessels are being filled are fortifying themselves against the return journey. Of children there are none to be seen. This is a flourishing house, and, rather than be bothered with the labour of "corking and sealing" the vessels and interrogating the deceptively ancient-looking youngsters as to their age, Mr. Publican will not serve any children under the age of fourteen years. The distinction between the "private" bar and the "saloon" bar is subtle. The same prices are charged in both. The customer whose desire is to escape the "mutable many" will patronise the former; the latter is affected by the "lads of the village" and their ladies. The saloon bar is the ante-chamber of the billiard-room, its *habitués* are mostly known to the landlord, and often address the barmaids by their Christian names.

As the hour of twelve-thirty approaches, preparations for closing are ostentatiously paraded; the potmen look to the fastenings of doors, lights are lowered, and cries of "Time, gentlemen, please!" grow more peremptory as the minute hand creeps towards its nadir. With the clock strike the customers are outside, the doors are bolted, and the policeman on duty disperses the reluctant groups and clears his beat of dawdlers against the visit of the inspector.

OUTSIDE THE "BULL AND BUSH," HAMPSTEAD, ON SUNDAY MORNING.

A CHRISTENING AT A WEST-END CHURCH.

CHRISTENING LONDON.

By SHEILA E. BRAINE.

BABIES may be all alike—to quote a piece of masculine heterodoxy—but anyone who looks into the subject will speedily discover that christenings differ. The tiny pilgrims just starting on life's strange and perilous journey have their feet set for them in this path or that. The Church, broadly speaking, receives them: but there are more creeds and churches than one, and, in consequence, varying modes of reception. London, city of the world, furnishes us with many examples in kind and in degree.

Let us begin at the top of the social scale, and find ourselves for the nonce among the highest in the land. Here comes a white-robed nurse, tall and elegant, with trailing skirts; she carries in her arms a royal infant, and a powdered footman precedes her. Arrived at the drawing-room, where an august party is already assembled, a lady-in-waiting takes the precious baby from her, and the christening service begins. She then presents him to the Queen, the chief sponsor, and her Majesty, at the prescribed moment, hands him to the Archbishop of Canterbury. The princeling is baptised with consecrated water brought from the Jordan, while the "font" is represented by a golden bowl of exquisite design, which, by the way, is used for all infant "royalties" born within the limits of the United Kingdom. Around it the sponsors are grouped, according to their rank. An ordinary baby contents himself with three, but the heir to a throne may have as many as a dozen, all told.

Needless to say, the hero of the day is always clothed in the daintiest and most costly of garments: nothing is too beautiful for him, He wears pure white, naturally, as we think; but less than half a century back another royal baby went through a similar ceremony in all the bravery of a silver cloth dress tied with pink bows, and an enormously long train. Any sum, say the authorities on such matters, may be paid for a christening robe trimmed with real lace.

Fifteen guineas is an ordinary price: one from the Paris Exhibition was sold by a Knightsbridge tradesman for fifty! Some families possess historic christening suits, which are

A NURSE: NEW STYLE.

preserved with the greatest care. A London-Scottish young lady was baptised in her grandmother's wedding veil and the robe worn successively by her father and two aunts.

The Chapel Royal, St. James's, sees many a christening in "high life"; so does All Saints' Church, Knightsbridge. A favourite time is shortly after luncheon. The guests then return to the house for tea, at which popular and informal gathering a splendid cake is sure to figure, with Baby's name and the date of his birth writ large upon it. Sometimes a Mamma of sentiment will save a slice for her darling to taste in after-years.

The ceremony at the church is neither long nor elaborate. The family and friends group themselves near the font. The godmother, when the time arrives, gives the baby to the officiating clergyman—a terrible moment for the young, unpractised curate—and the chief godfather replies to the question "Name this child." The clergyman either sprinkles the baby or pours a few drops of water on its face from a carved, silver-mounted shell.

The carriages convey the christening party back to the house, or, if the guests separate, they probably meet again at a grand dinner given in honour of the son and heir. Baby in full array and Baby's presents are on view,

while Nurse, all smiles, does not disdain any occasional offerings slipped discreetly into her palm. Very different is she from the "Sarah Gamp" portrayed by Dickens. As to the christening gifts, a simple silver mug is no longer the only article that suggests itself to the mind. Wealthy godfathers and "fairy godmothers" bestow a handsome sum of money, from £100 to £1,000, or arrange that the child shall have a certain amount of "pocket money," paid regularly on each birthday until his twenty-first. Here is a list of presents given to some lucky babies of both sexes: A clock, Irish loving-cup, gold bowl (from the King), perambulator, carriage rug, gold bangle, Louis XV. spoons, silver porringer of antique pattern, clasped Bible, prayer book and hymn book, any number of lovely embroidered robes, and real lace handkerchiefs and veils. A popular present is a tiny gold charm representing the sign of the Zodiac under which the child was born; this the little angel wears, hung round his neck for luck, by a fine gold chain.

No flourish of trumpets heralds the recep-

A NURSE: OLD STYLE.

tion of a "slum" baby into the bosom of the Church. No cake, no presents, no lace furbelows are for him! He arrives rolled up in an old shawl, and wearing a hood borrowed from a neighbour. In some parishes—at Poplar and Westminster, for example—there are evening christenings once a week, to fit in with the hard-working parents' daily engagements. Wander in some Wednesday night about half-past eight, and you may chance upon a curate, two women, and a baby standing round the font, in a silent, dimly-lighted church. Sponsors? Well, "Albert Edward" has a godmother, at any rate, although his godfathers are conspicuously absent; and, being a wise child, he sleeps placidly through the entire ceremony.

Sunday afternoon is a grand time for christenings in populous neighbourhoods. The officiating clergyman may find as many as half a dozen babies awaiting him, decked out as finely as their proud mothers can manage. One, disliking the whole proceeding, starts crying; the rest follow suit: and the parson's voice is drowned by a chorus of wails. Poor little souls, they already find life too hard for them!

Not unfrequently the clergy are called upon to bestow rather singular names in holy baptism. The parents have a leaning towards something flowery, as, for instance, "Dahlia Lorella"; or they desire to "date" their offspring, and so label them "Corona-

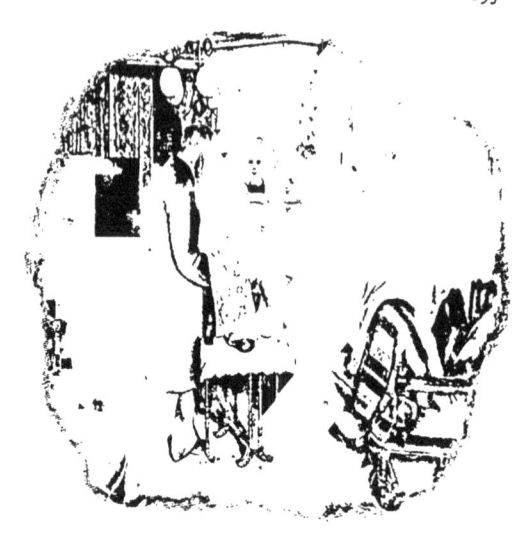

A SCOTTISH CHRISTENING IN LONDON.

tion," "Mafeking," "Magersfontein," or something equally terrible. Royal appellations are popular; hence we get the certainly startling "Queen Victoria" Jones, also "Princess Alice Maud Mary," shortened for common use into "Princess Mogg," and the less ambitious "Princess." The last mentioned was selected by a harassed father, because the relatives fought pitched battles about

A BATCH OF CHRISTENINGS.

the baby's name, and he decided that "Princess" could give offence to no one. In the register of St. Martin's-in-the-Fields we find "Alice Centurion." One small scrap of humanity had to be "Bill," for the reason that William and Willy were already there; while a certain wee Jack owned an elder brother John and a father also John.

The tall Scottish minister entering yonder house is about to christen a "bonny bairn," and the family and sundry friends are already seated round the drawing-room. They rise as he enters, in his ordinary attire, and the brief and simple ceremony commences. A white cloth is spread upon a small table, and the family punch-bowl, an old relic, serves for a more sacred purpose than the one for which it was originally designed. A trying moment soon arrives for the father: he has to stand, the rest being seated, while the minister solemnly and pointedly addresses him on behalf of the child, indicating his duties and responsibilities towards it. Then the mother places the baby in her husband's arms, and it is he who presents it to the minister.

Dark eyes, olive complexions, the murmur of a Southern tongue—signs are these that we have reached the Italian quarter of our all-embracing Metropolis. Entering the Italian church, Hatton Garden, one presently discovers, by the dim light of a dull afternoon, a couple of tiny *bambini*, probably from Saffron Hill, with their attendant guardians. Italians, be it remarked, choose their children's godparents most carefully, for the latter will henceforth rank almost as members of the family.

An old nurse, with strongly marked features, dressed in her native costume, carries Annunziata, aged five days, who is wrapped in a voluminous white shawl, tied round the middle, rather like a Christmas cracker, with a broad, red ribbon. Baby number two, small Agostino, wears a mantle, a much beribboned hood, and a cap with a blue bow. As he is to be christened first, these adornments are removed with speed.

The baptismal service used in the Roman Catholic Church is a highly symbolic one: we can but glance briefly at its most salient details. The priest asks, meeting the baptismal group, "Agostino, what dost thou demand of the Church?" and the sponsors reply, "Eternal life." The evil spirit is exorcised that it may come out of the child, the sign of the cross made upon the little one's forehead and breast, prayers are offered, and the "salt of wisdom" is put into its mouth. Arrived at the font, the priest touches the child's ears and nose; a burning taper is also placed for a second in the tiny hand, in token that it must keep its light shining before the world. The sponsors holding it over the font, due east and west, the priest anoints it with oil between the shoulders in the form of a cross. He next pours the holy water three times upon the little head; and, with a brief exhortation, the service is ended.

Wesleyans have no sponsors for their children, neither have the Congregationalists; with the latter baptism, although generally practised, is optional. Quakers do not christen at all, and the Salvation Army "dedicates."

A "dedication" is naturally of a military character. We are passing the barracks; let us enter the hall where an evening prayer-meeting has begun. Yonder stands the Captain of the corps, and the Adjutant and his wife, parents of the child about to be "dedicated." Behind them are rows of earnest faces, many framed in the dark blue bonnet we know so well. The little girl smiles in her mother's arms, recking not of future warfare, while her parents promise to train her up as a "faithful soldier" and to keep her from "intoxicating drink, finery, wealth, hurtful reading, worldly acquaintance." The Captain takes the child, the corps stand, and solemnly "Mary Greenwood" is dedicated to the service of God and the Salvation Army. He calls out, energetically: "Those who will pray for these parents and this child, and in every way they can help them to carry out the promises made this day—Bayonets—fix!"

"God bless these parents!"

"Amen!"

"God bless this child!"

"Amen!"

"God bless the Army!"

"Amen!"

The "volleys" rattle through the hall; the new recruit cries.

Does not this touch of nature make all our babies kin? And so, having brought them to this first stage on their earthly pilgrimage, let us take our leave of them.

I. A CHRISTENING AT THE ITALIAN CHURCH, HATTON GARDEN.   II. A SALVATION ARMY "DEDICATION."

COUNTY COUNCIL LONDON.

By FREDERICK DOLMAN, L.C.C.

THE London County Council has nothing like the Lord Mayor's Show with which to impress the Londoner in the street, and the annual dinner of its Chairman cannot yet pretend to the prestige of the Guildhall banquet. Yet during its existence it has acquired for London's millions a human interest and a living significance such as no other public body has ever possessed. In the civic activity it calls forth the Council's election every three years is comparable only with London's share in Parliamentary general elections.

On the other hand, it would be hard to find a provincial town which knows so little of its municipal rulers and the actual method of their daily work as does London of its County Council. At election time the Council and its work are the subject of hundreds of meetings, of thousands of newspaper columns, and millions of leaflets and pamphlets. At all times Londoners are constantly confronted with the letters " L.C.C."—at street improvement works, in the parks and on the bridges, on fire-engines and tramcars, and so on. But you might ask a dozen men in the street to direct you to the Council's meeting place without obtaining the desired information. London has not yet its Hôtel de Ville, like Paris or Brussels, to be regarded not only as one of the sights of the capital for its strangers, but also as the head-centre of municipal activity for its citizens. Perhaps this is largely the reason why Londoners, now well acquainted with the civic energy which is transforming the face of their great city, are at present apt to know so little of its source.

Of the hundreds who are crossing Trafalgar Square at this moment, I wonder what small fraction are aware that within a stone's throw —up a side street—are the headquarters of the largest municipality in the world, with a revenue exceeding that possessed by several of the European states. It would require some enterprise for any one of them to discover the "Entrance to Public Gallery" between the shops in Cockspur Street, although to a few earnest students of municipal affairs this is a place of weekly pilgrimage. As it is nearly half-past two on Tuesday afternoon, the County Hall's front door round the corner in Spring Gardens might be identified, after a few moments' observation, by the intermittent stream of members making their way to it for the usual weekly meeting at that hour.

It is a formidable programme of business which each member finds ready for him on his seat in the unpretentious but comfortable council chamber. There are over a hundred large pages in the "agenda," to be disposed of in the four hours and a half which usually represent the limit of the sitting! Nothing surprises the stranger in the gallery so much as the speed with which, at times, page after page of this agenda is turned over by the Chairman, amidst the silent acquiescence of the members. The stranger afterwards learns that practically the whole business of the Council is put before it in the shape of reports from its committees, which the members of the Council generally have already carefully read in the privacy of their homes, the agenda invariably reaching them by Saturday night's post in readiness for Sunday's leisure. Furthermore, the committees work so well that, as a rule, it is only on important matters of policy that their decisions are ever challenged in the open Council.

Nor is debate on these matters ever unduly prolonged. A fifteen minutes rule prevails at Spring Gardens, and the member who would speak longer than this time must receive the consent of the Council, whilst with the approval of the Chairman the debate can be "closured" at any time. Notwithstanding these time-saving expedients, the Chairman finds it necessary to travel through the agenda-

AT THE L.C.C. LICENSING SESSIONS (CLERKENWELL): EXAMINING A WITNESS

MONDAY, May 15th.		WEDNESDAY, 17th.	
Asylum Sub-Committee (Banstead), at *Asylum*	10.25	Education Sub-Committee (Teaching Staff—Section re Selection of Teachers and Instructors) at *Education Offices*	10.0
Education Sub-Committee (Special Schools), Linden Lodge Residential School Managing Committee, *at the School*	10.30	Fire Brigade Committee (View). (*Train leaves Charing-cross Railway Station* (s. e. & c. r.) *at*	10.22
Education Sub-Committee (Day Schools—Section re Examination), *at Education Offices*	11.0	Education Sub-Committee (Special Schools—Industrial schools Cases Section), *at Education Offices*	11.0
Thames Conservancy Board	11.30	Housing of the Working Classes Committee	11.0
Education Sub-Committee (Day Schools—Section re Vacated Schools), *at Education Offices*	12.30	Finance Sub-Committee (Education Accounts), *at Education Offices*	12.0
Building Art Committee	2.0	Education Committee, *at County Hall*	2.0
Education Sub-Com. (Buildings and Attendance) Accounts, at 1.30), *at Education Offices*	2.0	Improvements Committee	2.0
Education Sub-Committee (Special Schools), Aucrley Residential School Managing Committee, *at the School*	2.0	Finance Sub-Committee (General Accounts)	2.15
		Bridges Committee	2.30
General Purposes Sub-Committee (General)	2.30	Theatres Sub-Committee	2.30
Joint Committee on Underfed Children, *at County Hall*	2.30	Finance Committee	3.0
General Purposes Committee	3.0	Theatres and Music Halls Committee	3.30
Education Sub-Committee (General Purposes—Accounts at 3.30), *at County Hall*	4.0		
Public Health Sub-Committee (Cattle Inspector)	4.0	**THURSDAY, 18th.**	
Rivers Committee	4.15	Asylum Sub-Committee (Cane Hill), *at Asylum*	10.20
		Education Sub-Com. (Special Schools), "Shaftesbury" Training Ship Managing Committee, *at the ship*	11.15
TUESDAY, 16th.		Parks Committee (Visit to places in S.E. district). *Meet at Charing-cross Fire Brigade Pier at*	1.30
Ed. Sub-Com. (Day Schools), *at Education Offices*	10.30	Education Sub-Committee (Teaching Staff) *at Education Offices*	2.0
Education Sub-Com. (Special Schools), Drurylane Day Industrial School Managing Committee, *at the School*	10.30	Establishment Committee	2.0
Asylums Sub-Committee (General Purposes)	11.0	Main Drainage Sub-Committee (Accounts)	2.15
Highways Sub-Committee (Accounts, Stores and General)	12.0	Highways Committee	2.30
Housing Sub-Committee (Estates)	12.30	Main Drainage Committee	2.30
Local Government Sub-Com. (Street Naming)	2.0	Fire Brigade Committee	3.30
Parliamentary Sub-Committee (Thames Conservancy Bill, *if necessary*	2.0	Public Health Committee	3.30
Public Control Sub-Committee (Locomotives on Highways)	2.0	Parliamentary Committee	4.0
COUNCIL	2.30	Education Sub-Com. (Polytechnics and Evening Schools) (Accounts and Requisitions, 4.15), *at Education Offices*	4.30

FOUR DAYS' WORK: PAGES FROM A MEMBER'S DIARY.

paper at a high rate of speed, and as he proceeds it may be observed that first one member, then another, shows an anxious alertness, ready to strike in at the proper moment with his question or his challenge.

"Report of the —— Committee," calls out the Chairman of the Council. "I move the reception of the report," responds a voice from the front row of the semicircular benches on which seats are allotted to the chairmen of the committees. "That the report be received," says the Chairman of the Council. If it is the report of a committee, such as the "Highways" or the "Theatres," dealing with some subject of great current interest, there will be a bunch of questions for its chairman "on the reception of the report," and possibly a general debate.

The report having been received, its recommendations are enumerated. To any of these recommendations an amendment may be moved, the usual form of which is to refer it back to the committee "for further consideration," with sometimes a statement of the reason for this course. A show of hands, as a rule, decides the fate of such amendments, the decisions mostly confirming that of the committee. On the rare occasions when ten members rise in their places to claim a division, the division is taken by passing through an "aye" and "no" lobby as in the House of Commons.

Although the benches are always fairly well filled, the stranger in the gallery will notice much coming and going on the part of members. There is a constituent or a friend to be seen in the lobby, a book to be consulted in the library, or even a cigarette to be enjoyed in the smoking-room. After four o'clock the desire for tea begins to manifest itself. The Council's tea-room is an important feature in what may be termed the inner life of the L.C.C. Tea, with the kindred beverages that cheer without inebriating, bread - and - butter, and a dainty assortment of cakes form the only refreshments obtainable at Spring Gardens, and they are provided, together with the service of waitresses, at the councillors' own cost. Now and again the Council's sittings have been unduly prolonged, and on such occasions these edibles have, of course, proved wofully inadequate. The minority, it is said, once nearly starved the majority into surrender on an important question by

L.C.C. OPEN SPACE NOTICE BOARD.

keeping the Council sitting till long past midnight, sustaining themselves in the meantime on a pre-organised supply of provender from one of the political clubs.

But if the tea-room is deficient in its resources in such an emergency, it has at normal times an important influence on the good-fellowship of the members of the Council, and therefore on the easy working of the great administrative machine which is in their hands.

Apart from exceptional occasions, such as the Chairman's garden party in the summer, it affords the general body of members their best opportunities of becoming personally acquainted with each other. Over the teacups sit together in amity Moderate and Progressive who would otherwise remain strangers unless they happened to belong to the same committee. Over the teacups they learn to respect and even esteem each other without compromising their differences of opinion. In the tea-room, too, members entertain the visitors they have introduced to the Chairman's daïs, and it is often graced by the presence of ladies, whose animated talk is prone to sudden arrest on their catching sight of the awe-inspiring maps or plans with which the walls are usually adorned, the room being devoted to the labours of committees on other days of the week.

Yes, if you could see this room on the morrow you would begin to realise the vast amount of the Council's varied work, of which this weekly meeting is only a sort of synopsis, a synopsis which is again reduced to the smallest proportion in the newspaper reports, from which alone Londoners generally learn of their Council's doings. Probably ten or a dozen members of a committee of fifteen are seated round a long table, their chairman at the head, with a clerk and one or two other officials by his side. They are steadily going through a paper of business which may contain over a hundred items, listening to official reports, examining maps and plans, perhaps interviewing small deputations representing affected interests; then quietly discussing in an easy conversational style matters on which difference of opinion shows itself. The committee has been sitting for two hours, and may sit for two hours more. It is the Council in miniature, with the differences which privacy creates. On some matters, for example, speech is freer from the absence of reporters, and a useful part is taken in the

FIRE BRIGADE COMMITTEE STARTING ON AN INSPECTION.

deliberations of the committee by members who never have the courage to rise from their seats in the Council chamber.

If we leave this room and pass along the lobby, we shall probably find four or five rooms in succession similarly occupied. There are over twenty standing committees, and only six rooms at Spring Gardens available for their meetings. Some meet weekly, others fortnightly, and, including sub-committees, it is a common thing for sixty engagements to figure on the Council's printed diary for the week. Although, as we shall see, some of these are not at the County Hall, it is obvious that each of the six committee-rooms sees a great deal of service, whilst occasionally even the library and the smoking-room have to be invaded for purposes of joint deliberation. The largest of the committee-rooms, for instance, is this afternoon tenanted by the Theatres Committee, which is just now in consultation with a distinguished actor-manager respecting alterations in his theatre required by public safety. To-morrow it may be occupied by the Parliamentary or the Public Health Committee, the one busy with the preparation of the Council's legislation for the coming session, the other immersed in important details concerning the regulation of cowsheds, slaughter-houses, common lodging-houses, and the sanitary supervision of London generally. On another afternoon it will be taken possession of by the General Purposes Committee—the Cabinet at Spring Gardens, consisting mainly of the chairmen of all the other committees, and advising the Council on all matters of policy—or the scarcely less influential Finance Committee, which regulates its purse-strings.

In the County Hall itself there is room for only a small portion of the professional and clerical staff employed by the Council. This is scattered in about thirty different buildings, some of them very nearly half a mile away. If you have business with the Parks Department, for instance, you must go to 11, Regent Street; if you then desire to interview some member of the Chemist's staff, you must retrace your steps to Craven Street, only to find that you have passed on the way in Pall Mall the office of a gentleman whom it is necessary to consult on some architectural matter. There is no estimating the loss of time and temper which during a single week of County Council London is thus occasioned to officials and business men generally. Let us hope that with their expletives they mingle prayers for the time when the whole central staff shall be concentrated in a County Hall which shall be worthy of the Imperial capital.

This central staff, which maintains an excellent *esprit de corps* with the help of their own monthly journal and several recreative clubs, forms, of course, but a small proportion of the army of workers employed by the L.C.C.—an army now about 15,000 strong, or 35,000 if school teachers are included—whose operations extend all over the 118 square miles of County Council London, and a good distance beyond. In the illustration on this page are to be seen a few of the two or three thousand men—masons, bricklayers, navvies, and others—in the regular em-

L.C.C. STONEMASONS AT WORK.

ployment of the Works Department of the Council.

As I have said, members of the Council themselves have to travel far and wide in fulfilment of their duties. Let us accompany some of them on their journeyings.

It is about half-past nine on Monday morning when a little group of L.C.C.'s meet on the platform of Waterloo Station. They are members of the Education Committee, and are bound for Feltham, where is situated one of the L.C.C. schools for reclaiming boys from an evil life. It is an hour's journey in train and waggonette, followed by a tour of inspection and two or three hours' work round the committee-table, with an interval for luncheon provided from the school stores at the individual cost of each member. Once a month this visit is made; and every summer, at the annual sports, the whole Council has an opportunity of becoming acquainted with the school, while the best cricketers among them will probably engage in a match with the school team. The care of these boys takes members of the committee further afield than Feltham and Mayford, inasmuch as the Council has a home at Lowestoft for apprentices to the fishing smacks, whilst other boys are given their start in life on farms to which one of their legal guardians, out of regard for their welfare, occasionally pays surprise visits.

Most of the work of the Asylums Committee similarly involves its thirty or forty members in journeys out of London, the main body dividing themselves into sub-committees for regularly visiting the seven L.C.C. asylums in the country around the Metropolis. It is one of the largest committees, and at the same time the one for which there is least competition among the general body of the Council's 137 members. This is not simply because of the exceptional demand it makes upon the members' time — several of them often spend about half the week, I believe, in visiting asylums — but because of the nervous strain imposed by constant intercourse with hundreds of painfully afflicted people.

Every autumn the members of the Theatres Committee hold sittings at the Clerkenwell and Newington Sessions Houses, sitting one day to license places of entertainment north of the Thames, and another day to license those situated south of the Thames.

Nearly all the other committees have occasional "views" to undertake. During the summer the members of the Parks Committee spend some of their Saturday afternoons driving round to the Council's many open spaces, in order that improvements may be considered and difficulties grappled with on the spot. Once a year the Fire Brigade Committee inspects every fire station in London, driving through each district in its turn on one of the Brigade vans, and making one or two trips up and down the Thames in a Brigade tug.

L.C.C. WHARF.

Now and again the members of the Main Drainage Committee are conveyed from Charing Cross Pier in the Council's launch *Beatrice* to see the progress of work at Barking and Crossness, where the sewage of London is so dealt with before reaching the river that whitebait can now be caught as well as eaten at Greenwich, and there are rumours of salmon at Staines. Then the Bridges Committee may have to visit one of the ten Thames bridges which are under the control of the L.C.C. Then, again, the Housing Committee must occasionally make an expedition to Tottenham and Edmonton, in furtherance of its scheme for the establishment of a County Council town there with some 40,000 inhabitants; or possibly to some such place south or west of London, with a view to the purchase of another estate for the accommodation of overcrowded Londoners.

As for the officials of the Council, they are ubiquitous, although it is practically only the firemen that the general public ever recognise at their work. In one street surveyors will be examining an infringement of what is known as the "building line"—securing uniform width of road and pavement—for report to the Building Act Committee. In another representatives of the Public Control Department have stopped an itinerant coal-vendor and are testing his weights. This shop is visited on a complaint that the young women employed there are worked excessive hours or are unprovided with seats; that factory is being surveyed to ascertain whether it has adequate means of exit for its hundreds of workers in the event of fire. And so on through the whole range of social and industrial life in the Metropolis. There are important features of the L.C.C.'s administration, such as the schools and parks, to which I have only incidentally alluded, for they are dealt with elsewhere in this work. But in numberless relatively small matters, lost in the crowd of its larger activities, the County Council day by day has its part in Living London.

A SITTING OF THE LONDON COUNTY COUNCIL.

DYNAMO CLASS AT THE CITY AND GUILDS INSTITUTE (SOUTH KENSINGTON).

THE LONDON CITY COMPANIES.

By CHARLES WELCH, F.S.A

OF London it may be truly said that the past lives in the present. Turn whither we will, we find sturdy modern institutions, fully up-to-date and foremost in the ranks of progress, whose origin dates back to a venerable antiquity. Especially is this the case with those great public bodies, known to most Londoners in little more than name—the City Livery Companies. Some of their functions have become closely identified with our national life. Take, for instance, the term "hall-marked." How many of us realise that we owe this expression to the stamping by the Companies of the approved wares of craftsmen? What was once a practice with most of the guilds now survives almost solely with the Goldsmiths' Company, which carries out these duties by virtue of ancient charters and modern statutes, and without cost, either direct or indirect, to the trade or to the public. The ancient ceremony known as the "Trial of the Pyx," for testing the coinage of the realm, also takes place at Goldsmiths' Hall, under the joint direction of the officers of his Majesty's Mint and those of the Goldsmiths' Company.

Little is generally known of the inner life of these great corporate bodies. Let us take a peep behind the scenes. The Companies follow an ancient order of precedence which includes eighty-nine crafts. Of these seventy-seven only survive, but the gaps caused by the extinct corporations have not been filled up, each Company still retaining its ancient rank. At the head of the list are the twelve Great Companies, distinguished from the remainder by their greater wealth and importance. The relative importance of the Minor Companies, as the rest are called, is fairly well indicated by their position on the list, with but one or two exceptions. The Mercers are the premier Company, and an old dispute as to seniority between the Skinners (the sixth) and the Merchant Taylors (the seventh) is now only remembered by the wise decision of the Lord Mayor of the time, who ordered that each Company should every year invite the other to dinner.

The governing body varies in the different guilds, but usually consists of a Master, Bailiff, or Prime Warden, two or more other wardens, and a Court of Assistants the latter being elected from the general body of the Company who are known as Liverymen. Another class, that of the Freemen, have no share in the government, but possess a claim upon the charity of the Company. Substantial fees are payable to qualify for each of these grades, the first step being to "take up the Freedom." Those who enter by "patrimony," as sons of Freemen, or by "servitude" as apprentices of Freemen, are received at a lower scale than "redemptioners," who, as outsiders, have no claim upon the Company for admission, which they can obtain only by special consent.

The Master and Wardens wear gowns deeply trimmed with fur, and in certain Companies a hood is also worn. Some Companies provide silver medals for their Liverymen, and a gold badge for each of the Assistants; others present a badge to every Past-Master. These insignia become the personal property of the recipients, but the official badge of the Master, a jewel of far higher value, is solely for official use.

The election day, held on the feast of the Company's patron saint, is the red-letter day of the year, and very quaint are the ceremonies observed on the occasion. These vary, of course, in the different guilds. With some, the new Master and Wardens are crowned at table by the outgoing officials with the ancient election garlands. In other Companies the new officials are pledged by their outgoing brethren in the loving cup during the course of the banquet. Many of the Companies attend a neighbouring church in procession to hear a sermon before or after the election. The Mercers' Company has a chapel of its own at its Hall in Cheapside, where divine service is performed every Sunday throughout the year.

Each of the Halls has a court-room, where the meetings of the governing body are held, the Master and Wardens being clothed in their robes, attended by the Clerk and other officers in their official dress. Our photographic illustration opposite represents a sitting of the Court of the Cutlers' Company, at which the Company's apprentices attend to show specimens of their work.

Some of the Companies possess estates in Ireland which form part of the original Plantation of Ulster in the reign of James I. Two of the Companies, the Vintners and the Dyers, have important privileges on the river Thames, enjoying with the Crown the right of keeping a "game of swans." The Fishmongers perform a very useful public office in seizing all unsound fish brought for sale to Billingsgate.

Perhaps the greatest work which the Companies perform is in the cause of education. Their public schools have a world-wide reputation. To the Mercers Dean Colet entrusted his great foundation, St. Paul's School, which is now housed in a splendid building at Hammersmith. This Company has also its own school at Barnard's Inn. Merchant Taylors' School, which long stood in Suffolk Lane, is now more pleasantly accommodated at the Charterhouse. The Haberdashers are trustees of the Aske Schools at Hoxton and Hatcham, the Skinners have their famous school at Tonbridge, and the Drapers, Stationers, Brewers, Coopers, and other Companies have well-known and flourishing schools under their charge. The Ironmongers' and Haberdashers' Companies, though possessed of small corporate incomes, administer most extensive and varied educational endowments.

The University scholarships and exhibitions which so many of the Companies have in

OUTSIDE A CELL, BRIDEWELL HOSPITAL.

COURT OF THE CUTLERS' COMPANY: EXAMINING THE WORK OF THEIR APPRENTICES.

their gift are the means of launching many an earnest student of slender means upon a successful career in life. But apart from their trust income the Companies liberally support the claims of national education; a noteworthy instance being that of the Drapers' Company, which has bestowed upon each of the Universities of Oxford and London munificent grants of several thousands of pounds.

The City Companies were the pioneers in technical education, and jointly with the City Corporation founded in 1880 the City and Guilds of London Institute. Here, at the Institute's City and West-End colleges, young students receive at moderate fees practical as well as theoretical instruction in various arts and handicrafts. The Goldsmiths' Company for long had an Institute of their own at New Cross, and the Drapers extended similar support to the People's Palace in East London. The latter institution—already referred to in "Institute London"—combines general with technical instruction, and has a recreative side.

Many of the Companies also make independent provision for technical instruction in their particular crafts. The Carpenters hold lectures and classes at their Hall, and other Companies hold periodical exhibitions, at which prizes are awarded for excellent workmanship. The Clothworkers' Company follow their industry to its principal seat in Yorkshire, where they have established and support successful technical colleges. Another useful work is that of registering, after examination, duly qualified workmen, who receive certificates of competency, and in some cases the freedom of the Company. The Plumbers took the lead in this direction, and have sought legislative authority for compulsory registration. The Spectacle Makers' and Turners' Companies have also taken action on these useful lines.

Great as are the educational trusts committed to the care of the City guilds, their charitable endowments are even more numerous, and comprise almost every form of practical benevolence. The oldest form of provision for the aged and decayed guildsman was the almshouse. In many a quiet corner of the City until recently were to be seen the almshouses of the various Companies. Later on, the value of City land and the need of less confined quarters led to the removal of these retreats to more open sites.

Of the grants and subscriptions made by the Companies to our great national charities it is unnecessary to speak : the donation lists of these institutions show how greatly they are indebted to such munificence. An entire wing of the London Hospital was built by the Grocers' Company at an expense of £25,000. Some Companies administer trusts for special classes of sufferers — the Clothworkers and others have in their gift important charities for the blind. The Home for Convalescents, established by the Merchant Taylors' Company at Bognor, is free, excellently managed, and replete with every comfort.

Each Company has a marked in-

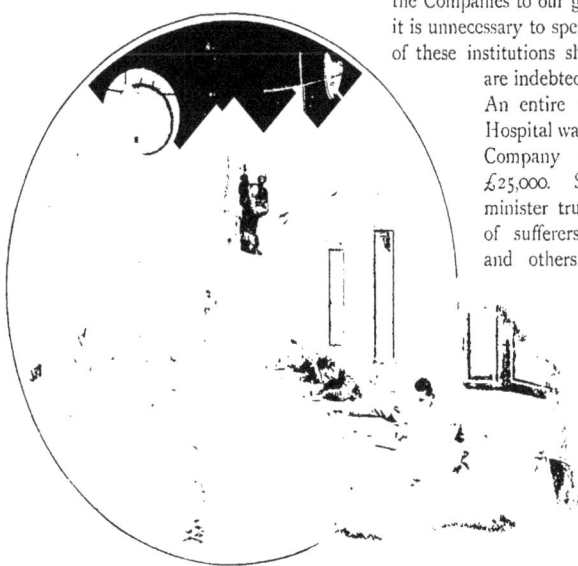

AN EXAMINATION AT APOTHECARIES' HALL.

dividuality, which comes upon the visitor as a pleasant surprise. At the election feast of the Broderers there is a Master's song, which the newly elected Master is required to sing. The Fruiterers present every new Lord Mayor with a magnificent trophy of fruit, and are in return invited to a banquet at the Mansion House. The Makers of Playing Cards present each guest at their annual Livery banquet with a pack of cards, the back of which is embellished with an elaborate artistic design. (On the next page is a facsimile of one of the designs.) The Clockmakers have a library and museum, both of which are deposited in the Guildhall Library. At Apothecaries' Hall the aspiring medical student can, after duly satisfying the examiners, obtain a qualification to practise medicine and surgery; here, too, the profession and the public can obtain pure drugs. The Gunmakers have a proof-house at Whitechapel, where they examine and stamp firearms.

The Stationers are strictly a trade company, and, like the Society of Apothecaries, have a trading stock, shares in which are allotted to their members in rotation. Their chief publications are almanacs, and among these is the authorised edition of the celebrated "Old Moore." Of much greater importance are the duties devolving on the Stationers under the Copyright Act. To secure the exclusive right of publication of any work it must be "entered at Stationers' Hall," This process, which is effected in the Registry, is illustrated on this page.

The Halls of the Companies are among the chief public ornaments of the City. Some of the minor Companies have never possessed Halls; many others, whose Halls were destroyed in the Great Fire of London, or subsequently, did not rebuild them; and

THE COPYRIGHT REGISTRY, STATIONERS' HALL.

the number of existing buildings of this kind is thus reduced to thirty-seven. In most cases these sumptuous structures have to be sought for, their street frontage being insignificant. This is especially the case with the Mercers', Drapers', Merchant Taylors', and Clothworkers' Halls, where one enters through a narrow doorway into a veritable palace. The gardens have almost all disappeared, but that of the Drapers, in Throgmorton Avenue, and the famous mulberry tree of the Girdlers, in Basinghall Street, still afford a refreshing sight in summer.

These stately homes of the Companies have the highest interest for the connoisseur, on account of their many historic and art treasures, some of which are of great antiquity, while others are masterpieces of modern art. To the former belong the specimens of ancient plate, illuminated records, tapestries, early paintings, and ancient armour. The latter include modern paintings, sculpture, porcelain, etc., found chiefly in the Halls of the more wealthy Companies.

The privilege of the Honorary Freedom and Livery is granted at rare intervals by many of the guilds to eminent statesmen, warriors, travellers, philanthropists, and others. Even ladies have been thus honoured by the Turners' and other Companies, whilst many of the guilds permit women to take up their freedom by patrimony. Twice in the year the whole of the Livery are summoned to the Guildhall—on Midsummer Day to elect the Sheriffs, and on Michaelmas Day to elect the Lord Mayor and other officers. They have also a vote in the election of members of Parliament for the City. Apprentices are bound at the Halls and encouraged by gifts and good advice, receiving also in some cases help to start in business. The disobedient and incorrigible are brought before the City Chamberlain, who, in his court at Guildhall, has power to commit them to a short term of imprisonment at Bridewell. Part of one of the cells in this Hospital is shown in our illustration on page 306.

The hospitality of the Companies is extended to all the most notable in our land, and to distinguished visitors from our colonies and from foreign countries. The Salters present each guest with a pair of little bone spoons, a survival, possibly, of the old practice which required all who came to dinner to bring with them their knife and spoon. At many of the Halls the guest is presented, on leaving, with a box of cakes or candied fruits, technically known as "service."

The position of the City Companies of to-day is unique, not only in the history of our own country, but in that of the world. Their existence, in the case of the most ancient guilds, for a period of from 700 to possibly 1,000 years; their past and present services to the country; the immense trusts of which they have been the chosen and faithful almoners; the independence and admirable fitness of their present condition; and the distinguished men who have adorned and still adorn their roll of members—in all these respects they present a combination of age, excellence, and modern vigour absolutely without parallel. Well may we join in the sentiment of the toast so often heard in their Halls, "May they flourish, root and branch, for ever."

A PLAYING CARD DESIGN (PLAYING CARD MAKERS' COMPANY).

LONDON GETS UP IN THE MORNING.

By GEORGE R. SIMS.

LONDON is a city that never sleeps, but a very large proportion of its inhabitants take a night's rest, and consequently have to get up in the morning. The process, simple enough in itself, has many attendant variations. There are lazy people who sometimes envy the domestic dog, who wakes, stretches himself, shakes himself, wags his tail, and is ready for another day of life; there are others to whom the morning ablutions and toilet are a delight, not to be hurried over or mechanically performed.

It is a wonderfully human picture — this rising of the people of a great city for the labours and pleasures of the day — that would greet our eyes could we, like Asmodeus, lift the roofs and gaze within the houses. Let us glance at a few of its details.

In the hospitals, the great palaces of pain, certain nurses and officers remain on night duty till the waking hour. Between five and half-past the sufferers who are asleep are gently roused by a nurse, and those who are able to get up begin to wash and dress. Then the stronger patients, those who are getting better, make their tea and boil their eggs and help to prepare breakfast for the cases who are too weak to help themselves. By seven o'clock the wards are all awake, the day nurses have come on, and everything is being prepared for the visit of the matron, to be followed by that of the house surgeon.

After the hospital is up, the patients who can get about pay little visits of sympathy to the bedsides of their weaker fellow sufferers. Pale faces appear at the windows, sunken eyes look out upon the daily life of the streets, and, in fancy, see far away to the home where dear ones are waking and whispering, maybe, a little prayer for the absent one fighting the battle of life and death.

But there are men, labouring men, whose waking hour is earlier than that of the hospitals. By four o'clock in the morning certain workers must be summoned, for the day's toil will begin at five— at the dock gate and in the great markets you must be afoot betimes. In the common lodging-houses there is frequently a "caller," who goes round and wakes the heavy sleepers. The man who lives in lodgings and has no wife is occasionally roused by a passing policeman, who performs the friendly act from the street.

The rising of the domestic servant is frequently one of the little worries of the good

MARY JANE DESCENDS.

housewife. She has generally a quick ear, and, tread Mary Jane never so softly, should she descend the stairs at a later hour than usual the mistress will hear her, and there will be "words" later in the morning.

Cook, in the ordinary household in which there is no kitchenmaid, is the first to rise, for she has to light the kitchen fire and prepare the kitchen breakfast. One by one the girls come down, as a rule listlessly, for domestic service lends itself to heavy sleep, and the household work of the day begins.

In houses where there is a nursery it is there that the first *joyous* sounds of a new day of life are heard. Young children, like the birds, have a habit of saluting the morning either with song or its equivalent. Romps are frequently indulged in before nightgowns are off and baths are ready. There is an urgent enquiry for toys directly the little eyes are open. Baby girls betray the maternal instinct in a demand for dolls, while little boys have been known to introduce, not only woolly rabbits and baa-lambs on wheels into the nursery bed, but have frequently emptied the entire contents of a huge Noah's Ark on the counterpane pell-mell with Shem, Ham, and Japhet, who have passed an open-eyed night in close quarters, their necks entangled in the hind legs of the greater carnivora. If, in a weak moment, Papa has bought the baby boy a trumpet or a drum, music will sometimes assault the parental ear at an hour when it is least soothing.

It is not infrequently Baby's gentle task to wake Mamma, especially if it is a first baby. When Baby has grown to the age of four or five he—if it is a he—occasionally toddles out of his bed and rouses Papa, bringing a new and favourite toy with him. The fond father, who wakes up with a terrified start to find a black kitten sitting on his neck, easily checks his wrath when he finds that it is his little son who has placed it there, and is eagerly waiting for Daddy to have a game of romps with him.

The family getting up in the morning where the children have to start for school before nine o'clock is to many a mother a daily anxiety. There is so much to be done in a short time; and when it happens also that Papa is a City man, who goes early to business, there is a double strain. Between her husband's comfort and the punctual despatch of the children with the maid, who sees them safely to the seminary, her time is fully occupied. Sometimes everything goes wrong. The servants begin it by oversleeping themselves. There is trouble among the children—sometimes a quarrel and tears. Boots at the last moment are found not to be ready; a school-book has been mislaid. Papa has found his razors have been used by Master Tom for wood-carving, and the shaving process has involved loss of time and temper.

But at last the children have been hastily despatched, with injunctions to hurry, for they are ten minutes late. At last Papa,

THE CHILDREN AWAKE.

with a piece of black sticking-plaster on his chin, has gone grumbling down the garden path on his way to the suburban railway station. Then the sorely tried wife and mother returns to the empty breakfast table, and has a strong cup of tea to soothe her nerves, and for a few minutes forgets her family cares, until the housemaid comes in to clear away. Then she takes the opportunity of expressing her views upon early rising.

In the getting up of the idle classes the variety is endless, for the riser has, as a rule, but himself or herself to please. The society belle may continue to take her beauty sleep long after the ordinary world is astir, and then enjoy the extra luxury of breakfast in bed; or she may be one of the bright, healthy English girls who are up betimes, and taking their morning canter in the Row between eight and nine a.m. The young gentleman who, living in bachelor chambers, is studying life from its late side, is not an early riser. His valet looks in occasionally as the morning advances, and finding him still sleeping retires discreetly. Such a young gentleman, when he wakes to the consciousness that another day has arrived to be killed, occasionally feels "hipped," and requires a slight stimulant before he rises and performs his toilet, and in dressing-gown and slippers lounges into his sitting-room and toys with a carefully prepared breakfast. His earlier toilet is not an elaborate process. He postpones the artistic touches until he is ready to saunter out and allow the fashionable streets of the West to become aware of his presence.

But the waking up is not all comedy even to the well-to-do and well dressed. The night is merciful to most of us in that it brings a little space of forgetfulness, but with the morning the knowledge of life returns. Many a beautiful English girl opens her eyes to the morning sunshine and finds no joy in it, or in the song of the glad birds that fill the air with melody.

A LATE RISER.

For her the course of true love has justified the proverb. There are jealous pangs gnawing at her heart, perhaps despair is in her soul. The scene of last night's ball comes back to her as the flood-gates of memory are opened. It may have been only a lovers' tiff, it may have been the parting of the ways; but it makes the waking hour a sad one, and the doubting maiden sighs with Mariana that she is weary, and she rises with a pale face and dresses listlessly.

The morning postman plays an important part in the domestic drama of "The Awakening." The envelope pushed into the little box with the familiar rat-tat, now in many districts supplemented by the vigorous ring —for knockers are somewhat out of fashion— may contain the best or the worst of news. Brought to the bedside of the late sleeper it may make his waking hour one of tragedy or flood the room with sunlight on the foggiest November day.

The letter may be eagerly expected, or anticipated with dread. It comes at last, and nearly always by the first post. If you are in doubt as to the view which the Fates have taken of the situation, you either tear the envelope open hastily with trembling fingers or you turn it over and over and then put it aside for a while, postponing the verdict as long as possible.

In many a little home the morning letter may mean ruin or salvation. The young clerk out of a berth, with a wife and child to keep, has sent in his application for a situation that has been advertised. He has mentioned his references; he has spent his last sixpence in postage stamps. When he

WELCOME NEWS.

wakes in the morning—lying late, as he has no work to do—his anxious wife stands by his bedside with a letter.

He takes it, but dreads to open it. Is it a message of hope bidding him call at a City office, or is it the stereotyped reply which some firms are courteous enough to send to applicants if they are not too numerous?

The wife waits; the man sits up, and, nerving himself for his fate, tears the envelope open. Tremblingly he unfolds the letter and scans the contents. "Thank God!" he cries, "Thank God!" There is no need to say more. The loving little wife's eyes fill with grateful tears as she falls on her knees and puts her arms round her husband's neck. The letter lies open on the counterpane; she can read the glad news. "Mr. —— is requested to call at the City office. If his references are satisfactory," etc., etc.

There are certain days in our lives when most of us wake with eager anticipation of the postman's burden. The birthday means loving greetings from relatives and friends long after it has ceased to mean presents, and, because it is still customary to consider the knocking off of another year of our allotted span as a feat to rejoice at, most men and women who have retained the "joy of living" wake smilingly upon their birthday morn and ask for their letters.

The waking of the dramatist on the morning after the production of his new play, of the actors and actresses who have taken part in it, is largely influenced by the previous night's reception; but all are anxious "to see the papers" which are brought to them with their morning tea. No matter what may be happening in the world, no matter how momentous may be the events of the day, theatrical folk have only one thought when they open the great journals. They scorn the leaders, and spare not a glance for the latest news. The criticism of the new play is the printed matter in which their interest is centred. They read notice after notice, sometimes with a smile, sometimes with a frown. On the nature of the notices, so far as they are individually concerned, depends the humour in which the player folk will get up in the morning.

There are times when the "paper in bed" makes half the country rise gloomily from slumber. The news of a disaster to England's arms, of a terrible accident at sea, of the death of a popular member of the Royal Family, affects the spirits of the whole thinking community. There have been days when all London has risen with an aching heart, and gone sadly and wearily forth to the day's work.

And there are days when the greater part of London rises gaily. These are the days

LONDON GETS UP IN THE MORNING.

READING THE PRESS NOTICES.

of national rejoicing, of street pageantry, of general holiday-making. The spirit of the gala day is infectious; even those who can take no part in it have a kindly sympathy with it, and get up with a sense of pleasure which has no part in the ordinary working day.

So vast is London, and so small the area usually covered by a public pageant, that early rising is the order of the day on most of these occasions. The police regulations compel the crowd to concentrate on the given points long before the hour of procession. Then the knuckles of the housemaid knock at the bedroom door at an unaccustomed hour, and there is no turning of the sluggard for the "slumber again." Habitual late risers are invariably the first to get up on these occasions. They make elaborate over-night preparations for not being late down, and are among the earliest in the streets. If the morning is fine and warm, they descant loudly on its beauty, and announce their intention of turning over a new leaf and enjoying the early hours of London's sunshine more fre-

quently. But these promises are rarely kept.

On Sunday morning the majority of Londoners take "an extra hour" in bed. There are good folk who go to early service, and many Roman Catholics who go to early mass. There are people bound for distant country trips who are up and about before the life of the day begins; but as a rule the servants have a little indulgence, and breakfast is later. The workers, enjoying the relief from labour, and accepting Sunday as a "day of rest," interpret the phrase literally, and take a portion of it in bed. The "getting up" is a slower and more elaborate process. The creeping hands of the clock inspire no terror of lost trains, the warning horn of the express 'bus will not sound to-day, and church, which is generally

THE BRIDE OF THE DAY.

close at hand, does not begin till eleven. In humble homes Mother is up and about long before Father; for the children must be dressed neatly and sent to Sunday school, with credit to themselves and their parents.

All the hopes and fears of life come home to London in its waking hour. Some of its children rise with their hearts elate and their nerves braced for high endeavour; others wake with a sigh for the days that are no more, and with grim forebodings for the future.

The bride of the day, her heart full of love for the man whose life she is to share, wakes for the last time in the old, familiar home. Some little mist may gather in her eyes as she thinks of the parting from those who have been beside her always until now, and she is filled with vague wonder as to how the new tie may mould and fashion the life that is to be.

But she has given her heart long ago, and to-day she is to give her hand. And so love overcomes all the pain of parting, and hope is in her heart, though the tears may be in her eyes as she looks round the little room for the last time, and begins the elaborate preparations that lead up to the bridal dress and veil and the little family circle of admiration, before she timidly goes down the steps to the carriage leaning on her fathers arm, and is driven away to change her name and be linked by a golden fetter to the man of her heart.

And there is one waking hour on which all thoughts are concentrated now and again as the days go by.

When the hour of doom is to sound for a fellow creature, the hour known and fixed beforehand, many a man and many a woman wake with a feeling of intense pity—not so much, perhaps, for the condemned criminal as for those who love him.

When a hanging morning dawns on London our thoughts go out to the condemned cell in which a fellow creature is waking from his last sleep on earth.

It is said that most of these unhappy ones sleep soundly until the warder approaches and, gently touching them, bids them rise and prepare for the awful moment that has come.

It is not good to dwell upon this waking scene. But, with all its horror, the mental torture for the victim is a question of an hour or two at most.

But for the mother, the wife, of such a man. Ah! God help them in their waking upon that fatal day. The pity of every human heart is theirs when the hour of doom strikes upon their listening ears, and they know that, far away from them, to son or to husband the awful end has come.

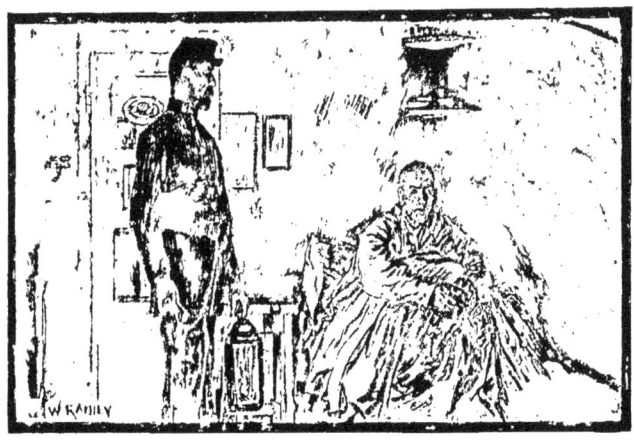

IN THE CONDEMNED CELL.

NET MAKING.

LONDON'S STREET INDUSTRIES.

By P. F. WILLIAM RYAN.

"SWEEP!"

TRADE followed the flag! Trade was a chubby fellow about the height of an umbrella, with an empty bottle clutched tightly under his arm. With his left hand he helped along a tiny mite who was as yet but a novice in the art of walking. The mite's left fist, about the size of a small tomato, was clenched desperately. It was an exciting moment; the eyes of the children proclaimed it. Fifty or sixty yards away was the man selling flags and windmills, his handcart surrounded by an eager crowd of juveniles. What a calamity it would be if the two arrived on the scene only to find his stock sold out! Their troubles were not quite over when, breathless, they reached the spot; for, though there were plenty of flags, there was still some danger that they might have to wait for their proper turn amongst a dozen customers. In the Borough you never wait for your turn. You make it, and take it. The elder boy was a staunch Imperialist. He handed over his bottle and accepted a miniature Union Jack reverently. The babe solemnly opened his fist and looked at his halfpenny. What would it be—flag or windmill, windmill or flag? His small soul was torn with doubt, yet they cruelly hurried him. Then he took a windmill, just because he wanted a flag, and toddled away broken-hearted to cry his big blue eyes out for his folly and his halfpenny.

The toffee-man enjoys beyond all his peers the admiration of the juniors amongst the rising generation. They would make him a Minister of the Crown if only in his flight to Downing Street he would forget to leave a deputy-warden of his stock-in-trade. The toffee-man manufactures his sweetstuff under

CRUMPETS.

SWEETSTUFF MAKING.

FLAGS AND WINDMILLS.

SALT.

BREAD.

the eyes of his patrons. In this respect he differs from all his rivals. In Farringdon Street, Fleet Street, the Strand, Ludgate Hill, and many other thoroughfares pedestrians are tempted with nougat and American caramels, Turkish delight, and other mysterious compounds set out on handcarts with some pretence at artistic effect.

Besides the street confectioners and fruiterers, who pander, of course, to mere luxury, there is a legion of men and women who make a living out of the sale of homely delicacies. Some of these are nearly as well known as though their names figured in beautiful gilt letters over a shop in Piccadilly or Oxford Street. Watercress is much favoured by Londoners, and the numberless hawkers who trade in it find a ready sale for their stock. The shrimp-sellers hardly command such extensive patronage, but they nevertheless cater largely for the metropolitan tea-table. In many quarters there is a brisk demand for muffins and crumpets; nor is there any lack of customers for fritters. The fish hawker is a regular feature of street life. In the eastern districts especially his hand-cart is a great aid to the humble housekeeper in varying the daily menu.

The baker, the milkman, and the saltman may not be popular idols, but from a commercial point of view their position is impregnable. The milkman labours under the imputation of slavishly imitating the early rising habits of the lark. A sleepy age might forgive him the plagiarism; what excites its wrath is the spirited reveille he performs with his tin cans on the area railings.

Most of those who cultivate a street industry adhere absolutely to one line of business. Take the men who hawk hats — and there are many of them — they never think of bartering any other article of dress. Almost any day one can buy a brand new silk hat for five or six shillings in certain streets. The seller is usually also the maker, which accounts for its cheapness. Its pattern might not be the theme of universal laudation at a church parade; but hats are worn at other places. Then there is the vendor of hats that have seen their zenith, and in the autumn of their days are glad to find a resting place on anybody's head.

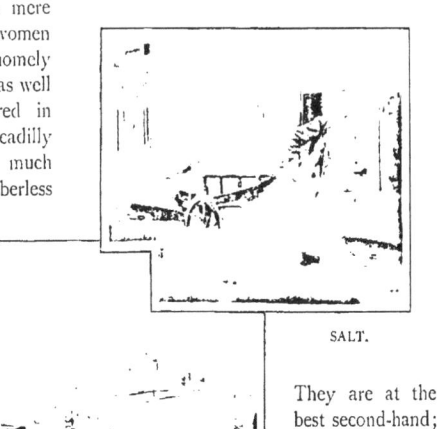

They are at the best second-hand; and at the worst, goodness knows how many hands they have passed through. But the best as well as the worst go for a song. Needles and thread and similar trifles for women's use are hawked from house to house in the poorer neighbourhoods, while many an honest penny is turned by the sale of plants suitable for suburban gardens.

To one man, at all events, London never metes out hard times. It is always the harvest of the chimney-sweep, whose familiar cry brings his calling within the category of Street Industries. One sees him everywhere, and the richness of his workaday complexion serves as well as an auditors' report to demonstrate his prosperity. On Sundays he often drives out with his family, happy in the consciousness that neither war nor pestilence can eliminate soot from this beautiful world. The window-cleaner is almost equally happy so far as business is concerned, for the climate is his faithful ally. Sometimes he is a permanent servant of one of the limited liability companies which exist for purposes of this trade. There is, however quite an army of window-cleaners who work for themselves. These are often Jacks-of-all-trades, ready to put in a pane of glass as well as to polish it.

The coal man is known by his cry. As he leads his horse through the streets he occasionally curves his hand round his mouth and indulges in a demoniacal yell, which is doubtless his professional rendering of "Coal! Coal!" Nobody understands him; everybody hears him! Another familiar street trader is the greengrocer, who carts his stock from door to door, and whose brisk business many a shopkeeper might envy. The china-mender is a less striking figure in the streets than the chair-mender. When the latter is at work a contingent of children belonging to the neighbourhood generally act as his overseers.

"SCISSORS TO GRIND."

Sometimes he is assisted by his wife, sometimes he labours in single blessedness. Occasionally the chair-mender is a woman—the widow, very likely, of one of the trade. The broken chair is usually taken to a quiet square or to a retired quarter of the pavement, and there operated upon. The industry is far from being as good as it once was.

The periodical visits of the scissors-grinder, with his impressive machinery, is an event in the more gloomy streets of the Metropolis. It could not well be otherwise seeing the fuss his wheel makes, not to speak of the sparks he sends flying when a knife bearing signs of long and arduous service is submitted to his tender mercies. Judging by appearances, the scissors-grinder is often one who has acquired a hankering after "cold steel" in the ranks of the King's army. Saw sharpening is much less showy, much less exciting. There are no sparks, and but a poor substitute in the form of a diabolical noise that might well set even artificial teeth on edge. To the butcher, however, it is a delicate operation, to be watched with the same solicitude as a Paderewski might bestow upon his piano when in the tuner's hands.

Street manufacturers are not numerous. Amongst them, however, must be reckoned

CHAIR-MENDING.

the old ladies who make holders for kettles and irons. The tinker is never at a loss for opportunities to practise his calling; and his wife, with the most praiseworthy industry, adds to the family income by making wire stands for flower-pots and similar trifles, which she hawks from house to house. That fishing nets should still be made by hand at a seaside village seems only natural; but to see them in process of manufacture in a London thoroughfare lends an unexpected suggestion of poetry to a prosaic scene. Greater dignity, however, belongs to the woolwork-picture maker, for he is an artist. With his needle and thread he launches coquettish yachts on frolicsome waves, and dots the horizon with armadas. The photographer is an

I. KETTLE-HOLDER MAKING.   II. SAW SHARPENING.

aristocrat amongst those who make a living in the streets. The engraver on glass finds his patrons mainly amongst publicans, though glass ware has now become so cheap that his services are little needed.

One's sympathies go out to the shoeblack more than to any other class of street industrialist, except perhaps the flower-girl. Little wonder; for his life is a hard one, his earnings are sometimes precarious, and yet he is always civil, and apparently content with a small payment. The shoeblacks, following the example of more important crafts, have trade societies. Of these the oldest and most important belongs to the City. Its members, like those of the Borough organisation, wear red jackets. Blue is the colour of the fraternity in East London. In Marylebone they affect white, and at King's Cross brown. Some of the more well-to-do members of the trade provide chairs for their patients, with convenient pedestals for the feet. To the average customer five minutes in one of these imposing chairs must be rather trying. It is probably for the purpose of assisting modest patrons to bear with equanimity the "splendid isolation" of the position that the proprietors sometimes keep on hand a supply of periodical literature. One remarkable member of the corps has a partner in the business—a cat. Since the days of her kittenhood she has been in the trade. A most worthy cat she is in all respects, her one fault being a pronounced spice of vanity. At a word of praise, such as one might let drop as a matter of course without any thought of flattering a reprehensible weakness, she arches her back and rubs against your ankles, purring in an ecstasy of delight.

Step-cleaners in the Metropolis—"stepgirls" they are usually called—are legion. It is a curious calling, but those who follow it no doubt prefer it, with all its drawbacks, to employment which would impose restrictions on their liberty. As a class they are in a sense alien to the hard-driven sisterhood of more mature years who offer their services as charwomen. The vendor of fly-paper is more than a business man, he is a humanitarian. He displays samples of his goods on his hat, a mode of advertisement that is frequently productive of painful surprises to the unthinking fly. Many humble workers eke out an existence by preparing firewood. The pulling down of an old building comes as a godsend to these people. The rotten timber is bought for next to nothing, and cut into small pieces. It is then hawked through the poorer quarters in a barrow, and sold by measure.

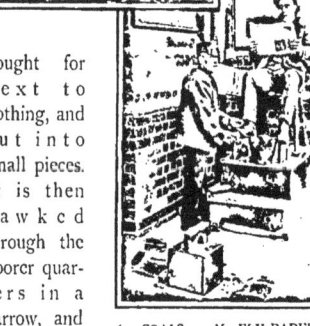

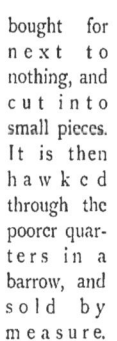

I. COALS.   II. FLY-PAPERS.
III. WOOLWORK PICTURE MAKING.   IV. SHOEBLACK.

The parts that are too tough to be sawn up are called "chump wood." There is firewood and firewood! It is a prosaic trade till

OLD IRON.

Christmas comes. Think of the logs flaming and crackling in the grate on a December night—*the* Night — when the blinds are drawn, and the light shines on the faces of loved ones, and transmutes to gold the mistletoe berries, and to globules of glistening crimson the ripe holly fruit. The Yule-log man is not there, he is out in the shadows; but he has thrown the glamour of poetry over that English hearth.

Perhaps the day is wet. Here is a salesman offering sacks to keep out the rain. This one is old and blind, and in other days was a miller. He is useful still; for, though some people are above facing the weather in a closely woven sack, there are carters and scavengers and errand boys who think little of fashion and much of a dry skin. A parcel has to be sent post-haste; you can purchase the services of a licensed messenger at the nearest corner. You drive up to your door in a four-wheeler. Before you have stepped on to the pavement a couple of rivals for the privilege of helping with your luggage have appeared as if by magic. The clock-mender is now a pathetic figure amongst the army of street dealers; his trade is no longer what it was. The man who buys old iron is one of the few who make a living on the streets by paying out money rather than taking it in.

What cannot you buy in London's highways? Here is a hawker with feather dusters on cane handles, and another with brushes of all sorts and sizes. There are artificial flowers of tints to make a botanist green with envy, and artificial butterflies of tropical brilliancy. A man with "counter cloths"— used for mopping up the liquor which overflows from customers' glasses—is disappearing into a public-house. At your heels is a locksmith rattling a hundred keys on a huge ring. The traffic in old leather bags and portmanteaux is limited. On Saturday nights you may see a barrow laden with them in the neighbourhood of a cheap restaurant or a big public-house. On Sunday afternoons in summer choice fruits are hawked noisily through the residential streets of the west. But in summer and winter, through

STEP-CLEANING.

GREENGROCER.

every night of the year, there is a delicacy on sale which shames the language of eulogy —the baked potato. There it is, big as a melon, and piping hot, its jacket of brown crisped in parts to big, shiny, coal-black blisters.

The children of Little Italy supply a fair proportion of those who trade in chestnuts and ice-cream. Often the Italian cannot speak a word of English. What does it matter! The coppers of his customers are sufficiently explanatory. In the City and the

BRUSHES.

leading arteries of the town business is good, but one can only marvel how the chestnut man in the quieter districts wards off starvation—sometimes, indeed, famine must press close upon his heels. There is a young Sicilian who rolls his barrow to one of the sleepiest of the central London squares. Why he should select such a pitch is a mystery. For hours the nuts on his fire crisp, and crisp, and burn; yet, except on Sundays, hardly a coin comes his way. In

CLOCK-MENDER.

the deepening gloom of a winter's evening, when the tide of life sets homewards, one sometimes sees a group of children gathered round him. They are not buying. They are gaping at him in silence, hypnotised by his pinched face, his great haggard eyes, his air of patient, abject poverty. The tattered dreamer, the wondering children, the battered furnace, form a strangely unreal picture, half buried in the shadows that swathe the square. The man is a helpless, hapless, stricken lotus-eater; the melancholy antithesis of the eager, alert, strenuous army—the tireless, dauntless army, of all ages and all nations —who wring a livelihood, copper by copper, in the fair way of trade from the countless simple needs of the World's Emporium.

OLD SACKS. YULE LOGS. LICENSED MESSENGER.

BIRD-LAND AND PET-LAND IN LONDON.

By HENRY SCHERREN.

A PET PYTHON.

LONDON is a paradise of birds. Here you may see, between January and December, a wealth of bird life which can scarcely be paralleled in any equal area in the British Isles. The Metropolis is one vast preserve; and there is no other city where such interest is taken by the people in the birds.

All have watched the gulls on the Thames, with their outlying flocks that spread into St. James's Park, making the sky white with their pinions, or flecking the river with silver-grey patches as they settle on its bosom. At the working man's dinner-hour there will be few among the crowds that line the Embankment who have forgotten their feathered friends. The gulls swoop down to the parapet to seize the food thrown to them in the air, the bolder ones coming so near as to be within hand's reach, but all fearless from past experience of their treatment. Here is, then, the link between man and the gulls. The birds have learnt that it is pleasanter to spend the winter on a sheltered river, where people provide them with food, than to forage on the sea-shore, when close-time is over, and the plume-hunter is on the look-out for "wings."

London has its share—its full share—of sparrows. They swarm everywhere; they nest under the eaves, in trees, bushes, in ivy and other climbing plants, and the predatory cat takes heavy toll of their young. They come to the window-sill for breadcrumbs, squabble in the streets for the corn dropped from the nosebags of the cab horses, and carry off dainty morsels from beneath the bills of larger birds. They soon learn to know their friends. A gentleman feeds those in Hyde Park and St. James's Park. The birds fly to meet him, circle round him, and have grown so tame that they will take food from his hand.

The London pigeons are as familiar as those of Venice, from which they differ in being the pets of the people, not of visitors. Illustrations on the opposite page show how they are fed outside the Guildhall and in Hyde Park. Similar scenes may be witnessed any day round St. Paul's Cathedral, where are two colonies — one frequenting the east and the other the west end of the building—that do not intermix. At the British Museum many of the regular visitors to the Reading Room make a practice of bringing food for the pigeons that come flying down from their resting places among the statuary of the pediment. Let me describe a pretty incident of which I was an eye-witness. The children of a boarding school were feeding some birds which were enjoying the feast, and hard by was a group of poorly-clad girls and boys, looking on with wistful eyes. A dainty little miss, after consulting her governess, left her companions, and pressed her bag of food into the hands of one of the astonished children. East and west were immediately united in the pleasant task of feeding the birds.

Among the strangest facts of London bird-life are the numbers and the tameness of the wood-pigeons which began to settle here about 1880. In St. James's Park, in many of the squares, and on the Embankment, they may be seen strutting about quite fearlessly heedless of the presence of man. This is in strong contrast to their wildness in the country. They are summer visitors—leaving

I. FEEDING PIGEONS OUTSIDE THE GUILDHALL.   II. GULLS NEAR THE THAMES EMBANKMENT.
III. FEEDING PIGEONS IN HYDE PARK.   IV. FEEDING SPARROWS FROM HIS HAND (HYDE PARK).
V. FEEDING THE DUCKS IN ST. JAMES'S PARK.

A BIRD SHOP ON WHEELS.

us in the autumn to return again in spring, and many nest here. Birds, and of course other animals, have means of communication of which man knows nothing, beyond the fact that it exists. A naturalist, passing through a West-End square, saw a solitary wood-pigeon. He scattered some corn on the ground, of which the bird picked up a few grains, and then flew off in the direction of St. James's Park. It returned in a few minutes accompanied by its mate. It had evidently imparted the good news that there were free rations for wood-pigeons within easy distance.

London is a great centre for homing pigeons, which so many people miscall "carriers." As one comes into town, especially on the east side, one must notice the dormer windows leading into the lofts of the pigeon-flyers. Not that pigeon-racing is confined to the East-End. The King and the Prince of Wales are among its patrons. At a race of the London North Road Federation thirty birds from the royal lofts were tossed with the rest; and at a show at the Royal Aquarium birds from the Sandringham lofts have been exhibited. The London homers fly *to*, not *from*, the Metropolis. Their power of finding their way back is due to training for condition and for knowledge of the route, over which they are tossed at constantly increasing distances. Even with this training a considerable percentage of birds is lost in long-distance races. Some of the London newspapers still employ homing pigeons to bring "copy" and sketches from Epsom and the 'Varsity Boat Race.

"Fancy" pigeons are largely kept, bred, and exhibited. At the Crystal Palace and the Royal Aquarium shows are penned the finest specimens of the numberless varieties. Here are heavily wattled carriers, snaky magpies, pouters swelling with the sense of their dignity, snowy fantails that emulate the peacock in display, and a host of other breeds, nearly every one of which has its special club, all governed by the rules of the Pigeon Club, which takes cognisance of matters relating to the "fancy" generally.

Rookeries, with the exception of the colony in Gray's Inn, are confined to the suburbs. Interference with the trees, as in Kensington Gardens, has driven the birds away. But one may be pretty sure of seeing a magpie in Regent's Park, the jay in some of the outlying districts, and an occasional jackdaw.

In all the parks the ornamental waterfowl are a great feature; and feeding the birds constitutes one of the chief pleasures of the children. The stately swan is conspicuous among the ducks and geese. The dabchick and moorhen have nested on some of the lakes; the kingfisher and mallard have been noted on the Regent's Canal; and the ringplover has been photographed on her nest within the postal district. From time to time the surplus stock of waterfowl belonging to the County Council is sold in Battersea Park.

The parks have become the home of a number of species of smaller birds that there find sheltered nesting places. In the County Council parks miniature aviaries have been erected, in which many brightplumaged species are kept, to the delight of the visitors.

Bird-lovers are social. In one of the large rooms at a famous West-End restaurant, after a modest dinner, the members of the British Ornithologists' Club discuss matters relating to birds, and exhibit rare specimens. The East-End, too, has its social evenings, devoted not so much to exhibition as to singing contests, in which the birds seem to take as much interest as their owners.

Pet-Land is an extensive region, with boundaries that cannot be strictly defined. Just as "one man's meat is another man's poison," so one man's pet may be, and often is, the abhorrence of his next-door neighbour. The man whom Shylock quoted as unable to abide the "harmless, necessary cat" was neither the first nor the last of his kind. Nevertheless, he may have had a Pet-Land of his own, though its limits were too strait to admit of Puss dwelling therein. To feline as well as to canine pets, however, I need merely refer, for they have been already dealt with in the article on "Cat and Dog London."

The providing of pets is a distinct calling. In many of the places where costermongers have their "pitches" may be seen a bird stall, usually with a pretty good stock. Here, at a reasonable price—perhaps from a perambulating dealer—one may buy a grey parrot, with an unimpeachable character as to language, a gaily-plumaged parrakeet, or a cockatoo. Java sparrows and other East Indian finches are here in plenty. The buyer who wants a British bird can be supplied, for the stock includes a jackdaw, a magpie, a jay, larks, starlings, blackbirds, thrushes, linnets, bullfinches, and a goldfinch or two. These dealers will also supply cages—gorgeous affairs, resplendent with brass and gilding—for their permanent residence, or small wooden structures in which to take the new pets home. When the purchaser declines to pay the few pence asked for a small wooden cage, the bird is deftly put into a paper bag, with the corners twisted up, and so carried off by its new owner.

From the street-dealers other pets may be procured—gold-fish for the aquarium; pond-tortoises, as surely carnivorous as the land-tortoises (mendaciously warranted to clear the garden of slugs) are vegetarians; green lizards imported from the Continent; the smaller lizards of our own country and their legless relation, the slow-worm; newts, brilliant in nuptial attire, with a waving crest all down the back; black-and-yellow salamanders from Central Europe; and tree-frogs, scarcely to be distinguished from the leaves on which they have taken up their position.

Larger and rarer pets are to be obtained from the shops where such things are made a speciality. Does the purchaser want a monkey? The dealer will show him a macaque from India, a green monkey from Africa, or a capuchin from South America, and might guarantee to deliver a gorilla within a reasonable time. Are lemurs more to his taste? Here are all sorts and sizes, from the tiny "mouse" he can carry away in his pocket, to the ruffed lemur, as big and as fluffy as a Persian cat. Would he like a suricate, or meerkat, as the C.I.V.'s learnt to call this funny little beast in South Africa? There are half a dozen sitting bolt-upright, like tiny mungooses, and

IN A BIRD AND ANIMAL SHOP (GREAT PORTLAND STREET).

328   LIVING LONDON.

CAGED.

scratching away at the wire-netting in vain efforts to get out. A few armadilloes are pretty sure to be in stock; and, if something specially "creepy" is wanted, there is no lack of snakes, or a few baby crocodiles may be produced for inspection.

In such a shop there is sure to be plenty of birds—Indian mynahs that "talk," the rarer parrots and parrakeets, the monstrous-billed toucans, and a host of others to be seen year after year at the Cage Bird Shows. There are special shops where the stock consists of canaries of various breeds—Norwich, Hartz Mountain Rollers, Lizards, etc. — fancy pigeons, poultry, and waterfowl.

Children affect guinea-pigs, rabbits, white mice and rats. Birds require too much attention for them, and will not bear the vigorous display of interest the average child takes in its pets. Guinea-pigs may be handled and rabbits carried about by the ears without ill-consequences; while mice and rats will thrive under conditions that would soon kill any cage-bird. A little girl of my acquaintance has a pretty pet rat, which is tame and affectionate. Immediately its cage door is opened it runs to her, climbs on her shoulder, and waits to be fed.

The goat is the pet of the children of the poor, and may be said to be, in some degree, their playmate. It has also another character—it is their draught animal; and some of them show considerable ingenuity in utilising an old box for a carriage and scraps of rope for harness.

There are not very many London dwellings in which a pet of some kind is not kept. Among the labouring classes who have migrated to town from rural districts larks and blackbirds are in high favour, and the song brings back memories of green fields far away. The poor are always considerate towards their pets, and many instances are known in which they have denied themselves necessaries that their favourites should be fed.

Everyone will recognise the first illustration on this page as characteristic of not a few London homes, especially in the suburbs. Some rail at the cruelty of keeping caged birds; but even in the case of those that have been deprived of their freedom there is another side to the question—the brightness these petted little prisoners bring into dull, grey human lives. That all caged birds are not unhappy is shown by the fact that some, when released, have returned of their own accord. They are well fed and cared for, and the loss of liberty is not too high a price to pay for such advantages, to which

FEEDING PET LEMURS.

BIRD-LAND AND PET-LAND IN LONDON.

must be added security from their natural enemies.

The fowls and ducks of suburban gardens are on the confines of Pet-Land rather than true denizens; but many fanciers make pets of their poultry, especially of stock birds whose progeny have won honours in the show-pen.

The monkey, from its intelligence and affection, is a king of pets, when its propensity for mischief can be kept within due bounds. If a census could be taken of the pet monkeys in London, the number would come as a surprise to most people. The temper of these animals is, however, somewhat uncertain; and some which are on their best behaviour with the master will scratch and bite the children or the maids. The Monkey-House at the Zoological Gardens is a sort of penitentiary for such naughty pets.

The second illustration on the opposite page represents a collection of pet lemurs and squirrel monkeys probably unequalled in this country. The animals are kept in roomy cages, with space for exercise; the house is just warm enough, with a current of pure air flowing through. They are well cared for by the man in charge, but their owner and friend would feel he had missed a pleasure if he omitted to visit them at least once a day

The lady to whom the 10-foot python shown on page 324 belongs is exceedingly proud of it, as she may well be, for it is a fine reptile, quite tame, and seemingly delighted to be handled by its mistress, and showing no sign of resentment when taken up by others. Every Friday it is treated to a swim in a large bath, and the next day it gets its weekly meal.

The care shown for wild birds and for pets of all kinds is repaid a thousand-fold by the pleasure derived from the consequent fearlessness in the one case and the affection in the other. A bond of sympathy is thus established between Man and the lower animals over which he has dominion. But the care of pets imposes obligations, and these will be best discharged if we resolve—

"Never to blend our pleasure or our pride
With sorrow of the meanest thing that feels."

A STREET BIRD STALL.

MATCHBOX FILLING (MESSRS. R. BELL AND CO., LTD.).

SCENES FROM FACTORY LONDON.

By C. DUNCAN LUCAS.

WE are early astir to-day. The residential west is like a city of the dead: not a blind is up; save for a few stragglers—a weary-eyed policeman or two, a white-faced night-bird in evening dress tramping to his rooms, and a sprinkling of loafers—the streets are deserted. The only sound that breaks the stillness is the clatter of our cab-horse's hoofs. *En route* to the east we pass the great City workrooms, affording employment to thousands of men, women, and girls—tailors, dressmakers, shirt-makers, milliners, tie-makers, makers of artificial flowers—too many, in fact, to name. Little by little the scene changes. As each mile is covered it becomes more animated. The drama of the day is beginning. London's toilers are turning out, multiplying minute by minute, and as the tall chimneys come into view we are plunged into a stream of hurrying humanity that carries everything before it. The humble homes are sending forth their wage-earners. A kiss on the doorstep, a wave of the hand, and the father or mother has joined the great throng.

It is a many-sided crowd, a crowd representing almost every nationality in Europe, and every kind of man, woman, and child. A picture of more violent contrasts you could not imagine. Extreme age walks side by side with adolescent youth, and rude health brings out in sharp relief the pallid features of the consumptive. Every turning helps to swell the tide, which sweeps on fast and furious until at length there is a diversion. We are now in a factory quarter of London, and the crowd suddenly scatters. A thousand eager souls race for this building, another thousand for that. The rest disappear through big gates as if by magic. There are factories for the preparation of almost everything that mortal man can desire — for tinned meats, jams, biscuits, pickles, cheap clothing, hats, babies' food, mineral waters, sweets, cakes, soap, matches, tobacco, pipes, jewellery, upholstery, leather, pottery—indeed it is difficult to call to mind a single article in everyday use in the manufacture of which the Metropolis is not concerned.

The average person has little idea of the immensity of London's Factory-land or of the vast number of people who find employment there. In its busy hives hundreds of thousands of workers are engaged day by day in performing some essential service to the British race; and it is not too much to say that if its factories were to disappear this big, ever-growing city would be bereft of half its strength.

Let us visit that huge place opposite, the yard of which is stacked with timber. A regiment of bright-looking women and girls arrayed in many colours have just trooped in. They are match-makers, and the factory belongs to Messrs. R. Bell and Co., of Bromley-by-Bow. Picture to yourself a gigantic room, clean and airy. To the right a couple of drums in charge of women are revolving, and on these drums are strands of cotton—a hundred of them, and each one 2,500 yards in length. On its way from one drum to the other the cotton is drawn through a pan of hot stearin until its coating of wax is of the required thickness. It is then put aside, and when it is sufficiently firm it is given over to the young woman on our left.

She is a fine-looking girl. Quietly dressed and with an air of responsibility about her, she is a young mother. Her husband is employed at the soap works hard by, and though some one has to tend the babies during the day she is happy—happy because there are two incomes to maintain the bairns in plenty. Her daily output is 2,500,000 match stems. Watch her. She has a cutting machine all to herself, and as the strands of

CREAM FONDANT MOULDING ROOM (MESSRS. CLARKE, NICKOLLS AND COOMBS, LTD.).

wax flow into the frame she presses her thumbs at a certain spot, and behold a hundred stems are cut. Her thumbs never weary. The stems ready, up they go to the roof to be dipped. A man stands at a slab on which is spread the composition—a thick paste. He takes a frame and presses it on to the slab, and in ten seconds you have 10,000 finished matches. If any one should suffer from the deadly "phossy jaw" this man should, for he has been dipping matches for a quarter of a century, but he breathes the air of Heaven—the kindly proprietors, who do not look upon their employés merely as so many machines, lay stress on this—and as a further precaution fans are kept going throughout the day to drive away the fumes.

No one is idle here. Big strapping girls are making wooden boxes at the rate of 120 gross a day : others are filling the boxes with matches at a speed that beggars description ; while over the way men are cutting timber for wooden "lights" with knives as sharp as razors.

If time did not press there would be much more to see, but we are due at Hackney Wick to witness 2,000 men and women making sweets.

The factory of Messrs. Clarke, Nickolls & Coombs supplies the sweet-toothed brigade of Great Britain with 2,000 varieties of sweets, and so agreeable is the stuff that in the course of twelve months from fifteen to twenty tons of it are consumed by the employés themselves. Step into this building by the railway where the workers are a hundred strong. Some are boiling sugar in great pans ; some are kneading a thick, jelly-like, transparent substance that we have never seen before. It is sugar and water. One woman is especially vigorous, and we admire her biceps. Presently she flings her jelly on to an iron peg and proceeds to pull it about with the strength of a Sandow. In two or three minutes it resembles a beautiful skein of silk. Later on it will go through a rolling machine, from which it will emerge a delicious sweetmeat.

There are few more curious sights than those that are presented at a sweet factory. On our tour of inspection we drop into the fondant room. It is full of grey-headed women. But they are not aged. Their greyness is merely starch. Wash away the starch and you have pretty young Englishwomen. These grey-faced damsels make the starch moulds into which the fondant material in its liquid state is dropped to be properly shaped. Walk upstairs and you have a contrast. An apartment is reserved for the exertions of half a dozen girls whose complexions are of a rich coffee colour. Brown as a berry, we put them down as thorough-bred Africans. But they are Cockneys, and brown only because they dabble in coffee and cocoa beans. They are experts in chocolate.

What an industry this is! Men and women, old and young, scrupulously clean, 2,000 of them, are working for dear life. Literally tons of sweets are in the process of making. Suddenly a bell clangs. It is the dinner hour. Labour ceases on the instant, and 700 women troop into the great dining-hall, where penny, twopenny, and threepenny meals are in readiness. There is some chaffing going on to-day, and on inquiry we learn that a chocolate specialist is about to be married. As she has been making sweets for five years the good-natured firm will present her with a five-pound note on her wedding day.

We will now introduce ourselves to the soap-worker. Stand on tip-toe—we are in the factory of Messrs. Edward Cook and Co., of Bow—and peer into that colossal pan. The perspiring individual by our side is the soap-boiler, and the tumbling yellow liquid that we see is soap in its first stage. There are a hundred tons of it, and the men are pumping it into an iron vessel. Passing through iron pipes into an adjoining room it flows into frames, where it remains for forty-eight hours until it has cooled. They are extra busy to-day. One lot of frames is already cold, and the men are attacking the soap—great solid blocks over half a ton in weight. These blocks are carried away, and busy hands will presently cut them up into bars.

Women, girls, and boys, as well as men, find employment here. It is a case of soap in every nook and cranny. One woman is engaged on toilet soap. As the slabs are pushed into the mill she adds the colouring

ONE OF THE CIGAR MANUFACTURING DEPARTMENTS AT MESSRS. SALMON AND GLUCKSTEIN'S, LTD.

matter and pours in the sweet-smelling scent. Round and round goes the mill, and presently the soap is thrown out in beautiful long ribbons. These ribbons are subsequently put into a machine which binds them. Tons and they make cigars all day long, from two to three hundred per day apiece. There is no busier spot in the universe than a tobacco factory. Scrutinise these men; read their faces. Doggedness is written all over them;

MARKING SOAP FOR HOTELS, CLUBS, ETC. (MESSRS. EDWARD COOK AND CO., LTD.).

upon tons of soap are in preparation. One group of workers is marking soap for hotels, clubs, shipping companies, etc. Not a moment is wasted. Study the face of that young bread-winner in the blue blouse. It is as clear as noonday that she is thinking of her home One of a little group, she packs up soap from early morning till dewy eve. And observe that lad over there. He is the sole support of a widowed mother. As a shop boy he might be worth five or six shillings a week, but here as a soap-wrapper he earns double that sum.

Glance now at our photographic picture of a corner of a department in the great tobacco factory belonging to Messrs. Salmon and Gluckstein, Clarence Works, City Road. In this room are employed some 250 persons —Englishmen, Scotsmen, Welshmen, Irishmen, Frenchmen, Germans, Scandinavians, Dutchmen, Belgians, Poles, and others— their fingers are never idle; their backs never ache. As soon as a man has finished his hundred cigars away he rushes to get enough leaf to produce another hundred. He earns on an average from £2 10s. to £3 a week. In the next room women are just as busy. These are stripping the stalks from the leaves; those are sorting the leaves for quality; to the right, men are employed in preparing the leaf for the cigar maker. In other rooms you find girls busily engaged in banding, bundling, and boxing cigars, which are then passed on for maturing. In an adjoining department cigarette making is in progress on a colossal scale, and many machines are here running at a high rate of speed, producing huge quantities of cigarettes hourly. Apart from these machines, very large numbers of men and women are engaged in making cigarettes by hand.

The whole factory is a beehive of activity

Yet despite the feverish movements, which form the chief characteristic of this splendidly equipped establishment, there is a pleasant sense of comfort about the place. Of stuffiness there is none; every room is well lighted and ventilated, and both men and women are not only interested but happy in their work. Perfection of organisation and consideration for the welfare and health of the employés are apparent throughout this huge and up-to-date tobacco factory.

Down at Lambeth, at Messrs. Doulton's, we have the artistic factory hand—the potter. The clay is brought by ship and barge from the pits, and when it has been crushed, washed, and mixed is passed on to the potter. Come into the potter's room. There he is at his wheel spinning round a piece of clay that is soon to be a tea-pot. He is a genius this fellow, and has innumerable differently-shaped articles to his credit. Close by a muscular little fellow is committing a violent assault and battery on a lump of clay. Dashing it down on a slab, he punches it for all he is worth. There is humour in his bright young eye; he belongs to a boxing club. He is not playing, however. He is "knocking the wind out of it," so to speak, so that when he hands it to the potter the latter will have no difficulty in dealing with it. From the potter's room we go to the turners' room. Here a dozen men are giving our potter's vessels—they have been put aside for a while to get stiff—the finish necessary for decorative purposes. Each man is working his hardest. The big fellow to our right is putting on handles and spouts; the small boys who look so chirpy carry the vessels away—on their heads—when they are complete and ready for ornamentation.

Downstairs are the studios. The one we stop at is tenanted entirely by ladies. Twenty of them are seated at a table. They are colouring and decorating the ware prior to its despatch to the kilns. The colours are all very quiet in effect, but will ultimately be developed by the firing. Now to the kilns below. One of them is as big as a house. It is choke-full of ware. Stokers are here, there, and everywhere, and the fires are at white heat. The kilns are unapproachable, so fierce are the flames; yet the jugs and the candlesticks and the teapots and every other sort of ware must remain in that fiery furnace for nine days. Such is the work of the potter.

By way of a change we will visit a babies' and invalids' food factory at Peckham. To-day at Messrs. Mellin's they are making enough food-stuff to fill a hundred thousand little stomachs for a month. The factory is a mass of food. British babies must be fed, and men and women are scurrying hither and thither intent on one purpose only—the nourishing of the young. Yet there is absolute cleanliness and, strange to say, scarcely any noise. The food is non-farinaceous, or starch free, and in the process of manufacture the wheaten flour and malt after saturation are transformed at a certain temperature and then strained through the finest of sieves and taken into vacuum pans

THE POTTER AT WORK (MESSRS. DOULTON AND CO., LTD.).

WRAPPING INFANTS' FOOD (MESSRS. MELLIN'S FOOD, LTD.).

of great capacity—five in number—in which the liquid is evaporated until the result is a fine powder. A great point of interest in connection with the food is that it is untouched by hand.

The next process is the most interesting of all; but we must see this for ourselves, so we will look into the bottling department. A number of men are standing at a narrow table. At the far end is the bottling machine. At the top is a hopper, and a conveyer feeds the machine which rotates and fills the bottles—four thousand in an hour. And the men? They are working like mad, for the bottles are being carried along the table by an endless chain, and each man has something to do and something that must be done in a second. One is putting a strip of cork into the mouths of the bottles as they travel by, another is dropping in the stoppers, a third is pressing the stoppers down, and so on. It is a kind of magic. Upstairs women are wrapping the food as fast as they can go. Baby is clamouring, and his appetite must, of course, be appeased, and at a break-neck pace too.

And now before quitting Factory Land let us glance at those who produce "Living London." The vast printing works of La Belle Sauvage are teeming with life. We will not wait to count the men, because their name is legion, but we will count the machines. There are forty of them in the basement, besides others in different parts of the immense buildings, and monthly magazines and weekly periodicals, presently to be scattered over the face of the globe, are being reeled off at the most furious rate. So great are the bustle and the din that it is impossible to hear one's self speak. Those machines over yonder are printing "Living London." The boys at the top, as agile as young monkeys, are slipping in the paper, one sheet at a time. Away it goes, round rolls the sheet over the type, and out it comes at the other end. It falls into a tray, and a clean shaven man, very wide-awake, having satisfied himself that it is perfect, it is left where it is until the tray is full. Before anything further can be done the ink must be allowed to dry, so the hillock of sheets is put into a lift and sent up to the next floor to the drying room. In this chamber "Living London" remains for a couple of days, when, the ink being dry, it goes away to a machine to be cut up into sheets of eight pages.

Ascend now to the fourth storey, to an

airy room which is full of women. Several thousands of sheets have just come up. This young woman with the jet-black hair is looking after a machine which is folding the sheets into four; her colleagues at the tables are folding them by hand. Further on we introduce ourselves to a battalion of British maidens armed with long needles. They are sewing the folded sheets together.

From the sewing department "Living London" proceeds to an adjoining room, where it is bound into parts. Observe that big man with the enormous glue pot. A pile of stitched parts of "Living London" is by his side, and he is smearing the backs with glue. As fast as each pile is finished it is passed on to another regiment of women, who fix on the outside covers: and then the copies are trimmed and tied up in parcels. How many hundreds of parcels lie before us one is unable to say, but presently an attack is made on them. A number of broad-shouldered men appear and pack them away in the lift, which conveys them to the ground floor, from which they are transferred to the publishing department, where for the time being we leave them. Returning early on publishing day we witness one of the busiest and most interesting scenes in the world of print. La Belle Sauvage Yard is crammed with vehicles. Newsagents' carts, carriers' carts, railway vans block up the entire space; while from the publishing office perspiring men and boys are hurrying out with stacks of "Living London" and other publications on their backs. One by one the carts and vans pass out with their loads, and "Living London" has started on its journey across the English-speaking globe.

Such is the useful life of some scores of thousands of dwellers in the great city. When the hands of the clock—how anxiously they are watched!—point to six, seven, or eight, as the case may be, comes the hour of release. The bells begin to sound, the streets are once more full, and the factory worker heads for home, happy in the consciousness that a good day's work has been accomplished.

PRINTING "LIVING LONDON" (MESSRS. CASSELL AND CO., LTD.).

LUNATIC LONDON.

By T. W. WILKINSON.

Under the Dome.

THE QUARTERLY MAGAZINE OF
BETHLEM ROYAL HOSPITAL

THE BETHLEM MAGAZINE.

FROM Whitehall the roads of Lunatic London radiate in all directions—to the "mental" wards in workhouses, to Bethlem and St. Luke's Hospitals, to private asylums and the more distant county institutions, to remote suburban solitudes where doctors, unknown to most of their *clientèle*, have charge of "single patients."

Whitehall is the hub, because there is situated the office of the Commissioners in Lunacy, under whose care the law places all who are certified to be mentally deranged. But a number of those found insane by inquisition — "Chancery lunatics" — are detained in private houses and chartered hospitals, and, being frequently seen by the Lord Chancellor's visitors, they are, as a result, most carefully looked after.

For those lowest in the social scale—pauper lunatics—the workhouse is usually the first place of custody. Bright, well-fitted rooms are here their quarters unless they become violent, when they are placed in a padded room. Padded room! The sound conjures up all sorts of unpleasant visions. But the newest type of such prisons is as comfortable as maniacal fury warrants. It is about three feet wide and seven feet high, and lined throughout—top, bottom, sides, and door—with perfectly smooth padded rubber, more yielding than a pneumatic tyre inflated for a lady's weight.

Lunatics not suitable for treatment in the workhouse are transferred sooner or later to the county asylum. They are sent away singly or in batches, and then London may see them no more, may never hear of them again. Sometimes a man is lost to the outer world for ever when he leaves the poorhouse gate, and never in more pathetic circumstances than when he is absolutely unknown. This is of a truth one of life's tragedies. A poor creature, found wandering, is brought to the workhouse by a policeman. "What's your name?" A stare or a guttural noise: no intelligible reply. "*What's—your—name?*" Still silence. Further questioning, then searching, then attempting to induce him to write are alike futile to discover his identity. Not a word does he utter, not a letter does he form on the slate. At the asylum renewed efforts are made to find out his name. It is all in vain. Who he is, whence he comes, to what circumstances his mental condition is due—these things are mysteries, and mysteries they remain to the end of the chapter. He continues to be a nameless lunatic as long as life lasts, and ultimately descends to the grave unknown.

Patients whose condition appears to admit of amelioration, and who, while belonging to a superior class to that confined in public madhouses, are yet unable to pay the cost of maintenance in a private asylum, are eligible for admission to Bethlem and St. Luke's Hospitals. Of the two charities the former is the older and more important, and, if no longer one of the fashionable sights of London, is nevertheless deeply interesting.

Enter it, marking as you cross its portals the notice prohibiting visitors from posting patients' letters without showing them to the medical superintendent—a rule made, of course, solely in the interests of the general public. At once you are struck by the blending of the old and new. The building itself, the third Bethlem, belongs to the first decade of the nineteenth century; its fittings and appointments are only of yesterday. In the board-room, you discover presently, there is a collection of shields bearing the names, crests, and mottoes of an unbroken line of presidents and treasurers of the hospital extending far back into the sixteenth century; in the wards the most modern methods in the care and treatment of the insane can be studied. Ancient as Bethlem is, it is the centre whence the latest knowledge pertaining to the medical aspects of lunacy are diffused all over the world.

It is now eleven a.m. The wards are nearly deserted, most of the inmates being in the extensive grounds at the back. Let us pause here for a moment. Down below, spread like a panorama, there is a slice of the gardens, with a maze of trees and shrubs and flower beds, among which females are

A CHRISTMAS ENTERTAINMENT AT ST. LUKE'S.

340   LIVING LONDON.

PADDED ROOM IN A LONDON WORKHOUSE.

winding in the sun. Nearer the building more are pacing to and fro; and over there others are resting on seats. With these male figures are mingled—figures of doctors, who are making their morning round.

A few steps, and we gaze on a companion picture, which includes men only. And now there is more life and movement, and the babble of voices and the sound of joyous laughter rise on the fresh morning air. Yonder the tennis courts—seven or eight in number—with their light-hearted players, and there the rackets courts. Not at all like prisoners are those men. And, indeed, some of them are not such in any sense whatever. Several could walk into Lambeth Road this minute, for they are voluntary boarders—patients, that is to say, who have come here of their own free will and without being certified.

In the background is another remedial agent, which looks from here like the apparatus of a lark-catching combine, but which is really an all-the-year-round cricket ground. The pitch is of asphalt covered with cocoa-nut matting, while the ball—which is an ordinary composition one—cannot travel far before it is pulled up short by a net. Play takes place on this pocket ground two or three times a week, summer and winter alike, and it has been the scene of a distinct novelty in English sports—a cricket week at Christmas.

To one of the female wards now. It is a long, narrow apartment, with a bright and cheerful air and a dominating note of comfort. Some of the female patients are occupied with needlework; in the middle distance a young lady is seated at one of the many excellent pianos that are scattered about the building; and beyond her another female guest is working and curing herself simultaneously by painting flowers on the panels of the door leading to the adjoining ward. The pursuit of art, as well as of music and literature, is encouraged to the utmost. Neither here nor at St. Luke's is it possible to carry out the rule in county asylums of finding most patients bodily work —though at the latter institution some of the inmates are employed at gardening, etc. —because the guests generally belong to the educated and professional classes. So the policy followed at Bethlem is the cultivation of music, painting, and literary composition. This practice, unlike that in operation in large institutions for the insane, does not effect a financial saving on the one hand, and, on the other, it necessarily affords no physical exercise. But the other reasons for which lunatics are employed—occupying the mind and restoring confidence—are fully attained.

To see the Bethlem system in operation let us take a peep into a male ward after dinner. Why, the place is a regular academy of fine arts. All the pianos are engaged; easels are scattered over the floor, with an inmate working away in front of each; and here and there a guest is bent over a table, pen in hand, and committing his thoughts to paper—writing, perhaps, for the quarterly magazine of the hospital, *Under the Dome*. He may be on the staff of that entertaining little periodical, which has its own art critic— who, of course, "does" the picture exhibitions —or one of the regular gentlemen who attend concerts and confer immortality on instrumentalists and vocalists. Or he may be (this is a frightful drop, but no matter) only an outside contributor, bent on submitting a poem or an essay to the editor in spite

LUNATIC LONDON. 341

of that gentleman's notice that he cannot undertake to return rejected communications. Altogether, the ward is the very antithesis of that conjured up by the popular imagination.

Pass now to the recreation room, noticing on the way the many pictures with which the walls are hung. Some are from the brushes of inmates, and are consequently interesting apart from their artistic merit, which in some cases is considerable. The most curious example is not in the wards, but near the main staircase. The subject is Father Christmas, but Father Christmas as he was never yet conceived by a sound mind. Scarcely recognisable is our old friend in the character presented—as a man of sorrows, with long-drawn face and tear-laden eyes.

But to the recreation room. Night is the time to see this delightful side of the hospital. Viewed from the back when a play is presented, it is like a West-End theatre on a small scale. From the orchestra—which is occupied by a band composed of doctors, attendants, and inmates under treatment—come the strains of the overture. Then there is a lull, broken only by the usual chatter, which presently ceases abruptly. Another burst from the orchestra, the curtain which has hidden the fine stage ascends, the characters in the "opening" are "discovered," and then all settle down with a buzz of expectancy. The play has begun.

Such is the scene on one night. On another there is a dance, on a third a "social" or concert, and so on. Entertainments follow one another in quick succession. And Bethlem was once a show place, where the morbid flocked to see its inmates in chains! Nowadays it merits the name by which it is known to many of its guests— Liberty Hall.

Grimy, forbidding St. Luke's is essentially the twin-sister of Bethlem; not so comfortable, perhaps, not with such fine grounds, but broadly a replica of the famous cure house. It receives the same class of patients,

has pretty much the same rules, and has the same system of wards.

Though it is not seen at its best and brightest soon after lunch time, we will stroll through it when the inmates are indoors, resting after their mid-day meal. Into a long room, windows overlooking Old Street on one side, doors leading into sleeping chambers on the other. Silence, absolute silence. The taciturnity of the insane, coupled with their self-absorption and their love of solitude, makes the patients seem more like lay figures than living, breathing men. Through one of the windows a man appears to gaze on the kaleidoscopic bustle and movement below—appears, because his eye is fixed as if he saw nothing and his face is marble in its impassivity. Near him a younger man, his gaze fixed on the ceiling with the same stoniness. To right and left men asleep or looking fixedly at nothing

CRICKET (BETHLEM).

GARDENING (ST. LUKE'S).

but a chair, the legs of a couch, or the floor. Over all an air of unreality. With one exception, the patients are automata. That exception, the only natural and life-like personality in the room, sits at a table—a greybeard, engaged in his favourite pastime of making copies, in water colour, of pictures from the illustrated papers.

Another room, where the worst female cases are associated. More movement and noise here, but not much. Yonder is a group of patients, with two attendants of neat, nurse-like appearance. In one corner a woman is to be seen standing like a pillar; in another a lunatic is in the attitude of prayer—outwardly, a rapt devotee; and close by a poor deluded creature is kneeling before a box of paints, some of which she has been sucking.

And here is a striking contrast. While a middle-aged woman is sitting in listless vacuity, her head drooping, her hands clasped in her lap, fit model for Melancholia, in the middle of the room there is another striding to and fro with regular steps over a fixed course—so many forward, so many back—muttering unintelligibly and raising her arms aloft with machine-like regularity.

How truly painful it is to study the faces of the patients in this and other rooms! The knitted brow of acute melancholia, the grotesque indications of delusion — here perplexity, misery, and fear, there dignity and exaltation — the fixed look of weariness indicative of the reaction that follows acute mania, are all present, with many other characteristic expressions. The rage depicted on some faces might make a thoughtful man apprehensive. What chance would the attendants have if a number of the patients banded together and attacked them? Yes, but by a blessed dispensation of Providence lunatics never combine; they have lost the faculty of combination.

Very different from the ordinary routine aspect we have seen is that which the hospital wears on St. Luke's Day. For then its little chapel is filled with inmates and officials, and a sacred concert is given, as well as an address, which is generally delivered by an eminent divine. Christmas also is a great festival at St. Luke's, having for many years been celebrated with much seasonable fare and fun.

With these and other red-letter days, frequent dramatic and musical entertainments, occasional dances, billiards and other games, and ample reading facilities, life in the hospital is not so dull and monotonous as thousands who pass along Old Street may imagine. Everything possible is done to rouse and amuse patients, and that in this the officials succeed is attested by the high percentage of cures—a percentage which, happily, increases every year.

Another part of Lunatic London remains to be noticed briefly. It is composed of a large number of ordinary dwelling-houses interspersed with private asylums, and inhabited by the general body of that section of the insane who can afford to pay for care and treatment. The tenants of the common-place residences are mostly doctors, who receive "single patients"—harmless, chronic cases, as a rule—for about two guineas per week, for the same reason that "paying guests" are received. Whether they all give adequate value for the money is a point which, interesting though it may be, need not be entered into here.

The other establishments, which are euphemistically known as "licensed houses," because they are licensed annually by the Commissioners in Lunacy, who have power to grant, renew, or withhold such licences in their absolute discretion, vary as much in comfort and charges as in size. Some have all the appointments of a good private house, and a patient may, if he or his friends choose to pay accordingly, have his own private suite of rooms and his own special attendant. And no doubt these proprietary asylums are, as a whole, well conducted.

NEEDLEWORK (BETHLEM).

PREPARING MODELS (MADAME TUSSAUD'S).

A COUNTRY COUSIN'S DAY IN TOWN.

By GEORGE R. SIMS.

MOST of us have country cousins. Sometimes they come to town. When they come in a family party they have, as a rule, a definite programme, and can be relied upon to "do" many of the sights of the Metropolis without your personal guidance. But the male country cousin occasionally comes alone—comes for a day—"runs up to London," having previously sent you a letter to say that he shall take it kindly if you will meet him and show him round.

In my mind's eye I have a typical country cousin. He is of frugal mind and not given to jauntings. But there is an excursion from the Lancashire town in which he lives—one of the so-called pleasure trips which take you from your home in the dead of night and deposit you in London shortly after breakfast time, giving you a long day in the capital, and picking you up again on platform 12 about midnight for reconveyance to the town in which you have a vote and a bed.

It is a country cousin of that kind I am waiting for this autumn morning at St. Pancras. Punctually at nine o'clock the long "excursion" by which he is travelling steams into the station. I grasp his hand, hurry him into a hansom, take him to my house, where he "smartens himself up" and has a hasty breakfast; and then we sally forth to put an amount of hard work into the fourteen hours' holiday that lie before us that would justify the charge of "slave-driving" against any employer who compelled us to do it for money.

First, because I live in Regent's Park, near Baker Street, I take my country cousin to the famous waxworks of Madame Tussaud.

At the great waxwork show, after we have made the acquaintance of kings and emperors, rulers and statesmen, literary and historic and scientific celebrities, and that great gallery of criminal notorieties who remain permanently underground, I have the good fortune to meet Mr. John Tussaud, the modeller to the world-famed exhibition. Here is a chance of taking my companion behind the scenes, and showing him something that the ordinary visitor would never see.

Following Mr. Tussaud into his atelier, we find several celebrities rapidly approaching completion. The figures have been built up, the features have been modelled—in many instances from sittings given by the originals—and now they are ready to have their hair on and their eyes put in.

In the wig department there is a stock of every shade of hair. Directly the correct nuance has been ascertained, the hitherto bald head is carefully covered. The parting is scientifically made, and the curling or waving, if any, is performed by an experienced *coiffeur*. Mr. Tussaud, as we enter his atelier, points to a reigning sovereign whose hair is at present much in the condition it would be after his morning bath. "We can't do his hair yet," says the artist, "because we don't know whether he parts it in the middle or at the side."

At that moment the assistant enters with a telegram in his hand. "The Emperor of —— parts his hair at the side, sir," he says, holding up the opened "wire."

Tussaud's have telegraphed to the Court Chamberlain asking for the information, and thus the parting of his Imperial Majesty's hair has been settled beyond dispute.

We notice that another figure, that of a woman who has just been tried and found guilty at the Old Bailey of poisoning her husband, is without eyes. The sockets are empty. Presently the eye specialist enters, in a blouse such as sculptors wear at their work. In his hand is a box containing eyes of all possible colours. Pinned to the figure is a memorandum on which are all the details of identification that used to be given on certain foreign passports. The eyes, according to this memorandum, are light blue. The specialist picks out a couple of eyes, and Mr. Tussaud steps back and criticises the effect. "Too dark," he says; "try a lighter pair." The eyes are removed, and a fresh pair tried. This time the effect is considered satisfactory. The eyes are passed. For years to come the visitors to Tussaud's will gaze into them, and perhaps wonder how a woman with such gentle eyes could have been guilty of so cruel a crime.

We should like to stay longer at Tussaud's, for my country cousin is intensely interested in this private view, but time is on the wing, and so must we be.

We hurry off to the Baker Street station of the Metropolitan Railway, jump into a train just as it is starting, the doors are closed one after the other by an acrobatic porter, and we plunge into the dark tunnel with "Bang! bang!! bang!!!" ringing in our ears. In a short time we alight at Mark Lane, and steering our way through the busy throngs of business men and workers we enter the charmed precincts of the Tower.

Every country visitor looks upon the Tower as one of the sights of London that must on no account be missed, though there are thousands of Londoners living within a mile or two of it who have never entered it. In "Living London" it has a special article to itself.

After an hour at the Tower we make our way out, and joining the great stream of dull drab humanity hurry to Cheapside; where, to show my friend a phase of City

THE ARTISTS' ROOM, PAGANI'S.

life, I take him into Pimm's, and let him elbow bankers and stockjobbers and City merchants and clerks at the famous luncheon counter. Here he eats with appetite a magnificent slice of game pie, and when he has drained the foaming goblet of ebony stout asks for another, and fills me with envy of his digestive powers. He would have taken his time, amid the rush of hasty snacksmen, but I have to tear him away, for the items on the programme are not few, though far between.

We now make our way towards the great amusement centre, and find there an embarrassment of riches. We are in good time for the afternoon performance at the Hippodrome, and it takes the fancy of my country cousin at once. I have to impress upon him the fact that unless we hurry we may fail to get a seat. The magnificent Roman chariot with the prancing steeds that crowns the edifice has caught his eye, and he is gazing aloft at it with open-mouthed astonishment, in the manner of a rural population paralysed by the unexpected appearance of a balloon in the skies above.

When at last I get him comfortably seated in a spacious fauteuil, he continues to gaze around him at the appointments of the building. The decorations attract him first, then the packed audience in the upper portion of the house. But when the splendid orchestra finishes the overture with a crash of melodious sound, and a bevy of charming young ladies, attired as courtiers of the days of Historical Romance, line up, and form an avenue of beauty through which the performers concerned in the first item on the programme enter, my visitor settles himself in his seat for a couple of hours' enjoyment.

He is delighted with the ring "turns," and the "turns" on the stage, but the climax of his excitement is reached when the entire arena is transformed before the eyes of the audience. The rolling up and wheeling away of the great carpet positively thrill him. When, as if by clockwork, an army of assistants obey the whistle of the ubiquitous stage manager, and a fairy scene is built up by a series of "Hey Presto's," he is doubly impressed.

When I tell him that sometimes, when a water carnival is the close of the entertainment, the whole floor of the arena sinks down several feet, and the space is rapidly filled by a small ocean of fresh warm water, he says, "I have heard about it. Some friends of mine at home came here and saw the plunging elephants. They talked about it for a month afterwards."

After the wonders of the Hippodrome have come to an end, and we are in the street, I suggest that we shall have some tea, and then go to the Coliseum. We make our way to Piccadilly, pass through a crowd, largely composed of ladies, coming away from a matinée at St. James's Theatre, take our tea at the Popular Café, of which he has heard and read a great deal, and then—I had anticipated this item of the programme, and secured seats earlier in the day—we join the eager crowds that are pressing towards the colossal building in St. Martin's Lane.

Again my country cousin gazes spellbound at the beauty of the appointments and the palatial magnificence of the house of enterment, at which you can secure an advanced and numbered seat for sixpence. The performance is beginning as we take our seats.

The song scenas my cousin thinks delightful, and he is greatly attracted by the white-garbed chorus sitting on either side of the proscenium. When he gets a scena from a grand opera, sung by grand opera favourites, he is silent. He has temporarily exhausted his vocabulary of admiration. But he recovers his power of speech presently, and remarks that it is the most marvellous show he ever saw in his life.

I tell him that this vast building is packed four times a day, and he accepts my statement, but wonders where so many people with nothing to do but amuse themselves can come from. I assure him that, vast as the population of the capital is, that is a question which Londoners very frequently ask themselves.

The big "sea piece" of the show, with the moving panorama, and the stage that seems a live thing performing miracles on its own account, brings my country cousin's enthusiasm to a climax, and as we pass out with the mighty crowd into the street, without the slightest confusion or difficulty, he grasps my arm and says, "It was worth coming to London only to see this. By

THE COLISEUM: FROM THE STAGE.

IN THE BRASSERIE, HÔTEL DE L'EUROPE, LEICESTER SQUARE.

Jove, I'm not sure I wouldn't like to go back again and see the next show—the one from 9 to 11. It's all different, isn't it?" "Yes," I reply, "every item is different. There's a double company. One company plays from 12 to 2 and 6 to 8, and the other from 3 to 5 and 9 to 11." "Four shows a day," he murmurs. "Well, it's wonderful. I suppose presently you Londoners will want a show that never leaves off at all!"

It is now eight o'clock, and in our hunger for amusement we have forgotten all about dinner, so I venture to suggest that we might find a place in the programme for a form of entertainment which, if not exciting, is always agreeable. My country cousin confesses that an idea of refreshment a little more elaborate than a cup of tea has been passing through his mind. So I take him to Pagani's, because I want to show him something that everybody who dines at a restaurant does not see.

By the courtesy of Signor Meschini, one of the proprietors, the world-famous little "artists' room" is reserved for us, and there we dine *à deux*.

A wonderful room this, and renowned over Europe; for here the most artistic of London's visitors and London's celebrities have written their names on the wall. Here in lead pencil are autographs that the collector would give gold for. Here are drawings made on the spot at the hour of coffee and cigars. The Italian prima donna, the world-famous pianist, the fashionable artist, the great humourist, the queen of tragedy, the king of comedy, have all contributed to the wall of celebrities. One day not long since a new waiter, eager to show his usefulness, began to scrub out what he called "the scribbling on the wall." Messrs. Pagani have in consequence protected the signatures of their world-famed patrons with thick sheets of glass. These have been obligingly removed for our photographer.

From Pagani's soon after eight o'clock we set out on foot. We pass down Regent Street, where, thanks to the sensible habit of some of the tradespeople of leaving the shutters down and the shops lighted up, the gloom of the desert no longer prevails after closing hours; and so across Piccadilly Circus, gay with illuminated devices, into the ever gorgeous Leicester Square.

First I take my friend into the Alhambra. Here we see one of the poetic and beautifully draped ballets for which the house is famous, and my friend, who has music in his soul, is loud in his praise of the magnificent orchestra.

There is many a tempting item upon the programme, but the hours are hastening on. Leaving by the Leicester Square exit, we stroll across to the brightly

AFTER A MATINÉE

THE EMPIRE PROMENADE.

glittering brasserie of the Hôtel de l'Europe, where at comfortable tables, amid jewelled lights, one can drink the long glass of lager in the most approved Continental manner, and listen to the strains of an admirable band.

Here are the citizens dark and fair of many capitals, little family parties, husbands and wives, lovers and their lasses, folk from the country slightly overawed by the surrounding splendour, and young Londoners complacently accepting the new advance towards the comfort and roominess of the Continental bier halle and café. My country cousin would gladly linger over his lager. But the hour of the Biograph is approaching at the Palace, and thither we wend our way.

The Palace is peculiar among the great theatres of variety. It has no promenade, and its stall audiences are frequently as fashionable as that of the opera, with here and there a tourist not in evening dress, who only heightens the effect of the surrounding toilettes.

The Biograph is the distinguishing feature of the Palace. It followed the living pictures, and has not disappeared; it looks like becoming a permanent feature of the programme. There are a truthfulness and a reality about the Palace pictures. They are always original, up to date. You can see the Derby run over again on the evening of the race; a Royal reception repeated within a few hours of its happening. The journey on a railway engine through Swiss valleys or Canadian snows gives one the feeling of travelling. When my friend has travelled by the express train of the Palace Biograph over the Rocky Mountains, and finds himself as the lights go up still sitting in his stall, he jumps up and exclaims, "Do we get out here?"

I reply in the affirmative, for still before us lies another palace of pleasure, the famous Empire. At the Empire we stroll about, for I want the man from the North to see something of Living London as it takes its evening pleasure in grand array.

To point out to him the famous men about town, the great financiers, the eminent counsel, the "club men," the racing men, and the literary and artistic celebrities who promenade in the grand lounge and chatter in the famous foyer, amid the rustle of silks and the flashing of diamonds, is exhausting, so I suggest that we should take two seats, for which we have already paid, and see the performance. We are in time for the finish of the grand ballet. All that lavish outlay and artistic taste can accomplish in the matter of adorning the female form divine is accomplished at the Empire. Nowhere in the world is the grand finale of a ballet presented with more costly and at the same time refined magnificence. The three great variety theatres of London—the Alhambra, the Palace, and the Empire—are unique; no other capital has anything like them. As a consequence, and also to a certain extent because the entertainment does not demand a great knowledge of the language, they always include among their audience a very large proportion of foreign as well as provincial visitors.

Soon after eleven the audience in most places of entertainment in London begins to make a decided move. At the variety theatres the stalls for some reason empty first, although one would have thought that the train and tram and 'bus catchers to the suburbs would have been the earliest to go.

But at ten minutes past eleven the house empties rapidly from all parts, and by half-past eleven most of the lights of the theatres and halls in the West-End of London have paled their highly effectual fires.

At a quarter past eleven, having given my country cousin a hurried peep into one of the bars found near Piccadilly Circus, and allowed him to feast his eyes upon the tempting display of lobsters and crabs in the famous front windows of Scott's, I assure him it is time to take a hansom. But we are outside the entrance to the Café Royal, and he suggests that, as he has a long journey before him, he shall be allowed to take his final refreshment seated comfortably on a luxurious lounge at this, one of the oldest and also one of the best-known café restaurants of London.

And so it is twenty minutes to twelve when at last I succeed in putting him into a hansom, which bears us swiftly to St. Pancras, where we find platform number 12 rapidly filling with the excursionists who have had a day in London, and are now going to have a night on the railway.

The clock points to ten minutes past midnight, the porters begin to shut doors, the rear guard waves the green lantern, and with a hearty "Good-bye" my country cousin is whirled away into the darkness.

And, having seen more of the amusements of London in one day than I generally see in six months, I go home to bed, and dream that all the shows of London are performing round me, and that I am vainly endeavouring to fight my way through the crowd of wild performers and seek refuge in a hermit's cell beside a silent pool.

A country cousin can accomplish an amount of sight-seeing in twelve hours without fatigue which would leave the ordinary Londoner a hopeless wreck.

"GOOD-BYE."

IN A REGISTRY OFFICE: SERVANTS SEEKING SITUATIONS.

SERVANT LONDON.

By N. MURRELL MARRIS.

MAID-OF-ALL-WORK.

"THERE are no servants to be had!"

The cry begins with the mistresses, it is taken up by the registry offices, it is repeated in the Press. Yet in London alone we have a great army of servants, who spend their lives waiting upon a still larger army of their fellow men and upon each other.

There are always servants for the rich. Money will buy service, if it will not buy faithfulness; it will buy plausibility, if it cannot secure honesty. In the humbler household, where the servant is truly one of the family, character becomes a matter of the utmost importance; and amid this great army the friendly, faithful domestic is still to be found. Servant London is an integral part of all London life, and the class which employs no servants most often supplies them. So huge is the panorama now unfolded, that only a few of its scenes can be given, only a few of its figures can be sketched in

When the great city wakes, the servants wake with it. Peep through the grey and curtainless windows of Westminster Hospital. In the servants' quarters the drowsy wardmaids and kitchen staff are dressing. It is only half-past five, and a raw winter morning; yet within an hour the great building will be cleaned down from top to bottom, and the

HOUSEMAID.

long procession of meals will have begun. No chattering over work, no exchange of amenities at the area steps; housemaid, wardmaid, kitchenmaid, cook — all are subject to rigid discipline.

Eastward the sun is rising, and the river glows a fitful red; eastward still, past the Tower, where the officials' households are waking and the soldier servants begin their day's work; east, and further east to the furthest edge of the city, where Greater London is now wide awake. Follow the river till you reach a desolate region lying below high-water mark, not very far from the Victoria Docks—a region where still the pools on the waste land are salt when the tide is high, and where thousands of grey-faced houses, built squat upon the reeking earth, lean towards each other for mutual support.

This is the servantless land.

These endless rows of expressionless grey houses, with their specious air of comfort and gentility, their bay window and antimacassar-covered table, are tenanted by two, it may even be by three, families housed in the four rooms. These are the people who "do for themselves." And here many of our servants get such guidance in housework as serves them for a training. Here are born and bred the sisters of the little "Marchioness," true "slaveys" in all but spirit, who recount the last battle with the "missus" with that dramatic instinct which never fails the child of the street. "And I give 'er as good as 'er give me, I did; and well she knows I won't stand 'er lip!"

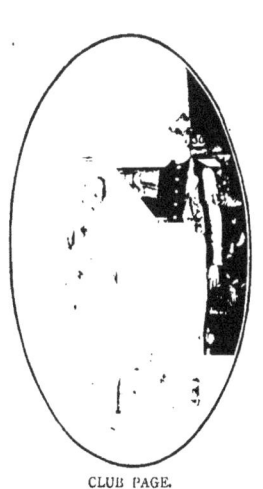

OUTSIDE A REGISTRY OFFICE (TOTTENHAM COURT ROAD): READING THE NOTICES.

Louisarann is fortunate; she left school in the seventh standard (says her mother proudly), and now the "Mabys Ladies" (Metropolitan Association for Befriending Young Servants) have been able to find her "a place—£8 a year all found, and no washin'." Lucky girl! Alice Mary, her sister, left school as ignorant as she entered it, but she too has found work. She has gone as "'general' to the public-house round the corner—father bein' an old customer, and the 'Pig and Whistle' mos' respectable." She minds the "biby" during the day, and perhaps takes a turn at "mindin' the bar" during the evenings.

Let us follow Louisarann to her first place. A lodging-house is "genteel," but life there is not very amusing. It is about six when, on a winter morning, a small shivering object, she creeps out of her dingy pallet bed at the back of the underground kitchen which is her home. A grated window shows the filthy pavement, the yellow fog, and the boots of the passers-by.

CLUB PAGE.

CLUB WAITER.

Hastily gathering her meagre wardrobe from the bed where she has piled it for warmth, she dresses herself, gives her face a shuddering smudge of ice-cold water, and draws on a pair of old gloves given to her by "one of the gents upstairs," to keep the soot out of her broken chilblains while she cleans her flues. Poor Louisarann is neither quick nor skilful, and she gets blacker and blacker as she works

She has only time to wipe off a few of the worst smuts before she is carrying hot water when she has a chance, and she gives an extra "shine" to the "drorin'-room gent's." He is a "real swell, and mos' considerut, the dinin'-room bein' a commercial gent," good-natured, but stingy as to tips. The gents are all right, "but it's the top floor widdy and me as falls out!"

To be rung up three pair of stairs just to be sent all the way down and up again for "an extry knife, as though hanyone couldn't wipe the bacon fat off on a bit o' bread, is one of the widdy's narsty ways." Louisarann has

IN A SERVANTS' HALL: AT DINNER.

up to the top of the house. Down she clatters, and snatching her brushes climbs up again to do the grates in the three sitting-rooms; then up and down she toils, carrying coal and removing ashes. Her mistress, half awake and proportionately cross, comes into the now warm kitchen to make herself a cup of tea and get the breakfast for husband and household. Upstairs Louisarann removes the dirty glasses and cigarette ends, gives a hasty "sweep up," and then, amid the appetising smell of frizzling bacon, toils again up and down stairs, staggering under the heavy breakfast trays. While all the hungry souls but herself are breakfasting, she cleans the rows of boots. She likes to do things well to snatch her breakfast—as she does all her meals—standing.

But the girl has pluck; she refrains from "langwidge," when "missus" is worse than usual, being determined to stay long enough to get a character. Behind all is the great consolation — the day out! To-day she makes her way through the thick and filthy fog to a great house in Berkeley Square, where her cousin Jane is housemaid, "second of four." Carefully the "slavey" feels her way down the area steps, and is admitted.

Jane is a little ashamed of her cousin's shabby appearance, so she takes Louisarann upstairs and "tidies her up a bit." The "slavey" looks round the neat room, and thinks of her bed in the back kitchen, and then and there makes up her mind to "better herself, for she wouldn't stay no longer, not if she was rose every month, she wouldn't." And Jane, sympathising, offers to step round with her to the registry office, if she can get off by-and-by, and speak for her. As they go downstairs, the "slavey" sees a young lady sitting by a fire in a pretty room, sewing, while a housemaid "takes up the bits." Jane gives an expressive shrug, but as the lady looks up says sweetly, "Good morning, mademoiselle." Jane wants to buy her next best dress from her ladyship's maid, who has all the "wardrobe," and who knows how to put on the price if one is not over civil. All day long the panorama of life below stairs unfolds itself before Louisarann's astonished gaze; and she reads with awe the printed rules regulating the work of the huge household. During dinner the butler takes the head, the cook the foot of the table; men sit one side, women the other. As the meat is cleared away, the butler and cook, lady's maid and valet, rise and sweep from the servants' hall. They have gone to the housekeeper's room for dessert and their after-dinner chat. The distinction between "room" servants and "hall" servants is rigidly maintained.

Customs in the big houses vary considerably, and in some great state is observed. Then the upper servants, among whom the groom of the chambers is numbered, do not take their meals with the "hall" servants. They are served in the steward's room, and supper at nine o'clock is really dinner in miniature. Each course which appears up-

COACHMAN.

stairs is repeated below for the "room" servants, even to the "second" ices, prepared by the still-room maids, and dessert of every kind. A glass of claret replaces the homely beer—occasionally something costlier than claret. The ladies are in demi-toilette, with evening blouses, and not seldom with gloves and fan; on great occasions the lady's maid appears in full dress, with ornaments and even jewels, a complete copy of her ladyship. Precedence is strictly observed, and the servants sit according to their masters' rank. The valets and ladies' maids staying in the house join the party in the steward's room. When there are a number coming and going, the presiding butler and housekeeper do not trouble about the individual names, but use those of the master for convenience. Thus the inquiry may be heard, "What can I pass your ladyship?" "Duke, what will you take?"

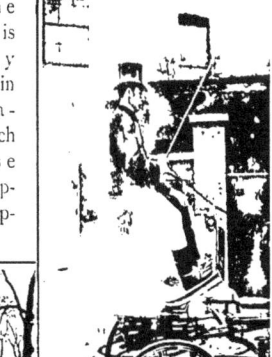

GROOM.

FOOTMAN.

Where do these servants all come from—

who supplies them? There are formal and informal registry offices. One coachman carries the news of Jones leaving to another; there are inquiries at the china shop, or the mistress "just mentions it" to her butcher, a most respectable man, who has served her since her marriage. There are also Servants' Homes, to each of which a registry is attached, and which may be termed, in fact, if not in name, Protection Societies, as the officials fight the servants' battles for them, recovering wages due and giving them that "character" without which they can never get a respectable situation. The difficulties of securing true characters are enormous — about one-half the mistresses are employed in obtaining servants' characters from the other half — and when obtained they are not always to be relied upon, for a mistress "does not like to have unpleasantness."

The law of master and servant also is sufficiently rigid, and prevents a mistress from recording suspicions which she is not able to prove.

Certain registry offices (especially the larger ones in the West End) have a black list, which is always kept carefully posted up and which records the history of the black sheep, male and female. Even as there is a trade in the writing of begging letters, so there is one in the manufacturing of servants' characters, and such a calling will prosper, in spite of all risks of detection and punishment, so long as a written character is deemed sufficient. What can there be to prevent the accomplice from impersonating the complaisant mistress who is losing a "treasure"? The Associated Guild of Registries does much to separate the sheep from the goats, but it cannot prevent the risk to servants who answer specious advertisements. There are "situations," with "good wages for suitable young women," which are not "places" within the accepted meaning of the word, and if the lights in Servant London are bright the shadows are black indeed.

A much-dressed lady is deep in conversation with the head of the registry office. She is the wife of a rich tradesman at Clapham. She keeps a cook-general, house-parlourmaid, and nurse. They are all very trim and neat, and the house-parlourmaid wears the latest thing in cap streamers. The nurse's white dress in summer and her grey uniform in winter mark her separation from the common nurse in coloured clothes. These servants have good places, and they know it, although the rule of "No followers allowed" is strictly adhered to. They serve their mistress fairly, though they do not care about her. The children are the bond between them; and "cook" is always sure of a kiss if she asks for one, for the children—as yet—are no respecters of persons. Next door to them lives Selina, grim and grey, who serves her old-maid mistress with a faithfulness proof against all temptations, but who rules her with a

SERVANTS' FIRE BRIGADE AT THE HOTEL CECIL.

SERVANTS' RECREATION ROOM AT THE ARMY AND NAVY CLUB.

combination of obstinate humility and rampant remonstrances. Yet her mistress, who sometimes sheds a tear in secret because "Selina is so cross," would not change her for all the streamer-bedecked parlourmaids in the world.

Across the road a young housemaid sings as she does her work. She has joined the Girls' Friendly Society, and a portrait of her "G.F.S. lady" is on the mantelpiece in her pretty attic bedroom looking over the Common. On Sundays she gets out to service regularly. She lifts her dress high to show the starched white petticoat beneath it, and as she carries her new prayer-book in the other hand she feels sure that soon there will be a desirable young man only too ready to walk out with her, and then she would not change places with anyone in the world.

Let us now enter one of the fashionable squares on a summer afternoon. Servant life is manifest on every hand. In the garden nurses are sitting under the trees; from the doors the children and nursery maids are driving off to the park, with the schoolroom footman on the box. A newsboy comes leisurely across the square, making it ring with his cry, "Hall the winners!" He knows his customers. The door of a great house opens. A powdered footman stands on the steps and signals to the boy; his face is anxious as he takes the paper. He is gone in a moment, and the house is impassive and undisturbed once more. A little later the butler comes out, and makes his way along Piccadilly towards Charing Cross. He drops in, say, at the Hotel Cecil for a moment, and hears news of the latest interesting arrival. He has several friends there, one a *chef* in the servants' kitchen, which provides for the wants of the staff of 500 persons; another a waiter in the banqueting-room. The latter is one of the hotel fire brigade, and the butler stays to witness a drill and practice. His master is a naval officer, so he next visits a friend, a waiter at the Army and Navy Club, who gives him the latest gossip; for in the recreation room set apart for the club servants the day's news is discussed with vigour over a game of billiards.

In connection with St. Paul's, Knightsbridge, is a Servants' Club which offers a variety of attractions. The Chesterfield Union, a benefit society for gentlemen's

LADY'S MAID LEARNING HAIR-DRESSING.

servants, meets on the ground-floor. Above are a couple of billiard tables and one for bagatelle, while in the basement are a skittle alley and a fine ping-pong table. The top floor contains a reading and dining room, where a chop and tea may be obtained at one end, and light literature at the other; here, too, smoking concerts such as are depicted in our illustration below are organised by the members.

A coachmen's club is to be found in the immediate neighbourhood of Berkeley Square, and the Duke of Westminster gave land for the Grosvenor Club in Buckingham Palace Road; but here, though there are a number of members who are servants, men engaged in other occupations are also admitted.

Hyde Park is the real recreation ground of West-End servants. Before the dew is off the grass the grooms are exercising the horses. Here is a grey-haired man, grown old in the service of "the family," now proudly superintending the baby horsemanship of the young heir on his diminutive pony. Behind him flies a young girl at full canter, her long hair streaming in the wind, as the groom thunders along after his delightful little mistress. As the sun grows hotter the "generals" bring their "bibies" to sprawl and sleep on the grass. The neat maid returning from a hairdressing lesson in Bond Street has an interesting chat with a gentleman's gentleman who has just turned his master out in first-class style, and is himself as near a copy of him as possible. In the late afternoon the magnificent coachman surveys with stolid pride his equally magnificent horses, as they sweep round into the Drive—"my horses," which even "her ladyship" cannot have out at will. As dusk falls sweethearts crowd the shady alleys of the Park or wile away an hour upon the Serpentine; and more than one of the cyclists enjoying the cool of the evening is a domestic servant.

"What!" exclaimed a visitor to her friend, "another new bicycle, and such a beauty?" as she looked at two machines side by side in the narrow hall.

"Oh, no! That is not mine; that is cook's—she says she can't keep in condition unless she has her ride every day."

The great wheel of life in London is for ever turning, and the hands which turn it are those of the servants.

SMOKING CONCERT AT A SERVANTS' CLUB (ST. PAUL'S, KNIGHTSBRIDGE).

THE PESTERING ACQUAINTANCE.

LONDON'S LITTLE WORRIES.

By GEORGE R. SIMS.

SOME one has said that a succession of little worries has a worse effect on the nervous system than one great big worry. Whether that be true or not, there is no doubt that the Londoner's life is beset with little worries, and that he manages to bear up against them with commendable fortitude.

The business man has a hundred little worries beside the ordinary and legitimate cares of his business. Let him be guarded in his office never so effectually the worriers will manage to get at him. They will waylay him in the street as he goes to his lunch, stop him on the steps of the Metropolitan Railway as he is about to dive down below for his evening train, seize his arm as he is stepping into his hansom or his brougham. As a rule these people have some slight claim of acquaintanceship or introduction, or the City man would make short work of them. The worrier generally succeeds in capturing his prey just when every second is valuable. There are heads of great business houses who face a commercial crisis with iron nerves, but are haunted day and night by the dread of being held up by one of the worrying fraternity.

While the business man is suffering in the City, his wife has frequently her little worries at home. In this catalogue the great servant question does not enter, for when a worry comes in that direction it is almost always a big one. The next-door neighbours are a fruitful source of a wife's little worries. The family on one side have dear little children who play at ball in the garden. If they would keep the ball on their own ground all would be well, but it is constantly coming over into some one else's. If you are the some one else and amiable, you don't object to your servant answering the pitiful little cry, "Please will you give me my ball?" say three or four times a day. But if the youthful pleaders cannot make anyone hear they will come to the front door and ring and ask permission to go into the garden themselves and hunt for the missing property. If it has hidden itself among the flower beds the search is not always conducted with dexterity of tread. When it dawns upon you that your neighbour's children are making your garden their daily hunting ground for lost balls, you lose your temper. One day you pronounce an ultimatum. You will preserve your flowers though a hundred balls be lost. Then you are looked upon as unneighbourly by the children's parents. They scowl at you when you meet in the street. Occasionally on fine summer evenings they make audible remarks to your disparagement.

A small vendetta grows sometimes out of this lost ball business. You find a dead cat in your garden path, and you credit it at once to the big brother next door. Occasionally you look up from your garden chair and discover the small children at an upper window making rude faces at you. A letter for you, left by mistake at your neighbour's house, is kept for two days and then given back to the postman. Unneighbourly messages are sent in when you have a musical evening.

Music enters largely into the catalogue of London's little worries. The piano next door is a fertile source of annoyance. In a flat it occasionally embitters existence. In most London houses there is a piano, and it must occasionally be played. But the hours of practice are, as a rule, ill chosen. A piano against a wall in terraces or semi-detached villas invariably plays into two houses at once. The next-door piano sometimes leads to the Law Courts.

There are three animals who contribute largely to London's little worries—the dog that barks, the cat that trespasses, and the cock that crows. The parrot is a rarer source of annoyance, but he makes up for it by being more persistent. To live next door to a screaming parrot would tax the patience of Job. People who have suffered under the infliction have often wondered why it was not included in the lengthy list of that good man's visitations.

The dog does not matter so much in the daytime; such noise as he makes mingles with and is lost in the general *brouhaha*. But when in the dead of night —the hour of sleep—he begins to howl, or to bark savagely at imaginary burglars, or to bay the moon, he is a source of discomfort to an entire neighbourhood. Many a father of a family forgets that his wife is awake too, when out of the fulness of his heart his mouth speaketh.

The cat worry leads to a retaliation of a more practical kind. It has been known to cause threats of murder to poor pussy. "If she comes into my garden again, madam," cries the indignant householder proud of his floriculture, "I'll shoot that cat!" There is a more terrible end than being shot. It is one to which poor Tom often comes through playing Romeo under the balcony of a feline Juliet. The Capulets in their wrath with the Montagus seek the Apothe-

"LOST BALL."

cary, and the dose proves fatal to Romeo, who, finding a tempting supper in Juliet's garden, partakes of it and crawls home to die. You may see at any time in London handbills offering a reward for information which will lead to the detection of the poisoner of a favourite cat. In the Dogs' Cemetery in Hyde Park a heartbroken mistress has buried her murdered tabby. Over its grave originally was an inscription which consigned to dreadful torture hereafter the heartless assassin. The inscription was considered out of order in a cemetery, and the lady was compelled to remove it. So she went to a Chaldean student and had the inscription translated into that language. There it now figures on Pussy's headstone. As no one can read it, it gives no offence. But the curse remains.

The parrot up to a certain point, when his language has been carefully selected for him, is amusing. But he begins to be the reverse when he is placed in the balcony to enjoy the sunshine of a summer's day. In his joy he becomes incoherent, and shrieks. When a jubilating parrot shrieks for a couple of hours at a stretch he is the little worry of an entire neighbourhood.

The begging letter impostor who knocks at your door and leaves a catalogue of

"I'LL SHOOT THAT CAT!"

his miseries, stating that he will call for an answer later on, is an infliction so widespread that he deserves an article to himself. He often works in connection with a gang.

The rush for the omnibus is a little worry which the fair sex appreciate more than the mere man. You can see a crowd of ladies at certain hours of the day standing at well-known street corners, and every face is anxious. For 'bus after 'bus comes up full inside and out. On wet days the anxiety is increased, for then "inside" is a necessity. To make sure of securing a seat in the 'bus is always an anxiety to a woman, when her time is limited, or she has to be at a certain place at a certain hour. When it is a case of the "last 'bus," the anxiety becomes tearful, almost hysterical. For to many a cab is a consideration; the difference between half-a-crown and twopence is sufficient to worry the careful housewife who has a limited income, the young professional lady, the governess, or the shop assistant.

In the winter time there are little worries with the domestic interior which disturb the whole family. The chimney that *will* fill the sitting room with a choking smoke is one of them. In the summer the chim-

"I WILL CALL FOR AN ANSWER."

ney, always a fertile source of anxiety, varies the performance by emptying its soot suddenly over the hearthrug and carpet, and reducing antimacassars and chair covers to a pitiful plight indeed. In the winter, when the frost sets in, comes the worry of the frozen cistern and the waterless home. When the frost is followed by a sudden thaw comes the worst worry of all —the bursting pipe. Then the household assembles hurriedly with cries of terror, as through the ceiling descends a sudden mountain torrent. The servants rush hither and thither with basins and buckets to collect the cataract, and a male member is despatched in hot haste for the plumber. In most cases the plumber is wanted in half a dozen houses at once and arrives when the last possible pound's worth of mischief has been done.

The chimney on fire, in addition to the mess and anxiety and the damage, means a summons and a fine. "Only a chim." is the official report at the fire station when the message for help comes through, but "only a chim." is very expensive to the London householder.

One of the worries to which all Londoners are subjected is that of having their pockets picked. There is not a day passes but a lady finds that while shopping, or travelling by 'bus or tram or by train, she has been relieved of her purse, which she invariably carries in a manner to facilitate its extraction by the expert London thief. When she returns to her home pale, tearful and excited, and gasps out, "I've had my pocket picked—my purse is gone!" the worry is shared by her family. Then there is frequently much anxious calculation as to what was in it. People who lose their purses are rarely *quite* sure what was in them. Sometimes there is intense relief to find that a five-pound note or a trinket had been left at home. Papa does not carry his money so recklessly as Mamma, but he occasionally loses his watch, or a pin, and be he never so well-to-do the loss is a worry to him. He regrets that watch and refers to it for many a month afterwards. If it is a gold one he registers a vow never again to wear anything but a Waterbury.

The lost umbrella is a little worry familiar to all of us. The umbrella stands at the head of the articles that Londoners have a habit of losing. It is left in cabs and trams and railway trains and on counters. It occasionally happens that you are utterly unable to say *where* you left it.

BEHIND THE SMOKERS.

The umbrella acquires a new value in the Londoner's eyes when he comes home without it. In the first hour of his bereavement he discovers that his umbrella was very dear to him. Few of us lose an umbrella with equanimity. It is always a passing cloud across the everyday skies of life.

In humble homes washing day is a little worry—especially to father. Mother's mind is occupied, and the feminine nose is not so delicate in the matter of the steamy odour which washing diffuses through the house. In the humble home, scrubbing day is also a trial to the male members. For this reason many respectable

"MY PURSE IS GONE!"

working-class fathers do not immediately return to the domestic roof when released from toil on Saturday afternoon.

Spring cleaning and house painting are little worries with which all Londoners are familiar. I hesitate to put spring cleaning in the catalogue. It extends over a period of time, and runs into so many "new" things in the carpet and curtain line which "we really must have" when the house has been done up, that it strikes the major rather than the minor note in one's "troubled lot below."

The latchkey occasionally leads to a little worry. Sometimes we go out without it when we are supposed to have it with us. This always happens when its possession is most sorely needed. Paterfamilias is going to a City banquet, or to dine at his club, and won't be home till late. The household retires at its usual time. About one o'clock the head of the family returns from the festivity in a hansom. He pays the driver and dismisses him, then puffing calmly at his cigar puts his hand in his pocket for his latchkey. It isn't there. There is nothing for it but to knock. It is no good ringing, because the bells ring below, and everyone is upstairs. So he knocks, gently at first, then, seeing no light moving about, he knocks again and presently loses his temper and bangs furiously. The whole neighbourhood probably hears him before his own people. But eventually he sees a light, and inside the door he can hear a nervous hand manipulating the chain.

The forgotten latchkey is a little worry that wise men have decided to avoid. They now carry the useful and convenient article on a chain attached to their braces.

There are Londoners who suffer systematic annoyance from the unfortunate peculiarities of the locality in which they have made a home. Brown is in a constant state of fever owing to the proximity of certain church bells, which he declares ring without ceasing. Jones is the victim of a steam whistle, which at some large works hard by his happy home makes hideous disturbance at an unearthly hour in the morning and at intervals during the day. Robinson is the victim of "vibration," a railway passing near his residence, his windows are perpetually rattling, his house occasionally "shudders," and when a limited mail passes in the night his bed (the expression is his) "rocks him" not to sleep but out of it.

Street noises have become such maddening minor worries to Londoners of late years that the law has been invoked. The old London cries are no longer prized for their quaintness. The street hawker is ordered to moderate his methods by the passing policeman, and the newspaper boy gets fourteen days for announcing another "great railway accident" or a "shocking murder" to the homestaying householder.

There are little worries of the outdoor walk with which all Londoners are familiar. Orange peel and banana skins on the pavement are so worrying to pedestrians that special police notices are issued with regard to them.

The Londoner who doesn't smoke is constantly finding a worry in the Londoner who does. Since the fair sex and the "pale young curate" have socially elevated the top of the 'bus and the roof of the tram there has been continual outcry against the outside smoker, who puffs his tobacco into an eye that looks upon it unsympathetically. On some 'buses and trams in the back seats only may pipe, cigar, or cigarette be indulged in. The tobacco smoke worry has been relieved to this extent.

There is another little worry which many Londoners have endured for years almost uncomplainingly, that is the worry of trying to buy a postage stamp after 8 p.m. in a suburban neighbourhood. It occasionally leads to another little worry, namely, a letter of no particular interest, for which you have to pay the postman twopence.

That the area merchant—the gentleman with a bag on a barrow—who calls at your area door to barter with your cook is a worry is proved by the large number of London houses which now exhibit in bold display the printed legend "No Bottles," sometimes in conjunction with the warning hint "Beware of the Dog."

Against this worry one can always barricade one's doors, but there is a worrier from whom there is little protection. The whining beggar who follows nervous women in the lonely street after nightfall is not easily disposed of. If the beggar is a man he has only to look villainous and to talk gruffly to levy his blackmail. If the beggar is a woman she sometimes obtains her object by pleasantly referring to the fact that she has left the bedside of a child who is suffering from scarlet fever, small-pox, or some other infectious disease. There are nervous ladies who, after being accompanied for a few minutes by such a woman, not only bestow alms in their alarm, but rush home and disrobe and subject their clothes to a disinfecting process before they wear them again. For the worrying beggar with the scarlatina child always takes care to rub shoulders with her prey.

These are but a few of London's little worries, but they are a sample of the mass. They are inevitable in the complex life of a great city. On the whole they are borne philosophically by everyone—except the people personally affected by them.

A WHINING APPEAL.

LONDON'S WASH-HOUSES AND BATHS.

By I. BROOKE-ALDER.

GREAT as have been the improvements to London, and numerous the benefits bestowed upon its inhabitants during recent years, there is probably no item of advancement more noticeable than that which concerns provision for cleanliness. Time was when to find a fitted bath-room in an otherwise elegant private house was the exception, and when a swimming bath was a well-nigh unknown luxury to dwellers in the Metropolis; but nowadays quite modest houses boast their hot-water furnished bath, rendering the all-over wash an easily acquired feature of the daily programme; and almost every district owns its public bathing establishment, comprising under one roof several grades of baths—private and swimming.

But besides these noteworthy signs of grace, immense progress has been made in regard to wash-houses, or laundries, where, under the new order of things, the public is provided with accommodation and every time-saving appliance for the washing of clothes and household belongings. For the rapid increase in the facilities for cleanliness thanks are due to the various Borough Councils and to the liberality of certain philanthropists, who, in conjunction with the (ordinarily) grumbling ratepayers, have provided the means to this satisfactory end. The modern public baths and their adjacent wash-houses are the natural result of the gradual adoption of an Act of Parliament relating to this subject. The comprehensive scale of their enterprise can be gauged by realising the extent to which they have been adopted in the Metropolis and its suburbs. Their far-reaching influence for good can,

IN A PUBLIC WASH-HOUSE (MARYLEBONE ROAD): WASHING.

LONDON'S WASH-HOUSES AND BATHS. 365

MEN'S PRIVATE BATHS (HORNSEY ROAD BATHS AND WASH-HOUSES).

however, only be adequately judged by those who are familiar with the daily life of Living London, in its many phases, from the lowest upwards.

To such a well-informed Cockney the consideration of "how London washes" would provide a fairly exhaustive review of Metropolitan existence. He would see in his mind's eye the various representatives of hard-working poverty washing their meagre scraps of clothing; the moderately prosperous members of the tradesman class enjoying frequent hot baths; the vast numbers that stand for energetic youth taking lessons in swimming, or joining in aquatic sports; and the smaller detachment which impersonates leisurely wealth indulging in the various kinds of comparatively expensive baths, such as medicated, electric, vapour, spray, and Turkish.

The first visit to a public wash-house is an experience that is not easily banished from the memory, especially if it take place in a poor locality and on a popular day. Shoreditch, Hackney, Bermondsey, Westminster, Soho (Marshall Street, Golden Square), are fruitful examples, and Friday and Saturday notable days. Marylebone runs them close. It is remarkable that as the week progresses the class of person who brings her possessions to the wash-houses deteriorates. By some unwritten law or unpublished code of manners the orderly members of the local community almost entirely monopolise the first half of the week, whilst the last three days belong to a gradually descending scale. The exceptions to this almost invariable rule are furnished by those whose wage-earning employment leaves them free only during the "early closing" hours of Saturday. On Monday come demure dames, primly precise of bearing, arrayed with an almost awe-inspiring neatness, even to the full complement of buttons on boots and gloves, and the exact adjustment of the chenille spotted veil. Behind these worthy matrons is borne by an attendant the brown paper

IN A PUBLIC WASH-HOUSE (MARSHALL STREET, W.): FOLDING AND MANGLING.

enclosed consignment of linen destined for the soapsuds. Tuesday sees a reproduction of such dignified processions, with, perhaps, less dignity as the afternoon advances. By Wednesday all pomp and vanity have disappeared. Washing is frankly carried, tied up in a sheet by the laundress herself, the great bundle protruding from the shawl that serves her as hat and mantle combined, or it shares a crippled perambulator with two small children. To Tom and Sallie the weekly sojourn in the wash-house ante-room, " 'long er Mrs. O'Hagan's Pat and Norah," while their mothers do the washing, is the most delightful of outings!

On entering such a laundry from the street, or a cool stone staircase, the immediate impression is of overwhelming heat and discomforting clouds of steam; but that soon passes, and one is conscious of a lofty, well-ventilated room, divided from end to end by rows of troughs, separated into couples by six-feet high partitions. In each division stands a woman washing; at her feet a pile of dirty clothes, and behind her a basket of clean ones. Her arms are plunged elbow-deep into one of the two troughs of which she is temporary proprietress. Water in plenty, hot and cold, is hers for the turning of overhanging taps, whilst the conversion of the rinsing trough into a copper is as easily accomplished—by opening a steam-containing valve. Her "wash" completed, she carries her basket to one of the men in charge of the row of wringers situated in an adjoining room. A few moments of rapid water-expelling whirling whilst the laundress "stands at ease," and the clothes are returned to her almost dry. She folds them on long tables near at hand, and puts them into a mangle, many of which machines are, it should be stated, now worked automatically. Should she wish to iron her finer items, she has but to take ready-heated irons from the stove hard by. Would she air her clothes she hangs them on a "horse" and pushes it into a hot-air compartment.

And for all this luxury as laundress the authorities charge but three-halfpence an hour! Soap and soda they do not provide, nor do they limit her to any given number of hours; so she may stay from 8 a.m. to 8 p.m. should she feel disposed. The average attendance at each wash-house of the Metropolis is from two to three hundred persons every weekday.

It is curious to notice in the most crowded districts how many nationalities are represented by these people—a blonde Swedish girl helping a dusky daughter of the South to get through a heap of ironing, or a broad-nosed Russian grudgingly lending a piece of soap to a sharp-featured Polish Jewess. Strange peeps into home tragedies can sometimes be gained, as when the overworked looking eldest child comes clattering up the stone staircase bringing to its mother for a little while, the few-weeks-old baby; or when the half-sober husband lounges in to bully the price of another drink out of her. She is the breadwinner, it seems.

The price charged for hot baths and use of towels is twopence, fourpence, and sixpence, according to class and locality, and half each of these sums for children. All such private baths are kept scrupulously clean, and the cabins in which they are fixed are furnished with a seat, hooks for clothing, and, in the case of the best, a strip of carpet, mirror, and brush and comb. That these liberal conditions are appreciated is testified by the fact that they are used by between fifty and seventy thousand persons at each institution annually. At Westminster they tell a tale of a certain flower-seller which is well worth quoting: Every Saturday evening, week in, week out, comes this girl, clad just as she would be when crying "Penny er bunch" on the kerb-stone. She enters from the street by the "wash-house" door, and proceeds to a private room, where she takes off all her clothes but her skirt and jacket, and puts her front locks into curlers. Then she hires a trough, mangle, etc., for an hour, submits her underwear to the cleansing process, finally hanging it up to air; that done, she buys a ticket for a twopenny hot bath, bathes herself, puts on her clean clothes, combs her fringe, and for the expenditure of threepence-halfpenny emerges as good an imitation of "new woman" as anybody else could compass at any price!

For those who can afford a "first-class" bath a comfortable waiting-room is provided, with fire and a goodly supply of newspapers. It often serves as a sort of House of Assembly to a certain set of local worthies, who

TURKISH BATH (JERMYN STREET): SHAMPOOING ROOM.

WATER POLO MATCH (WESTMINSTER BATHS).

TEACHING SCHOOLBOYS TO SWIM (KENSINGTON BATHS).

count on the opportunity thus afforded to meet neighbours and discuss the affairs of the nation.

That swimming should at last have come to be regarded by the School Board as a necessary item of education is a fact on which we should heartily congratulate ourselves. Thanks in the matter are undoubtedly due to the persistent efforts of a few private enthusiasts as well as to the energy of such philanthropic bodies as the Life-saving Society, the Swimming Association of England, and the London Schools Swimming Association.

Practical testimony is given to the seriousness of the modern views of the situation by the provision of free lessons in swimming at the public elementary schools. All the summer large detachments from the various Board schools, in charge of masters or mistresses, present themselves daily for lessons at several of the baths. Funny scenes occur when the children take their first plunge into so large an expanse of water! Some of them decline to leave the steps at the shallow end, or cling desperately to the rail that runs round, only gaining courage by very slow degrees and after having been carried about by the patient instructor. But such alarms are gradually conquered, and the children become as much at home as ducks in the water, and willingly take part in various sports and life-saving instruction, their competency as swimmers and life-savers often being the means of rescuing playmates from drowning in the course of holiday expeditions. It has even happened that a child has rescued his father.

In order to bring the benefits afforded by the swimming bath within the reach of most young folk the ordinary twopenny entrance-fee is reduced to a penny for schools; and that the art of natation may be more generally acquired many University men and others generously give their services as instructors and also pay for the bath. There are, for instance, associations formed amongst the Post Office *employés*, telegraph boys, shop assistants, poor boys and girls in Homes, and others, all of which are encouraged by well-known enthusiastic experts, and meet for practice and instruction.

The swimming clubs of London number about two hundred, and are composed of members of every class—boys and girls, young men and maidens, representing all the various grades of well-being. In several instances their formation resulted from the initiative of some of the large employers, such as Messrs. Cook, Son and Co., of St. Paul's Churchyard, whose care for the physical development of their clerks and others has had the happiest effect both mentally and physically. The "Ravensbourne" is the designation by which Messrs. Cook's club is known; and, thanks to the excellent work done at its weekly meetings, its annual display at Westminster Baths draws great crowds of spectators—friends of the competitors and members of similar associations.

Another popular meeting is the free public display held every summer at the Highgate

Ponds by the Life-saving Society, at which as many as 30,000 spectators assemble.

A curious lack of knowledge of self-preservation is disclosed by our soldiers, it having been found necessary to teach swimming to thousands of the Guards. They learned the art at St. George's Baths, Buckingham Palace Road, and it was amusing to note that some of the stalwart fellows, absolutely dauntless in other circumstances, showed an almost childlike timidity in facing so unaccustomed an experience. How well their quickly acquired courage and ability in dealing with water have served them has since been remarkably demonstrated.

Although the feminine portion of the community is making undeniable progress towards the popularising of swimming, it is found somewhat difficult to interest the poorer classes of girls in this art. Broadly speaking, they do not care for gymnastics of whatever sort in anything like the degree that their brothers do. This they prove by their disregard of the opportunity for exercise provided all the winter by the covering in and fitting with gymnastic appliances of some of the swimming baths. But the same remarks do not hold good in connection with the sisters of our public school boys, University men, and so on; they are veritable mermaids! Ambitious mermaids, too, with a very decided intention to rival all comers in proficiency and grace. Thanks to their comprehensive love of frame-developing sports, their achievements in the water are of no mean order. To see them at their best one should belong to the Bath Club, a luxurious institution in Dover Street, Piccadilly, once the town mansion of Lord Abergavenny, where, whilst enjoying all the advantages of an ordinary social club, one has the run of every variety of bath—Turkish, shower, douche, swimming, etc.—provided on the premises. This popular and well-managed establishment is frequented by both ladies and gentlemen, who claim the use of the baths on alternate days. There are 2,000 members, of whom 500 are of the gentler sex.

The swimming bath at this club is unique in its accessories, having suspended over the water, besides several diving boards and Newman's water-chute, not a few gymnastic appliances, such as trapeze and travelling rings. The contests at the Bath Club, either for the men members or their feminine relatives, always attract a large attendance —spectators filling the gallery and thickly surrounding the bath edge. The variety of costumes worn by the ladies — some of mermaid-imitating scales, others of gaily striped materials—and the floral decorations of the place provide a very attractive spectacle.

The height of luxury in the way of taking a bath is attained by the Turkish variety. It is practised in perfection at the Hammam (or Turkish bath) in Jermyn Street, St. James's. It costs four shillings, and it takes two hours; but nothing yet invented by Londoners, or annexed from abroad, has ever come near

TURKISH BATH (JERMYN STREET): COOLING ROOM.

the delicious experience or the restorative quality of the Turkish bath. One enters, a world-weary wreck, tired from travelling, working, pleasuring, maybe, rheumatic; one sits, or reclines, in a succession of hot-air rooms, each of the eight hotter than the last —varying from 112° F. to 280° F.—until a sufficient perspiration has been attained. Then one is conducted to the shampooing room, and, whilst reposing on a marble slab, one is massaged by light-handed attendants. That process is followed by a series of brushes and different soaps; and, after a variety of shower douches and a plunge into cold water, the bath is complete. A sojourn in a lofty cooling room, a quiet smoke, or a light meal, and one sallies forth a new being. A visit to the gallery of the attendant hairdressers makes perfection more perfect.

This bath is patronised by gentlemen only, but many districts now boast their Hammam, open to both sexes—among others, Charing Cross, Earl's Court, Islington, Camden Town, Brixton—at all of which the price is extremely moderate, some even descending to one shilling.

The vapour bath (obtainable at the Marylebone and a few other public baths) is an excellent substitute for the Turkish should limited time be a consideration. Various medicated baths are also used by a section of Londoners—such as pine, bran, sulphur—to cure certain ailments, as alternative to foreign springs, etc., whilst electricity is impelled through the water at the request of some others. This sort of bath is occasionally used in conjunction with the Swedish system of treatment (massage and exercises by means of mechanical appliances), now much practised in the Metropolis.

Given the desire to wash, the means are certainly not lacking in Living London.

LADIES USING THE CHUTE (BATH CLUB).

AWAITING THE ARRIVAL OF MINISTERS TO ATTEND A CABINET COUNCIL.

SCENES FROM OFFICIAL LIFE IN LONDON.

By L. BRINDLE.

IT has been said, and with very good reason, that the things that impress one most in London are the things that one does not see, which one cannot see, but of which one has a tolerably accurate knowledge if a student of such matters, derived and assimilated from a hundred sources in the course of many years.

Royalty, Parliament, the City, all these are in truth wonderfully impressive, and we see them, or something pertaining to them, almost every day of our lives in London. But all the time there is something else which we feel among us, but which we never see unless we are more than usually favoured mortals. In London, especially when some country visitor is with us, we often feel a sense of pride and importance which may be partly accounted for by the ostensible wonders of the capital and partly by the common instinct to which Dr. Johnson gave utterance when he remarked to Boswell, "I will venture to say there is more learning and science within the circumference of ten miles from where we now sit than in all the rest of the kingdom." Yet even with all this there is a balance still to be accounted for, and I think that if most of my readers will examine their own minds on the subject they will agree that it is made up of that other instinct which consists mainly of one's appreciation of the fact that here in London we are pulling every day the strings of the Empire, the greatest empire which has ever existed. We do not see these strings, nor do we see anybody pulling them—seldom indeed do we catch a glimpse of the dignitaries who perform this awe-inspiring task. But we know that it is done, and we know furthermore that there is not a nation of the world but has just as much appreciation—it may be admiring appreciation or it may be bitter appreciation —of this great and all-important fact as we and our country visitor have. We walk with him along the western side of Whitehall, and we point out to him the solid and stately structures which make this such a noble thoroughfare. And it is here, within an area of but a few acres after all, that these strings are for the most part pulled. To-day a Minister in one of

A RECEPTION AT THE FOREIGN OFFICE

these buildings dictates an instruction to one of his private secretaries; an hour later the message which is the result of it is speeding its way along thousands of miles of the ocean bed. To-morrow our great pro-consul acts upon the order which he has received, and the news of the significant departure in policy is cabled back to every newspaper in London, to every newspaper in the world—more than that, to the chancellery of every Power; and the foreign Ministers knit their foreheads and bite their pens and scowl when they read this news, and understand that Downing Street has advanced another point. One of the big strings has been pulled again.

And, again, there is a crisis in some home affair which is of urgent importance to the well-being of a very large number of people. It may pertain to the care of an industry, or to the soundness of the people's education, or to any other of the thousand questions which ever and again are troubling the public mind. Interested persons hurry now to Whitehall, and there are long conversations in the rooms of Ministers, after which the interested persons, with their minds all in a state of doubt and trepidation, go their way. A few hours later an order is promulgated from the seat of authority, and, as likely as not, the trouble at that moment is at an end. One of the smaller strings has been pulled. We never see the pulling of these strings, but we feel each and every day that it is being done here in London as it can be nowhere else, and somehow this grand, this exalted official life that is being lived in the Metropolis permeates the atmosphere which we breathe and gives us a quickening sense of pride and importance.

But now, though we have said that none of these things are visible, we will avail ourselves of a more than usually special permit—which we will say at once would be granted to no person alive, save the King and his Ministers—and will take brief glimpses at some of the scenes which are enacted in Downing Street and other places curtained off from the public gaze. When we come down to a cold analysis there is much that is quite ordinary in these scenes; but they inspire a vast amount of awe notwithstanding. To all outward appearances a meeting of company directors is much the same as a meeting of kings, but they are very different meetings after all. So it is with these scenes.

What meeting, for instance, would one regard with greater interest and curiosity than a meeting of the Cabinet, fraught as it often is with the destiny of the nation? This is so well realised that, especially on a cold damp afternoon in the middle of winter when the Ministers gather themselves together from the four points of the compass in Downing Street for the first time since the beginning of the autumn recess, there is quite a big crowd to see them going in, one by one, to their solemn deliberations which have regard to the programme of the forthcoming session of Parliament. Some come on foot, some in hansom cabs, others drive up in their own well-appointed carriages, and Ministers have even been known upon occasion to ride up to a Cabinet Council upon their cycles. It is the same with other Cabinet Councils, which are held in frequent succession after the first one, but it is in this that the public interest is keenest, because it marks the awakening of official life after the autumn siesta. The people see the Ministers come and see them disappear under the archway that leads to the great quadrangle, and then as far as they are concerned, the Cabinet Council is at an end, for they witness no more of it, and only the most meagre paragraph report of its doings, and that usually mere speculation, ever finds its way into the papers.

A wonderful secrecy is preserved with regard to all that pertains to these meetings. They are usually held in a room on the ground floor at the Foreign Office, and in white letters there is painted on the door of it "Private." The furniture of the room is not elaborate, and there is little to distract the attention of Ministers from the business in hand. The Prime Minister takes his seat at the head of the table, and the other Ministers place themselves round the board as best suits their convenience, but in no set order. Then the door is closed, and upon no pretence whatever may any outsider gain admission to the chamber until all is over. The Prime Minister has an electric bell at his elbow, and if need arises he summons a departmental official or a servant to the room, but he does so as seldom as possible, and when the outsider is present the deliberations are suspended. Ministers may bring with them the private Government papers which have been addressed to them, and of which they have need, and there are also upon the table documents that have been printed in the private Government printing office, and which are endorsed "Most Secret. For the use of the Cabinet"; but they may produce no paper for the making of notes for their own use as to the proceedings of the day. It is a strict rule that no minutes of any kind whatsoever shall be made of the business which is discussed, each Minister having perforce to content himself with his mental impression of what takes place. This is all for the sake of secrecy. The business may be comparatively trivial, and may last but half an hour; or there may be laid before this meeting of the executive Government a threat of war or a proposal for peace from some foreign country, and for hours and hours the Cabinet may sit with anxious faces and minds which hesitate between two courses upon which depend the future of our Empire. Ministers have even been known to be summoned to a meeting of the Cabinet when Big Ben hard by has been striking the midnight hour, and have remained in conference until the daylight has streamed through the windows upon their ashen, worn-out countenances.

But there is another great Council of the State, about which we are privileged to learn even less. The only report which we are ever allowed to read is the simple one contained in the Court announcements, which may run thus:—

"His Majesty The King held a Council at Buckingham Palace to-day at 12 o'clock. There were present:—The Archbishop of Canterbury, the Duke of Devonshire, K.G. (Lord President), the Duke of Norfolk, K.G., and the Marquess of Cholmondeley."

That is all. It is a Privy Council which has been held in this case, and it usually assembles in one of the royal residences, the King, of course, presiding. There are many members of the Privy Council; but as a rule only Ministers, certain great officers of the Household, and sometimes the Archbishop of Canterbury, are summoned to the meetings.

A COUNCIL AT BUCKINGHAM PALACE.

A summons to the whole Council is sent out only upon the most extraordinary occasion. What the functions of the Privy Council precisely are it is hard to say; a Privy Councillor himself would have difficulty in answering such a question. But in theory it is what the Cabinet is in practice. Its real practical value is as a necessary medium between the throne and the executive Government, and so we may imagine at these meetings the King and his Ministers chatting over points in matters of State, or perchance discussing details of some ceremony which is soon to take place. The Privy Council is thus of service; but perhaps the general sentiment concerning it as a whole, as apart from its divisions, is that it is a very good reserve council, which might conceivably upon occasion be of the greatest utility. The Privy Councillor, whom we see in our fancy with the King, has taken an oath that he will "advise his Majesty to the best of his cunning and discretion," that he will keep the King's council secret, that he will help and strengthen the execution of what shall be resolved, and, amongst other things, that he will observe, keep, and do all that a good and true Councillor ought to do to his Sovereign Lord. Besides the King and his Councillors there is admitted to the apartment the Clerk of the Council, who has also to take a most solemn oath that he will reveal nothing of what is discussed.

These are the Councils of the chiefs; consider the latter now in their own departments where they are certainly not less interesting, and only a trifle less private. There are two of the ministerial offices that help to make up the great quadrangle to the left of Downing Street, which possess deeper interest for the curious outsider than most of the others, and these are the Foreign Office and the Colonial Office, the work of each of which is of vast and enduring importance.

Observe the Secretary of State for Foreign Affairs at work in his own room. As befits the apartment which is reserved for the man who deals direct with the heads of all other Governments, it is luxuriously furnished. There are beautiful, morocco leather-covered chairs, and there is a particular one of them upon which scores of ambassadors have in turn been wont to sit when they have called upon the Minister to discuss some matter of urgent international importance. There is a writing table in the room with a number of pigeon-holes attached to it, labelled "Home Secretary," "Minister of the Colonies," and so forth. It is not too much to say that here are contained the secrets of an empire. At the Foreign Office

A DEPUTATION TO THE COLONIAL SECRETARY.

AFTER A NAVAL DISASTER: ENQUIRERS AT THE ADMIRALTY.

upon occasion his Lordship will hold a great reception, and there will come to it the Corps Diplomatique, and many other persons of high degree, presenting an imposing and even showy spectacle.

There are perhaps fewer displays of magnificence in connection with other great departments, but they are scarcely less interesting. The Foreign Office may deal with the world; but at least the Colonial Office, on the other side of the great archway, concerns itself with all that part of the world which we have the pleasure to call our own. Wending our way up the wide and handsome staircase, having some business with the Colonial Secretary or one of his subordinates, we are ushered by an attendant into a waiting-room overlooking the quadrangle, which is pleasant enough in its way, but which is principally decorated with maps with big blotches of red upon them. This is indicative of the business of the office. Probably there are many other persons waiting in this room, even some with dark skins who form a deputation to the Minister from one of those far-off lands which are under the British sway. Within, the Colonial Secretary is hard at work with more maps around him. Everything in the room suggests work, hard work, and heavy responsibility.

In another department there is the Home Secretary on duty. He, too, is a very busy man, controlling as he does most of those insular matters which more closely affect the comfort and prosperity of people at home. Ordinary folk understand the functions of the Home Secretary better than they do those of the Foreign Minister. Some of them may have heard that he has in a little room hard by his own a telephone by means of which he may speak direct to New Scotland Yard at any time without a moment's delay upon a matter of life or death. It is really so.

A little further down Whitehall there is a building, one of the Government group, at the sight of which all but millionaires are often apt to experience a curious creepy feeling. This is the Treasury, which is presided over by the Chancellor of the Exchequer, and whence the income tax and all other taxes come. It is the headquarters of the national finance, and when folk want to grumble whilst there is yet time—as they invariably do—at the taxes they have to pay, they repair to the Treasury in deputation form, and talk the matter over with the Chancellor. But whoever he be, the Chancellor is invariably a shrewd man with a cold heart, and the deputation in departing is not often a merry one. Elsewhere there are the Education Office, the Board of Trade, the India Office, and others, the precise characters of which are indicated in their titles. There is an office for everything and everywhere.

There are still two which have not yet been mentioned, but in regard to which public interest is always keen; at special times exceptionally so. The War Office

THE INDIA OFFICE
FROM ST. JAMES'S PARK

SCENES FROM OFFICIAL LIFE IN LONDON. 377

and the Admiralty, controlling as they do the mighty forces of the Empire on land and sea, have in due season news to give which will make London throb with pride, and which will at the same time cast a perpetual shadow over many homes that were once the happiest in the land. There may be a report that a British warship has foundered, and there are groups of terror-stricken mothers and wives and sisters—perhaps male relatives also—in the comfortless corridors of the enormous building which lies between Spring Gardens and the Horse Guards. Looking from one of the windows the King, with a brilliant staff of War Office officials, may perhaps be seen distributing the medals of victory to his soldiers upon the Horse Guards Parade, but these poor creatures in the Admiralty can hardly think at such a time of the glory of arms. A soothing word may be spoken by one of the officials attired in a blue uniform with an anchor on his cap, but what consolation is that?

In the War Office itself the Secretary of State is assisted in the multifarious duties he performs by the distinguished men who form the Army Council. In imagination one may see a line of red and khaki spreading from the War Office to the uttermost ends of the Empire, and with our preliminary reflection in mind the War Office then is a convenient spot to terminate a tour through secret places which have told such a tale of the great imperial body of which London is the mighty throbbing heart.

PRESENTATION OF WAR MEDALS ON THE HORSE GUARDS PARADE: ARRIVAL OF THE KING.

SATURDAY NIGHT IN LONDON.

By A. ST. JOHN ADCOCK.

FOR persons who live above a certain social level Saturday night has no particular features to distinguish it from any other night of the week; but for the vast majority of those who live below that serene altitude it is the most important night of the secular six: it means to them pretty much what a coming into port means to the seaman or a harvest-home to the farmer.

The City emptying itself much earlier than usual on Saturday, outgoing trains, 'buses, and trams are crammed to excess between one o'clock and five; then, from six to eight, incoming trams, 'buses, and trains are equally burdened, for many who went out early are returning now with friends, sweethearts, wives, or, at pantomime time, with small excited members of their families, in a hurry to add themselves to the extra long Saturday-night queues stretching away from the pit and gallery doors of the principal theatres.

Now, too, when there is a chance of escaping observation in the darkness, the pawn-shops are at their busiest: shrinking figures, mostly of women, flit in and out by obscure side-doors, some on a regular Saturday night errand to redeem Sunday wearing apparel that is as regularly put away again on Tuesday or Wednesday when the domestic treasury is again exhausted; others carrying household articles sufficiently mortgageable to raise the price of to-morrow's dinner, a husband being out of work, or delayed on the way home exhaustively refreshing himself, and not expected to arrive with any considerable salvage of his week's wages.

There are insignificant, comfortable people who sent a servant out to do their shopping this morning or ordered their Sunday requirements of tradesmen who call at the door, and this evening they will go, perhaps, to some little party at the house of a friend, or give a little party of their own; or, during the summer and autumn, they may make an afternoon excursion up the river to Hampton Court or down to Greenwich, and come back

SATURDAY NIGHT IN KING STREET, HAMMERSMITH.

SATURDAY NIGHT IN LONDON.

BRACES.

pleasantly tired, just in time to share a 'bus or a railway carriage with jovial amateur cricketers or footballers homing from a Saturday's match.

In the main, however, Saturday night is given over to the great weekly shopping carnival of the poor, and of all such as live carefully on limited incomes. They do their marketing, from custom or necessity or for sheer preference, in the very last hours of the last day of the week, and they do most of it in those boisterous, cheerful, plenteous, cornucopia-like thoroughfares where costermongers are still allowed to congregate and compete with the shopkeepers.

Of course, the genteel business ways of the west know nothing whatever of that carnival. In that region shutters are up early, and when Berwick Street and other arteries of Soho are congested with stalls and buyers and sellers, and doing a roaring trade in every sense of the phrase, the select shops of Oxford Street, Regent Street, and Piccadilly are, nearly all of them, closed and enjoying a foretaste of their Sunday sleep.

Broadly speaking, Saturday night's trade follows the costers, and finds them all over London: it finds them south under the arches and littering the streets around Brixton Station, in the Old Kent Road, on Deptford Broadway; up north in Phœnix Street, in Chapel Street, Islington, in Queen's Crescent,

Kentish Town; away west straggling for a mile or more along Harrow Road, or in King Street, Hammersmith; eastward in Chrisp Street by the docks, and nowhere in greater variety, more breezily good-humoured, or attended by a more cosmopolitan crowd than in Whitechapel Road.

On the way thither, through Aldgate, we pass Butchers' Row and the uncommonly miscellaneous line of stalls facing it, where business has been steadily increasing ever since noon. Some of the butchers have put up intimations that they make a speciality of "kosher" meat, and other signs are not wanting that we are in the neighbourhood of the Ghetto: round the side-streets are Jewish hotels and restaurants; in the High Street there are bakers, printers, all manner of traders who have announcements in Hebrew characters painted on their windows; a Hebrew theatrical poster appeals to us from a hoarding; dusky foreign Jews pass in the crowd chattering in a barbarous Yiddish.

As we push farther east the crowd becomes denser and livelier: an incongruously blended multitude in which abject squalor elbows coquettish elegance, and sickly misery and robust good-humour, and frank poverty and poverty decently disguised, and lean knavery and leaner honesty, drunkenness and sobriety, care and frivolity, shabby home-bred loafers and picturesque, quaintly-garbed loafers from over sea, all hustle or loiter side by side, in one vast, motley, ever-moving panorama

BOOTS AND SHOES: TRYING ON.

By this we are past the Pavilion Theatre and on the broad pavement that sweeps down to Mile End Gate. Up between flags of the pavement sprout stunted trees that drip dirty tears in the foggy weeks of winter and with the coming of spring break into a pleasant laughter of dusty green leaves. They are girdled with iron railings, and betwixt and before and behind them costermongers' stands and barrows are scattered in great plenty.

There are fruit and vegetable stalls, there are fish stalls, haberdashers', stationers', tailors', toy, jewellery, butchers', cutlery, boot, hat and cap, and unmistakably second-hand ironmongery stalls, all along to Mile End Gate; and, to add to the crush and the tumult, enterprising shopkeepers have rushed selections of their goods out of doors and ranged them among the stalls and set assistants bawling in wildernesses of furniture and crockery, or chaunting incessantly amidst clustered pillars of linoleum and carpet like lay priests in ruined temples.

The stalls and these overflowings of the shops are intersected by stands where weary marketers may solace themselves with light refreshments in the way of whelks liberally seasoned with vinegar and pepper, cheap but indigestible pastry, toffee, or fried soles; and there are ice-cream barrows that dispense ices and ginger-beer in summer, and in winter supply baked potatoes and hot drinks. Intersecting other stalls are a cripple in a wheeled-chair manipulating a concertina; a man with a tray suspended round his neck selling "electric" pens; an enormous brass weighing machine that soars up glittering and catching light from all the surrounding naphtha lamps till it seems itself a thing of fire; a galvanic battery and a "lung-tester," both popular with boys, who take shocks from the one and blow into the long tube of the other with a joy in the results that is worth at least twice what they pay for it; and, with a naphtha lamp all to himself, a sombre, wooden-legged man presides over a seedy collection of umbrellas stuck in a ricketty home-made stand and holds a specimen umbrella open over his own head as if he lived at the best of times in an invisible shower.

And buyers are stopping to haggle with the sellers; loafers and lurchers go by continuously; passing by also are rough artisans in their working clothes out shopping with their wives, and dainty fascinating young Jewesses dressed in ornate imitation of the latest West-End fashions and escorted by dapper young Jews in tall hats, resplendent linen, and suits reminiscent of Piccadilly.

Stand aside and see them passing; and here, passing with them, a couple of jovial sailors, arm-in-arm, flourishing their pipes and singing lustily; a wan woman in rusty widow's weeds leading a child in one hand and carrying her frugal marketings in the other; a young man wheeling a perambulator with a baby and some beef and a cabbage in it, while his wife, a keen, brisk little woman, chaffers at the fish stall for something toothsome to take home for supper; dowdy women, Jew and Gentile, in faded bonnets, or bright-coloured shawls, or with no other head-covering than their own plenteous hair; three dandy soldiers making a splash of red where the throng is drabbest; a sleek Oriental, astray from the docks, in his white linen costume and white turban or crimson fez; a lank, long-bearded Hebrew in an ample frock coat and ancient tall hat, moving in profound meditation, with a certain air of aloofness separating him from the surging, restless mob, as if the sanctities of the Synagogue and his newly-ended Sabbath still wrapped him about in an atmosphere of unworldly calm.

A few paces farther on, and here is a weedy youth swathed in a white apron shrilly inviting attention to a pyramid of pigs'-trotters on a board on trestles against the front of a public-house, in the saloon doorway of which a pair of musicians are manufacturing music with a diminutive harmonium and a tin-whistle, while outside the smaller public-house near by gossiping men and women with no taste for either music or pig's-trotters lounge drinking in the open air.

Across in the New Cut, and Lower Marsh, Lambeth, there is the same crush and uproar, the same smoky flare of innumerable naphtha lamps, the same bewildering miscellany of stalls, but the customers and idlers are, on the whole, more poverty-stricken, more depressed, more common-place. There are

SATURDAY NIGHT IN WHITECHAPEL ROAD.

flower-stalls and second-hand book stalls here, as there are in Farringdon Street and Shoreditch High Street; there is a sedate optician's stall with wilted old ladies and gentlemen pottering about it at intervals testing their sights at different-sized letters printed on a card and sparing a trifle from their week's addlings to treat themselves to new pairs of spectacles; there is a misanthropic-looking man sitting on a stool in the gutter with piles of muffins on a small table beside him; and there are the road is blocked by an eager concourse of girls and young and elderly women, and peering over their agitated shoulders we focus with difficulty a low, improvised counter buried under stacks of ladies' jackets, blouses, dresses, shawls, while four feminine hucksters, one at each corner of the counter, hold up articles of such wearing apparel for inspection and cackle persuasively in chorus. They do the thing better in such a place as Hoxton Street, for there the roadway is left to every other description of stall, and the

INSIDE A BIG PROVISION STORES (HAMMERSMITH).

usual hawkers wandering up and down with toasting forks, boot-laces, braces, song-sheets, and meat-jacks with wooden legs of mutton turning on them to illustrate their uses.

In nearly every market street to-night there are cheap-jacks selling crockery, and quacks vending corn-cures and ointment, and in some, notably in Stratford High Street and Deptford Broadway, there is occasionally a male quack, or one of the gentler sex, who, to create a sensation and gather an audience, will plant a chair in the public eye and extract the teeth of penurious sufferers gratis.

Half way through one Saturday market trade in women's clothing is carried on in skeleton shops, the fronts of which have been knocked out so that passing ladies may stray in without hindrance and wallow in second-hand garments that hang thickly round the walls and are strewn and heaped prodigally about the floors.

In other streets we have side-glimpses of brilliantly-lighted interiors opulently festooned and garlanded and hung with cheap boots and shoes, and, thus environed, men and women, affluent with Saturday's wages, examining and selecting from the stock, or a small child on a high chair having a pair of shoes tried on under the critical gaze of

CHINA.

its father and mother and the shopman; or, especially in such localities as Leather Lane and Whitecross Street, where boot-stalls abound, a similar scene is frequently enacting in the open air, with the diminutive customer perched, for "fitting" purposes, close to the stall.

In all the tumultuous market streets, and in broad, centre thoroughfares where there are few or no costermongers, big drapers have a passion for Saturday clearance sales that no woman who loves a bargain is stoical enough to ignore; and provision shops and mammoth general stores, in a cheery glamour of gas or electric light, are simmering and humming like exaggerated hives. Smart servant-maids in some districts, and in all practical housewives, domesticated husbands, children, singly or in pairs, and furnished with baskets and pencilled lists of their requirements, flow in and out of these emporiums in apparently endless streams.

While the Saturday saturnalia is thus at its fiercest and gayest and noisiest throughout the main roads and market streets, in grimy, quiet byways of Whitechapel there are snug Hebrew coffee rooms and restaurants, re-awakened after a Sabbath snooze, wherein Jews of divers nationalities are gossiping over coffee and wine and cigarettes, or beguiling the hours with dominoes and card-playing. In other dim, sinister byways there is, here and there, in an obscure room behind some retiring hostelry, a boxing match going forward for the delectation of an audience of flashy, rowdy sportsmen and their down-at-heel hangers-on; likewise, about Whitechapel and Bermondsey, Southwark and Soho, in shyer, furtive dens that are overshadowed always by fear of a police raid, there are feverish, secret gamesters gathered round the green tables. In the neighbourhood of Soho — much favoured by exiles from all countries —they are more numerous and of superior quality, and in some exclusive, elegant, equally secret clubs you may gamble with bejewelled gentry whose losses on the turn of the wheel or the cards are far from being limited by the size of a week's salary.

Meanwhile, theatres are full; and music-halls; and Saturday dances, singsongs, and smoking concerts in assembly rooms and over public-houses are liberally encouraged. When people begin to come out from these entertainments, the crowd that is still abroad marketing is of a poorer, hungrier stamp than that which enlivened the streets an hour or two ago. Stalls are beginning to disappear, and those that remain are mostly refreshment stalls, or fruit and meat stalls that are trying to sell off their surplus stock by auction.

Fruit stalls in Whitechapel Road have a special weakness for finishing up in this way—a way which is common to the meat shops and stalls in all the market streets

OUTSIDE A PUBLIC-HOUSE.

everywhere. The large cheap butchers' shops in Bermondsey and elsewhere make a practice of "selling off" by auction all the evening, but elsewhere it is the custom to adopt this course only after ten o'clock.

Then, after ten o'clock, you may see feminine butchers hammering on their stalls with the blunt ends of their choppers, and shouting and cheapening their primest beef and mutton as frantically and as successfully as any butcher of the sterner sex who, goaded to frenzy by the approach of midnight, is pedestalled on his stall, or on the block in his doorway or the sloping flap outside his window, and is lifting meat boastfully in both hands, offering it at absurdly high prices, and yet selling it for ever so little a pound to whomsoever will buy.

Rain or snow will thin the streets by keeping folk at home or driving them to the nearest shops, or to such roofed paradises for the small trader as the Portman Market off Edgware Road. But to-night has been fine, and everything at its best.

And now 'buses and trams begin to fill with laughing, chattering myriads returning from the theatres, and with shop assistants just emancipated. Laundry vans are coming back from delivering the last of their washing; in thousands of lowly, decent households busy mothers are ironing the last of to-morrow's linen on a corner of the supper table, or the whole family are seated to a rare but inexpensive feast at the latter end of a hard week.

Twelve strikes, and the public-houses close, not without brawling and a drunken fight or two; but the last stragglers will soon be making for home; the last stall will soon have packed up and gone away; the latest shop will be putting up its shutters, and all the flare and fever and flurry and wrangling and business and merriment of Saturday night will be quieting down at last under the touch of Sunday morning.

SELLING MEAT BY AUCTION.

PRINTED BY CASSELL AND COMPANY, LIMITED, LA BELLE SAUVAGE, LUDGATE HILL, LONDON, E.C.

SIMS, G.R.

Living London.

DA
684.
.S59
v. 4

ImTheStory.com

Personalized Classic Books in many genre's

Unique gift for kids, partners, friends, colleagues

Customize:

- Character Names
- Upload your own front/back cover images (optional)
- Inscribe a personal message/dedication on the inside page (optional)

Customize many titles Including
- Alice in Wonderland
- Romeo and Juliet
- The Wizard of Oz
- A Christmas Carol
- Dracula
- Dr. Jekyll & Mr. Hyde
- And more...